NO ORDINARY GREEK ODYSSEY

BOOK ONE - WHERE THE BLUE TRULY BEGINS

SUZI STEMBRIDGE
Contributions &
Photography by
Simon Stembridge

Komboloi Press

For my family who helped me create this volume: For Simon who was mostly responsible for Chapters 8, 11, 17, 21, 22 and 24 and for Oliver and Heidi who in these early adventures were so often there.

And for all those who offered advice encouraging us to launch our travel businesses, Greco-file Ltd and Filoxenia Ltd, in the early years of their creation, 1986-1989. Particularly I would mention: Noel Josephides and Dudley der Parthog of Sunvil Holidays and Yannis and Maria Georgidakis of the Minoa Hotel & Yannopoulos Travel in Tolo.

In memory of Max Turner June 1942- April 2020

**

Additional contributions by Oliver Stembridge
and Heidi Stembridge

Also by Suzi Stembridge

GREEK LETTERS QUARTET:

GREEK LETTERS Volume 1 Before
GREEK LETTERS Volume 2 And After
GREEK LETTERS Volume 3 The Eyes Have It
GREEK LETTERS Volume 4 Much More Than Hurt

THE COMING OF AGE SERIES:

CAST A HOROSCOPE –
Winner of a CHILL WITH BOOK Award
THE SCORPION'S LAST TALE
BRIGHT DAFFODIL YELLOW –
Winner of a CHILL WITH A BOOK Award
THE GLASS CLASS

THE PUPPY WHO DIDN'T LIKE RAIN

All books can be read independently of each other.

This volume is the first volume of
The Memoirs: NO ORDINARY GREEK ODYSSEY

Cover picture: Monemvasia at early light
Black & white photographs mostly by Simon Stembridge;
line drawings by Psyche (Suzi Stembridge);
other illustrations acknowledged individually.

The beginning of a meander through Greece

Sixty years of travel on the back roads and high seas of Greece

A way of life in the twentieth century but how much will survive?

LIST OF LOCATIONS &
DATES OF OUR VISITS

Introduction

This book has evolved from years of travel, at least 60 years, but it takes the extraordinary events following the 2020 quarantine of almost the whole world due to the Covid-19 outbreak, to persuade me to publish these memoirs. Even as we were writing these words, before the Coronavirus, we knew we were living at a special time and I hope that those who read this account will judge it as an historical account which in its own way documents a way of travelling which now belongs to an era – BC – Before Coronavirus.

Most of the material has been garnered from diaries, notebooks, photographs, papers and our own company's travel brochures, material produced mostly before the internet and this volume probably harvests about twenty-five percent of that which is available.

Time will tell whether we can complete a second, or a third, volume. An alternative title could well have been, "Oh look, it's for sale!" Eventually, through the generosity of friends, we did achieve the dream of owning our own little corner of Greece for a few years after we retired. But this is definitely another tale!

PART 1

This was, and is, GREECE

CHAPTER 1

Athens, Rhodes, Lindos -
& Crete ever-so briefly

April 1960

I am in Athens....My nostrils still tingle from the heavenly smell that greets me as I swing up the heavy cast iron inner handle of the aircraft cabin door and release it so the scent from the thyme-covered Mt. Hymettus floods in; heat and dust and the most evocative smell ever.

I am a rookie air hostess, and this is my first 'long haul' flight. Almost my first flight.

An oil painting about three-foot by three-foot painted on hardboard is hanging on the wall of the taverna where we dine on my first night in Athens. I want to buy the painting.

The proprietor of the restaurant says if I and my aircrew come back to eat there the next evening, he will ask the artist. We come back,

"Are you sure you want to come here, Suzi?" my Captain asks me as we approach the threshold. "Are you sure that repulsion at the thought of the slaughter of small birds with a dish of roast thrush proudly misspelled and chalked on the menu doesn't put you off?"

But it was the same story, "come back tomorrow, Avrio."

So yet again we come back, and I often wonder if the artist missed that wonderful primitive art as much as I still enjoy the sheer vibrancy of its amazing blue background, curiously effective for a night scene.

Most sobering to recall is that the Athenians we meet in 1960 as we dine in the Plaka, are only a decade away from the enormous trauma of not just of World War Two but also the Greek Civil War which tore Greece apart.

The Plaka is still a village with its nineteenth-century houses, steep stepped cobbled streets, the Acropolis towering over us, the waiters dressed in black and in the picture the dark shadows of the musicians cast in the moonlight and the old woman on the balcony shouting to the trumpet and to the bouzouki players to cease their noise; all the people around us, both in the picture and on the street part of the history.

It's an impulsive buy for a twenty-year-old air hostess and impossible to achieve had the aircrew I am with not assisted and helped me stow the painting in the hold of the small chartered aircraft which is accompanying us around Greece, as is the way in 1960 when it is uneconomic to bring the plane back with an empty leg at the beginning or vice versa at the end of the season.

Musicians below the Acropolis

The painting of the Athenian musicians, brilliantly lit by moonlight, follows me from lodging to flat to starter home to family home, always in pride of place, with the lined-old-before-their-time-faces of the musicians staring across the room. They talk about 'in living memory', and these tales are within our living memory, yet it sometimes feels like yesterday.

There is no doubt in my mind that flying as an air hostess has made me what I am. The pilots that fly the planes in the small airline I join are mostly hangovers from the Berlin Airlift, and during 1948 to 1949, they fly the tiny Vickers Vikings and larger Viscounts with the same bra-

vado they had used in the thrilling and dangerous missions into the marooned West German
capital. Some of them had trained and even
flown in the last months of WW2.

These memoirs are of the travels of un-
apologetic young Europeans. Privileged travels
which in the 1960s, 70s, 80s and even 1990s
would still uncover areas where few other than
genuine travellers and explorers had ventured,
even in parts of Europe. We were fortunate to
experience the thrill of real discovery, even on
family holidays and later as part of a way of life,
a business. Although curiously, both Suzi on her
first ever flight, and Simon's first long haul air-
flight was to New York. To this add Bermuda and
Trinidad for Suzi, these pages are dedicated to
our experiences in Greece, often with our family.

In 1960 I am well aware that I am privileged to fly to Greece and not only that but as aircrew we will stay in some of the best hotels, (often superior to the accommodation used by our passengers) and have ample time to explore the places we visit.

We walk up to the Acropolis and wander at will among the breathtaking remains, and it is with a sense of awe that we climb up the shallow steps to the Parthenon and from the centre of the temple we can look around and sense the enormous skill the architects employed.

"The columns were designed to swell in the middle to create an optical illusion of being totally straight," Vic, our captain tells us. We hang on his every word; he clearly knows what he is talking about. Outside he points upwards to the remains of the frieze above the entablature, "this frieze was Phidias' finest work," he says, "the pity of it is that our Lord Elgin stole it, and most of it is now in our British Museum in London."

"I've heard of Pericles," I say, glad I have something to add. In truth Theseus and the Minotaur are about the only Greek heroes I can recall. But I feel stirred and wonder if the passion that our Captain is sharing is the start of another interest.

"And so you should, Pericles was Phidias' boss, possibly the greatest of all the Athenian fifth century BC statesmen, but without the genius of Phidias's skill as an architect, sculptor and painter and the resulting Parthenon then perhaps Pericles would not have become the legend he has."

"Despite Lord Elgin, there is still plenty to amaze us," I say, "but it breaks my heart that so little of the frieze survives in situ."

"There are those who say that Lord Elgin actually preserved the marbles from looters. When he arrived most of the pediment was lying in ruins after the bombardment of the Acropolis when the Ottomans stored their ammunition within the temple."

"There are always two sides to every story," said Maurice, our first officer.

Not sure I agree with him, I think "but they were not really ours for the taking."

We cross over to the Erechtheion. The statues of six maidens acting as columns and holding up the entablature are very weathered. "Pollution and weathering are always a problem where marble is concerned," says Maurice. "I just hope someone removes them to a museum or something.

From the Album 1960. The days when you could wander at will on the Acropolis.

Nowadays we can go to Syntagma Square in Athens and wonder if a lot has changed.

Okay, the traffic no longer swirls around the square but rushes through at the lower end, there are not the number of cafes, I am sure, that there used to be with waiters dashing across the street, precariously balancing trays of coffee and pastries.

But a visit in October 2018 challenges many recollections not least of the street where I had spent my first night in Greece, my first adult night in a hotel on my own, in May 1960.

With our back to the Parliament Building, we would walk down to the right-hand corner where a narrow street, Karagiorgi Servias is now crammed on both sides with boutiques and small brightly lit shop windows, walk on down to where the street narrows further, turn left slightly and there it is: one of the oldest churches in Athens, the Church of the Panaghia Kapnikarea. Nothing to jog my memory as to the name of the actual hotel here, excepting a first edition of the Blue Guide to name it and place it as the Attica-Palace.

Strange how as you grow up with a village, a town, a city, little seems to change but from 1960 to 2018 Athens has greatly increased in size, particularly as the buildings also grow upwards, and old photographs emphasise what was merely collections of houses beneath the Acropolis in 1834 by 1900 has become a sophisticated small city with hotels and elegant wide streets and squares.

Sixty years earlier Athens offered much that Central Athens offers at the Millennium, wide streets, narrow roads, the ancient village of bustling Plaka, expensive shops in Kolonaki and Ermou, except in 1960 visitors could climb up to the Acropolis and wander in and around the Parthenon, without hindrance, without crowds.

Another climb is to the top of wooded Lycabettus hill in the centre of Athens which does not enjoy the facility of a cable car to the top of its 277 metres until 1965. It is all fantastically familiar.

Rhodes

Rhodes has only itself to blame for its touristic popularity but in 1960 it is unspoiled, quiet, primitive in parts and stunningly beautiful; the old walled town and ancient castle overwhelmed by the fabulously intricate and brilliantly white architecture of Mussolini and the Italians, who are still occupying the island as late as 1947.

The promenade with its splendid finery is lined with not one row of low green garden bushes but also with a parallel row, they define the waterfront. And did these green leaves glisten and if so, did they wear the red rose of Rhodes, the beautiful hibiscus flower?

We have walked into the town from the prestigious Hotel des Roses, on its own beach where we have just spent a very welcome hour, swimming and sunbathing, drinks brought to our deck chairs by a very courteous and bronzed waiter.

After a rather alarming flight from Athens to Rhodes we feel we need to relax, and this fits the bill. Perhaps this evening during supper our flight deck crew will unwind and let me know exactly what had been the problem with the rather curious landing, when we had appeared to have touched down and clearly had not for there was a repeat landing.

The Nea Agora in blatant Turkish style captures the eye and within its walls the market for fish and vegetables is fascinating. The windmills on Mandraki Harbour are perhaps closely sited to the point where once there was the ancient Colossus of Rhodes.

It is May. We have one full day on Rhodes. We are modern aircrew, no longer shackled by thoughts of RAF daring-do but still living life to the full. Are we going to explore the old town or hire a car and drive around the island? Will the roads be paved or merely rough tracks, should we go east or west? A compromise is reached, we start off down the west coast, passing by the smart Miramare Bungalows on the seashore, towards the little airport of Maritsa *(the international airport until 1977)* where our small Viking plane had landed and had been parked, and turn east to climb up the narrow lanes over the hills towards the east coast.

This might be foolhardy, but the two pilots, freshly released from the Berlin Airlift have been reared on adventure and excitement and they accept the advice of the concierge at the Hotel des Roses that to take the main road through Kolimbia to Lindos is simply too, too easy!

As we pass the airport, finally our Captain casually mentions our perilous approach to the runway two days previously. Apparently at this airport the tarmac rises and falls over a small hump and this with a huge crosswind had caused our Viking to lift up again as we landed and without power! It needed their combined skill to glide back down to the runway again.

It would be fanciful to suppose that perhaps because the guys are pilots they had seen the lie of the land we are now about to explore, during our approach, (too busy for that,) but now we are climbing up the mountains through the pine forests and unbeknown to us bypassing the must-see tourist attraction of the coming years: the Valley of the Butterflies at Petaloudes, where a subspecies of the Jersey Tiger Moth overwhelms the deep moist valley in their thousands during the early summer months, creating an unprecedented desire to see this unique sight, which will forever cause concern to environmentalists due to visitor numbers.

Our experience is different, unused to the summer heat and trundling slowly in our tiny hire car on the rough shale roads, we are thirsty. Totally lost we reach what we judge to be the crest of the hills, then coming out of the forest we come into a clearing where a small settlement includes a house with two or three tables with chairs arranged as we imagine a small tavern might do. Drawing up and hesitatingly scrambling out of the car we look for confirmation that this might indeed be a small cafe.

An old man and woman come from within the house and beckon us to sit down outside, but what to ask for and how to do it? The old man whistles and a small boy appears and is despatched faster than he can ask his grandfather for instructions. Meanwhile, the grandmother re-appears with a huge fruit cake from which she cuts generous slices and places them before us on small white plates.

Within five minutes a young man appears, broad-shouldered and immediately he opens his mouth and drawls his welcome, in the thickest of American accents, we know our thirst will be quenched. Nor can he wait to tell us that we are the first tourist-visitors to his village, and he is proud to welcome us. And the cake, the remains of which our new friend, Manoli, tries to press upon us for our journey, serves to remind us that the Greeks have only just celebrated Pascha, their Greek Easter festival.

With farewells that would have been appropriate were we saying goodbye to an old friend departing for Detroit itself, we set off on a flat level track. Cedar trees are bent double by the winds, Eucalyptus trees sometimes shredded and bedraggled by the wind, past olive trees in groves, and as we lose height, coming off the mountain plateau, of course, we are looking for the sea. Sea as blue as I have ever seen. Sea that is matched in clarity and expanse by the sky itself. And there way below us is the coast. From this height, the horizon drawn by the sea is a deep dark blue, the line of infinity drawn by the sky nearly white until the whole merges together.

"Where would we land if we sailed as far as we can see?" I ask naively.

"We would reach the Suez Canal," says our Skipper, without hesitation. We are flying on romance and as we reduce our altitude through bony rocks the habitation on the coast takes shape. Even in spring there is sparse vegetation, despite the clumps of red poppies and the rainbow colours of other wildflowers.

"We are heading for Lindos, the ancient acropolis dating back to six or seven hundred BC which picturesquely dominates its fourteenth century village," our Captain adds, he could appear to know everything. "Streets with cobbled pavements and courtyards that are surrounded by the high walls of the white cubist houses, a wonderful sight if you can glimpse the black and white mosaic pebble courtyards and the colourful walled gardens." But our rough track brings us down the mountain and doesn't allow us to catch our breath with a first view of the amazing natural harbour of Lindos until we are nearly upon it!

Then like the curtain of a proscenium arch drawn back in part, the revelation of the old city above the palette of green and blue swirling sea colours is divulged and the little white squares making a thin line, almost insignificantly, girdling the topography of the citadel and its shoreline, splitting it in neat halves.

Lindos, always to be in our dreams of perfection, where the perfect circle of the bay is shattered to allow a single entrance for the triremes of old and the envious and competitive merchantmen of the City of Rhodes were forced to build five harbours, it is said, before the superior harbour at Lindos could be replicated in a settlement to the north and allow the one at Lindos to be finally relinquished.

From the 1960 Album, top: Lindos village & Pallas beach, bottom right and left: two village street scenes.

Our little hire car is parked beyond high walls under a great plane tree and we are anxious to wash off the dust of the long rough journey over the rugged roads of Rhodes island, cool our warm skin with a swim through the swirls of vivid blue, turquoise, and aquamarine salty water and we dash down to the beach. Salt notwithstanding, I am swimming like a mermaid and make my first headlong swoop to swim underwater, spluttering, laughing and stumbling, as I come up for air. Not the way to show elegance! `

Our meal in Mavrikos, even then boasting as Lindos' oldest taverna *and nowadays still with old olive trees in situ in the main restaurant and apparently with a Michelin star,* is just a simple roast chicken, totally delicious with a Greek Salad and of course an introduction to the local Rhodian wine, crisp and light and moreish which has to be limited by our driver. Ex war-time RAF pilots are not known for their restraint in alcohol consumption, but this crew is on edge, so far from a phone or telex message; after all, where the passengers are at leisure definitely does not mean that the aircrew should be! On these country roads, we are a long way from our hotel base. It is clear our exploration of the beckoning white village streets crowned by the ancient acropolis and the massive fortifications against the Ottomans by the fourteenth century castle of the Knights of St. John is going to be limited to a short excursion of the narrow main street before it begins its ascent towards the carved trireme at the foot of the acropolis. The ancient temple and classical columns and Byzantine church of St. John all somewhat confusingly in plain sight at the top of the outcrop are clearly out of reach.

We hesitate in the square as we come out of the taverna, our vision blinded by the bright sunlight. We walk slowly in the heat across the square to the ancient tree under whose branches our car is parked, taking in the view that with obvious regret we must leave. A young man watches us as we open the car doors, allowing the pent-up heat to escape.

"Are you going so soon?" he asks. "You musts see my mother's home! She's very happy to have peoples see her lovely home. We have Lindian pottery, white lace for sale. You musts come this way!" His speech reflects the way that many Greeks add an unnecessary 's' when speaking in English.

"Then we shall," says our captain, "if your mother's house has a painted ceiling and a courtyard with a mosaic floor."

"It does," says the lad. The house is not close, but we follow happily along the narrow street, up the shadowed steps, taking one turn and then another in the silence of the siesta, until we come to a closed heavy blue wooden door with a large wrought iron knocker. Pushing it open we follow the dark-haired young man.

"In the morning, many of these houses open their doors so you can see the beauty of our living." We venture inside the archontiko, shaded from the heat and bright afternoon sun. Off the courtyard, with its fine mosaic black and white pebbled flooring, are several rooms, their doors are open, it is hard to say whether each is set out as a museum or a spotless living room, white lace cloths and tableware, in one room, beautiful Lindian pottery on wall dressers in another. Lindian rugs, mostly red and beige strips, some more red than brown, others more beige than deep red hang above a platform which is clearly a bed. More casual heaps of pottery, carpets and lace are artfully arranged, and our wonder quickly becomes embarrassment when the old lady with her white fringed and beaded kerchief totters towards us with a sweet smile but an unexpectedly forceful grasp on my hand.

It is obvious we are not the first 'tourists' to be invited to meet the young man's 'mother' and not the first to buy ornately decorated blue, white, orange, green and burnt sienna plates, packed with white cotton lace between each plate to protect it on its journey to foreign parts.

I am sad, it taints what I felt had been genuine hospitality in the kafenion on the mountain plateau and at the taverna at lunchtime. Perhaps our obvious horror at their attempts at a hurriedly arranged 'shop' dissuades the family from other attempts to hoodwink future visitors. As we withdraw the captain points out a beautiful painted ceiling and we leave with some dignity. Compared to our route over the mountains our road back to the city through orchards and agricultural fields is more straightforward, although we have scarcely set our course west than our progress is stopped, as a tortoise ambles across the road. Three-wheeled vehicles splutter their

way along the track, each cart packed with vegetables behind the driver, set in the direction of
the market.

We probably arrive back in the city in the
nick of time. A telex is awaiting us, which the
first officer passes to the Skipper with an arched
eyebrow.

"We are to leave the Maritsa airfield at 6
pm: destination Beirut. An hour to pack and get
ourselves to the airport!" I am becoming accustomed to the life of aircrew. Beirut is fascinating, cosmopolitan and sophisticated. It is just
one of the many European and middle-eastern
stop overs that are often combined with our
Mediterranean flights. *Beirut such a wonderful
city in the 1960s, destined to endure so many catas-
trophes in the coming decades.*

Crete

We stay one night and mid-afternoon we are
back at Beirut airport to pick up twenty passengers to transport to Crete, not even a full plane
load, which generally holds thirty-three passengers. It's a very short flight.

As I pack up the bar box making sure it is
locked ready for landing, check the galley is tidy
I go up to the cockpit to confirm with the captain that everything safely stowed. "Make sure
that your passengers are correctly fastened in
with their seat belts and have no loose parcels,"

he says. "This is still a grass airstrip in Heraklion, best not to take chances in case we skid!"

If I look amazed, he just laughs! I realise that nothing is going to surprise me anymore. As the plane isn't full, I take a seat at the back sitting next to the window. This is where I like to sit, although we are always supposed to use the windowless galley jump seat. I am learning sneakily that if I put something on this seat before the passengers embark it often remains unoccupied. Indeed, it is a grass airstrip and no sooner have we landed than we bring the plane to a standstill against a security fence after a very short taxi. Before I stand up to open the door, I can see a vast amount of people their faces pressed against the fencing. But as I open the cabin door, I know they are all clapping! And as soon as the door is open and swung back, I can hear the cheers and the clapping. It seems that the town has turned out to welcome us.

Tango Victor: one of the fleet of Tradair's Vickers Vikings. We were very proud of the fact two of the Vikings were ex Queen's flight aircraft.

We are due to leave from Crete with nearly a full complement of holidaymakers. Once they are boarded, I shut and lock the cabin door and count them, as they struggle with their seat belts and settle themselves into their new environment, to ascertain their number matches the manifest and walk up the fuselage to the cockpit to tell the captain that our end is ready for him to taxi out, which we duly do.

I strap myself into my galley seat opposite the aircraft door when suddenly there is a sound of banging on the door, not a polite knock but horrendous racket. What am I to do? Can they hear the cacophony on the flight deck? This is not the time to hesitate I tell myself; it must be urgent. Shall I open the door? I unbuckle my seatbelt and hurry up to the cockpit, all the passengers looking alarmed. As fast as I can report my concern, the first officer leaves his seat and hurries back down to the door. I follow. As he unlocks and opens it, with no time wasted, a huge black-bearded Cretan in long brown Cretan boots with his full white breeches tucked into the boots and a rough spun black waistcoat over his none too clean white shirt, leaps into the aircraft.

Terrified I stand back as he rushes forward claiming one of the two empty seats at the rear left of the aircraft. "Athinai! Athinai," he shouts and from under his voluminous clothing he pulls a knife. He is making bird flapping signs with his arms. "Rhodos, Rhodos, Athinai!"

I step back as the first officer shuts the door and calmly makes his way back to the cockpit and then the plane is moving. The man smiles and suddenly looks content.

I sit back on my galley seat afraid and unsure what to do. But then the plane stops, after what seems a long time the Captain now rushes down the cabin looking as fierce and authoritative as he can and stops by the intruder.

"Open the door," he shouts to me. Shaking and fumbling I comply. There the airport policeman and three burly assistants push some steps in place and hurry up into the plane.

"Come on Yianni," says one of them in Greek.

In English he says to us, "this is his favourite pastime!" He puts his finger to his head, indicating a person who may be a little wanting in common sense.

"Once he was taken on an aircraft to visit a cousin in Athens. Now, whenever he can, he stands at the perimeter fencing, just watching the planes. But twice he has managed to get through the fence with the passengers, hoping to board. This is the first time he has dared to try to get someone to open the aircraft door before take-off!"

"He was damn lucky the propellers didn't slice his head off," remarks the Captain. And to me he said, "we all need to learn from this. In America, there is a new word called 'hi-jacking'. It is becoming commonplace when terrorists and other non-desirables want to exercise their power, they simply have to compromise the crew of an aircraft to get them to fly them anywhere they will be welcome. We all know one bullet through the skin of the aircraft and we will be sunk."

In later years, we will return to Greece's southern islands, particularly the Dodecanese and Crete for other trips, business and family holidays. These gave us plenty of time to absorb its magnificent history, and that of Rhodes was particularly visible. We can appreciate that in 408BC Rhodians created their new capital, and much later the imposing Castle of Knights, the ancients in the name of progress shunning the older citadels of Lindos, Ialyssos and Kamerios, left as crumbling sites for us to wonder over.

We would have time to enjoy the wildlife, the partridge, badgers, hares and the flowers, broom, myrtle and euphorbia, and so much oleander and hibiscus reinforcing the appellation: The Island of Roses.

Lindos which will become so hugely popular, often a sophisticated destination, holiday home of Pink Floyd, will never recreate the freshness of that first awesome visit.

My travels as part of an aircrew will also bring me many times to Athens, Crete, and many other parts of the Mediterranean beyond Cyprus to Damascus, the Pyramids and Valley of the Kings in Egypt, as well as Jerusalem, Jordan and the Dead Sea, but when I marry I find my heart has taken root in Greece.

As well as my first visit to Rhodes there are other islands in the Dodecanese group that provide off the beaten track excursions to wonderful unusual and isolated beaches. Of these Astipalea has to take pride of place, but Symi, Patmos and Leros and Karpathos are worth more than a line or two, and so indeed this will happen.

We make a rule that if we can approach a new island by sea on a ferry we will do so, and so often our journeys start in Athens. Athens, for us always a town of some personal adventure, whether it is Greece winning the UEFA European Cup and attending the closing ceremony of the Olympic Games – all in the same year, 2004 ...

I nearly forgot, of the many visits we made as aircrew in the early 1960s there is one which should be recorded! Staying at the beautiful Hotel Acropole Palace opposite the National Museum of Athens a particularly fidgety captain announces we should check out of the hotel forthwith. His reason: "he did not like the chandelier in the lobby!"

What I think Skipper Frank meant is that he and the first officer on a lunchtime excursion whilst the rest of the crew delighted in the museum's displays had been chatting up some sea-faring folk. So, with his crew loaded into two taxis and the cab drivers instructed to drive to Tourkolimano we are on the move! Once in the delightful little port the Skipper walks purposefully towards a small swanky yacht and is warmly greeted by a seaman. "This, I am told by this good fellow here, is the yacht that Elizabeth Taylor sailed the Greek Seas!"

"I expect he tells all his customers that," says someone quietly! Even so with all of us safely aboard we did sail over the ink dark sea through the night and arrived in a lovely little harbour at breakfast time. I have since not been quite sure where the island was, but I do remember that we were asked if we wanted to visit the very famous temple over the hill, which says to me now that it was probably Aegina.

CHAPTER 2

Corfu

August 1965

O ur Honeymoon is spent in southern Corfu, and in August!! Here we expand on the trend established on my first trip to a Greek island, the early trip to Lindos on Rhodes because from the first few days on that idyllic island of Corfu we have the urge to explore off the beaten track on dirt roads, to cross over the mountainous hinterlands, to discover Palaiokastritsa hidden in its perfectly formed bay lapped by blue seas and find its other beautiful embryonic pristine bays, to eat a perfectly cooked lobster by the sea and then to drive up to the monastery, and then to Bellavista for its sunset.

To travel as far north as we can in 1965 where the police checkpoint stops us travelling further (since we have no authorised residents' pass), but before we are halted to enjoy the fabulous beauty of the coastal road to Nisaki under the forbidding gaze of Mount Pandokrator.

Talk to anyone today and they seem to have no knowledge of the no-go area we encountered in 1965, north of Nissaki, the internet too has not been forthcoming, but two books: The Corfu Incident, by Eric Leggett and The Eagle Spreads His Claws: a History of the Corfu Channel Dispute and of Albania's Relations With the West, 1945-1965 by Leslie Gardiner, suggest that a mine sweeping incident in the Corfu-Albanian channel near Sagiada, in 1946, a year after the end of World War 2, set off two mines, the first of which killed over thirty British sailors of a Royal Navy 4 ship flotilla and caused a stand-off given that very little would calm the Albanian dictator Enver Hoxha's nerves, that would last for over twenty years...

Link relating to the Albanian confrontation: https://www.historynet.com/cold-war-corfu.htm

In 1956 as a student of Chemistry A-level at Huddersfield Technical College I sat next to Skender Zogu, first cousin of Leka Zogu, Crown Prince of Albania, later 'King of the Albanians' his life spent mostly in exile.

We will flirt with the Albanian border

throughout our trips to Northern Greece. So perhaps this is the place to develop these Albanian flirtations, but we never achieve an ambition to cross that border.

The AITO - the Association of Independent Tour Operators' - day trip to Albania, to which eventually we were admitted as members, gives us our biggest opportunity to actually extend our waltz with the Albanian frontier with a planned visit on a day trip along with some of our colleagues. But at the last-minute, we fail to take the excursion to Sagiada, north of Igoumenitsa, although on a later date we do drive up to the frontier here, of course, and have a nosey. So, we miss the opportunity to leave the drab almost empty harbour village and be escorted by road with vetted Albanian guides to even more drab and impoverished villages, hosted to simple food and attempt to return.

Nothing such as a smooth return journey is easy in 1996. And hey-presto the next we know is the failure of the excursion to come back to Corfu in time for the AITO Conference's annual dinner and after much consternation, the relief felt when they finally arrive travel-worn and grubby, several thousand drachmae lighter, having paid their ransom monies.

We are glad that we had taken the advice of our chairman and not ventured into this beautiful, wild, impoverished and unruly country on an illogical pursuit of a new tourist destination. Those that did, were ahead of their time. But we are also *relieved when our colleagues make a safe return because we had volunteered to look after the elderly husband of one of the adventurers who had not wanted his spouse to make this excursion anyway.*

It is a lesson in human care: how to calm someone who is fearing the very worst.

The trip to Lakes Prespa and beyond to Vrondero, in the far north of Greece, many years later, is even scarier. And we put ourselves directly in harm's way. As if Psarades on Lake Prespa and Pili on Lake Mikro Prespa are not remote enough we have to press on to Vrondero! The way the shepherds and farmers look at us should have said enough; cautioning us not to press on to the border post on a truly remote road: three obviously tourist persons in a hire car are bound to attract attention in 1994.

We can't turn the car around fast enough as we catch sight of the heavily guarded border post and if a hire car has a tail, firmly tucked underneath its wheels, ours did and we beat a hasty retreat. We are clearly not like many of the pick-up trucks we have seen, perhaps armed with Kalashnikovs about to roar through the checkpoint with gallons of smuggled petrol on board!

More lessons learned. And how near is the border at Kakavia Bridge near Konitsa? Seeing refugees tramping along the main road from Konitsa to Ioannina, shoeless, doesn't whet our curiosity enough to challenge us to go to see. Nor is it to be our only encounter with shoeless refugees.

Borders for Greece have always been very

powerful: Fyrom (Northern Macedonia,) for Bulgaria, Alexandroupoli for near journeys to what Greek maps can still call Constantinople, the islands of Lesbos, Chios, and Samos for Kusadasi, Kos for Bodrum, Symi and Rhodes for Marmaris, and Kastellorizo for Kas, and then Cyprus...

Our divergence here so early into our story is to illustrate the spirit of exploration that has dominated our travels, and whilst we never got closer to Bulgaria than Sidirokastro near Serres, (a large and prosperous town with several good hotels where late one night we were failing to find a vacant room), or the memorable occasion when coming out of Thessaloniki at rush hour a young voice from the back of our car urgently announces "Dad, Athens left, Bulgaria right' just as we are to about enter the inescapable right-hand filter on the roundabout!

We flirt with all these proximities. It adds to the mystique, the romance, the inescapable fact that Greece is Byzantine and European, and when she chooses, Middle Eastern. In our travels undoubtedly, we will return to Macedonian and Northern Greece.

Pelekas & Corfu Town

But now it is August 1965 and there is a brutal intensity to the heat. We are restless and a small map of the island picked up in the bookshop introduces us to a vast network of narrow unpaved roads that could take intrepid travellers over forested mountains, on cliffs above seascapes or simply to the sophistication of Corfu Town.

One late afternoon we leave the luxury of our reed thatched honeymoon bungalows at the Miramare Beach Hotel at Moraitika in, of all things, a tiny Fiat 500 Miramarette, an underpowered roofless two-seater. Due west of Corfu Town, the road rises up off the plain to reach the attractive village of Pelekas where colour-washed houses cluster around the narrow winding streets which climb up towards the Kaiser's Throne.

We are here to watch the sunset and gaze down at the enticing almost inaccessible beaches of Pelekas and Myrtiotissa below and almost as spectacular the view to the east over the island to the Citadel of Kerkyra (Corfu). Beyond this, the mountains of Epirus don't hold back on their allure.

But first, in the centre of the village teetering over the steep cliff which drops down to the sea, thick with vegetation, there is a high wall. In the centre, a stone arch, its grey-white stone blocks rising to an apex with the keystone boasting a beautifully carved crest framing the opening in the wall with a gate through which we can see a very old fine pink mansion with pale green shutters and beyond this bottle green painted wrought iron gate there is a doorway with a matching arch. We peer through the iron bars taking in the age of the house, is it Venetian? To the side, there is a lush and overgrown garden and glimpses of the seaway below.

On the gate, there is a For Sale sign in Greek and in English, which of course is why we are taking such an interest! We write down the name of the agency.

Unable to wipe the vision of the pink mansion from our thoughts the next day we are in Corfu town, but the beauty of the town, the elegance of the arcaded Liston and the confusing number of streets, not to mention the heat undermines our mission and we succumb to a refreshing tsintsin birra (ginger beer made to a special Corfiot recipe) in one of the famous cafes.

The early nineteenth-century Liston, comprising of two rows of buildings along the Esplanade, and apparently named for the list of wealthy and notable families allowed to walk in the shade beneath its arches, was inspired by the Rue de Rivoli. Across the large green, doubling as the cricket pitch, the horse-drawn cabs known as Victorias, the horses' heads shaded by wide

43

sunhats with a ribbon of colourful flowers, advertise for trade with a pleasing tinkle of a bell.

However, we need to attend in the afternoon to watch a cricket match, and then only when British or Maltese cricket teams are in town, but a rehearsal for a band concert in the bandstand enlivens the atmosphere. Beyond the huge open space of the Esplanade the imposing Royal Palace with its classic Regency architecture stands in front of the Venetian fortress.

The one of us with the deepest pockets is unable to contain their curiosity and has been behind the Liston to locate a telephone booth. Now back there is news, the owners of the pink mansion want £2000 for the house and grounds. The grounds extend, probably a thousand feet, down to the coast!

We are to keep the image of this amazing property in our thoughts for the rest of our life. £2000 in those times would purchase a very nice small house in which to raise a family in England. But even if we had convinced ourselves it was a wise buy, we would have had our parents to persuade – that was the case in those days – that to buy and relocate to Corfu, less than a week into our marriage would be a sensible decision. And this decision notwithstanding that I had just sold my own small business before we got married, again that was the case in those days!

Additionally, had we bought at this time, it

is more than likely that a few years later during the Colonels' Junta rule, that our property being foreign-owned would have been confiscated and appropriated by the regime.

The waiter not unusually called Spiro, at the Aegli Restaurant where we take a lunch of bourdetto (traditional Corfiot fish stew) who spoke English asks us if we have paid our respects to the local saint – Saint Spiridon.

To many islanders he is more important than God although strictly speaking he is not a local and is said to have been born in Cyprus. I have to say that we are very impressed by the beautifully engraved silver casket, the very large silver icons behind and the profusion of silver lamps strung above. With the sweet smell of incense encouraging us we light a candle, taking our cue from the old folk queuing up in front of us. The first of many candles we will light in over fifty-five years of travel to Greece.

Agios Gordios

Two quiet days on the beach and we are ready to be on the road again. The roads in the south-west of this beautiful island where even the cypress trees are ingraining themselves into our souls, look easier, on the map, to explore.

We don't count on the roads being even steeper, narrower and rougher than the roads in the centre. Keeping the sun to our left and a westering feel to the sky we come to a col where behind us we can see Kerkyra city and in front of us in the west we are looking down to a perfect long pale beach, way below. It is stunning; and although the road down looks precipitous, we are fired up.

A small wooden sign, points west, with the words: Agios Gordios. A headland to the left gently slopes down to the sea from the heights of the mountain, complete with an almost perfect conical islet. Only a few dwellings seem to inhabit this nirvana. The shoreline isn't perfect, white waves roll in with some irregularity.

We stop the Miramarette and pull out long-sleeved shirts and hats, it is hot, and we are burning in the open car, but it takes some time to negotiate our way down to the foot of the hill. I notice a small praying mantis, which my spouse who is knowledgeable about these things says it is called a St. George's Horse. The beautiful tiny green slender creature with its thin lengthy legs and small triangular head is captivating.

"How do you know that?" I ask.

"I read about it, it could have been in a Gerald Durrell book," he answers.

"That's the one!" The Durrell books, particularly Lawrence's are one of the pegs that our engagement was founded upon.

The track is steep, and very rough but it brings us down to the middle of the beach. We can see no one else on the beach but there must be farmers in the fields, this is a large farming area. We park the car and walk onto the beach, two hundred yards further on partly hidden in the long vegetation is a small hut, set out to attract attention with a couple of tables and some chairs.

As we approach, we are obviously not going to be allowed to walk past unnoticed!

"Kalimera, Yassas!" We respond with a nod and a weak wave, as the hesitant British do.

"Avga!" The voice booms from an old chap, almost bent double and tottering towards us. "Kotopoulou?" The voice tries again. And the old fellow starts to beckon us forward.

Well, we have to eat, so we nod at each other and follow him into the tiny shack and through to the yard at the back. A dozen or so hens are running around, pecking as hens do and clearly enjoying their life. "He is asking us if we would like chicken to eat."

"Well that would be very nice, there doesn't seem to be much alternative unless we drive back to the town." We acquiesce and smile which says yes.

"Banio, banio!" The old fellow points towards the sea and makes swimming movements - as best he can - with his arms. He could have easily been mimicking a flying chicken, but we assumed the bathing mime is the most likely.

We enjoy the soft waves, come back to the

shore and lay on our towels until we have dried off. When we walk back towards the hut, the table has been covered with a red checked cloth, (reassuring, he has obviously done this before) and there is a shiny red tin vessel filled with red wine, two glasses, two knives and forks. Again reassuring, we are sitting at a 'taverna' and not just enjoying the hospitality of an old farmer.

We are on honeymoon and this is about as romantic as any beachside lunch can be. We talk between ourselves, of course. We talk about the house that we saw for sale in Pelekas, but we don't reach a conclusion, just married, fancy-free, why not move to live in Greece?

We finish one jug of wine and another had appeared before two plates of golden steaming chicken and chips have been placed before us. As young people, whose childhood memories go back to WW2 the aroma from this wonderful plate of food takes us straight back to those days soon after the war when chicken was a rare treat. It is safe to say the tasty memories of this meal have remained with us with throughout our life.

We pay the few drachmas our host will accept, but he is not finished! Grabbing me by the hand he leads us both towards the hut, putting his hands together lifted under his cheek he mimes sleep, "Siesta! Siesta?"

One glance at the ramshackle bed and its dirty blankets and as quickly and as politely as we can, we back off, expressing as many thanks as our lack of language allows us to do.

Moraitika

We are on honeymoon and the protective spirit is at large, from the taverna owner at Moraitika to where we have walked for supper who insists on lending us a torch to walk back to our cottage in the grounds of our hotel, protection against the beautiful dark night skies free of all light pollution. An arm around his new spouse we amble home towards bed but guess what? He, who is always polite and correct, insists on taking back the torch to the kindly taverna owner, leaving his new wife alone.

One hour later, and a couple of Greek brandies better off, the same taverna owner delivers the other half back to the bungalow on the back of his scooter! Is this a good way to start married life?

Palaiokastritsa & Sgombou

Another evening after a trip to Palaiokastritsa, try learning that when you are new to the Greek language, we stopped at La Lucciola Inn at Sgombou, on the road between Corfu Town and Palaiokastritsa. We noticed its sign as we drove past in the morning.

Crazily the half lobster we enjoyed at lunchtime in the beautiful bay of Palaiokastritsa in the under-named Tourist Pavilion with its stunningly beautiful location on the beach had not completely satisfied us or perhaps we are drawn to the equally intriguing small restaurant in the centre of the island.

The cockerel we order for our light supper is outstanding, phenomenal in the words of our guidebook which recommended it, not a hint of overcooking and beautifully deep with the glistening pink of the flesh that falls off the bone. With it came dolmades, vine leaves coating moist and tasty elongations of rice, and a perfectly dressed tomato and onion salad. As we dine under the vine-covered trellis there is the hypnotic hoot of a scops owl and as the early evening turns to dusk the sound of the buckling tymbals of the cicada still clattering, the only accompaniment needed to our romantic evening.

What will be our memories of this day in the years to come? Always the perfect semicircle of St. Spiridon's Bay at Palaiokastritsa, the monastery dazzling in the pitiless sun, its shady courtyard and the Corfiot bell tower standing guard over the soft pink tiles of the courtyard and the sentinel green trees, cypress, olive trees, against the sea-cliff path around the monastery. The soft white flesh of the lobster, sweet and juicy, and then after lunch the final dip in the azure blue sea, the water as clear as a grotto with small fish swimming beneath us. We recognise it is a perfect experience.

The drive across the island is magnificent, shaded in many places, it is not tarmacadamed until it reaches the Tsavros crossroads and we are aware of this as our little 500 cc open-topped Miramarette just trundles along at less than twenty miles an hour, pulling into a parking space in Corfu Town, more for a rest from the concentration needed for driving than the need for an evening coffee; we have still some way to go before we will reach our honeymoon lodgings!

Years later with our children, we are to return to Corfu to spend seven family holidays at various locations in Corfu in this area.

Ipsos, Kavos, Nissaki & Lucciola

The coming of children curtails our travels until the youngest is two years old. Then for the next seven years we return again and again to Corfu and through the seventies we can marvel at the quiet beaches and beauty of this island. We stay mostly in Ipsos either at the old Mega Hotel or in traditional villas on the road to Aghios Markos, behind The Pig & Whistle.

We can walk to this tiny restaurant where Andreas will ring a huge goat bell as each new customer comes in or leaves. Famously on one occasion, we compliment him on a particularly tasty lobster and cunningly this seems to give him licence to misinterpret what we have said and to bring us a second lobster. These are not tiny lobsters; we quickly become over-faced but cats beneath our feet save us losing face.

We are not aware that our first visit, as a family, coincides with Greek Easter, and nor are we even aware initially that the Orthodox Easter is usually a different date to the Protestant Easter. Red painted eggs are given to us, wherever we stop to eat, and the children quickly latch onto to the game of knocking one pointed end of an egg against your opponents' red hard-boiled egg until those with an uncracked egg is declared the winner. Kyria Koula is our saviour. Every morning she comes to preside over Michael's House, a traditional and very old stone house with wooden floors and a wrought-iron balcony entwined with wisteria, built over a working olive press. She may not have any English words but lacks none in Greek and her enthusiasm leaves us in no doubt of her meaning! She loves the children, our four years old daughter with her golden hair, our two years old son with his curls, are both quickly ingrained in her heart. The children's widowed great-aunt, our much-loved Aunty Mary, brought along to enjoy our company but also to babysit occasionally immediately bonds with the gentle beauty of Kyria Koula, they are of an age.

Not sure that the children's mother will

have enough cooking skills Kyria Koula prepares meals for the evening, artichoke hearts gently poached with broad beans in water and lashings of olive oil.

Most 'villas' come with maid-service; we have inherited an institution. Not only Mrs. Koula but her son who runs the olive press and the rest of her extended family become an integral part of our family. He has a little English and understanding that we live in England his immediate question is "how many cows, you have?"

Given that we live on a small farm in Yorkshire, the question doesn't faze the children. "Ten", says our daughter.

That number seems to satisfy him but there is a look of disappointment - as if for a farmer in England this is not a high number!

There is one morning towards the end of our stay when the press is set in motion. A great big stone wheel with an arm running through the centre of the stone turns around a trough as baskets of olives are thrown in and then the mash of the pressed olives is taken and put between dark stained mats and steaming hot water poured over as the mats are squeezed harder and harder.

One of our excursions takes us south to Kavos and to the still relatively unspoilt hinterland behind Messonghi and Lefkimi. Another brings us to the beautiful southwest coast around Maltas and Aghios Georgios, where beautiful Greek women with huge hats ride astride their donkeys.

We come to Kavos when George's taverna serves lobster, (there is no shortage at this time, nor are they prohibitively expensive) and the beach is a great swathe of pristine golden sand. There are few or sometimes no other beach-combers at all, and yes, I am talking about Kavos: but in the late 1960s and early 1970s.

About fifteen years later, we are to return. Amazingly George remembered us. Sadly, he said he would give his soul to return to those early days of his taverna. He and his wife hate what Kavos had become.

The paved tarred roads go as far south as the Achillion Palace and Benitses on the east coast, but only a few kilometres outside Corfu Town in the opposite direction.

Elsewhere on the northern and western by-ways and in the south, the roads revert to shale and sand. When the army leaves the northern protected area and the threat of the Chinese or Albanians invading recedes, not completely but enough for the two sides simply to glare at each other, another world explodes on our senses. A high cliff road, with beaches that can be approached slowly down even rougher tracks to hamlets or small taverna on the seaside, runs up the north-east coast from Ipsos, one of Europe's most attractive coastlines.

As the children grow older, we meet more

families who return to the Ipsos area year after year. We travel with grannies or other families and it feels like home. The narrow beach, the quiet road running behind, the shallow seas for swimming and the few small hotels behind are perfect for family holidays.

Our youngest, an inveterate thumb sucker is amazingly 'cured' at a stroke by Marcus-of-the-hat whose smooth persuasion stops this habit, where years of parental disapproval had failed.

One early May, Michael Wegg, whose 'house' we had rejected in brochure perusing process, in favour of an alluring house situated right on the rocky coast at the stunningly picturesque Nissaki, cowering under the huge peak of Mt. Pandokrator, comes to our rescue when unexpectedly we meet him in the bar of the Mega Hotel.

The seaside house is not just damp, it is wringing wet and simply not fit for family habitation so early in the season.

Michael Wegg is a tour operator who spends his summers in the same locations to where he takes his clients, and although we have not booked the Nissaki house through his company, he simply steps in and offers us a brand-new villa, for free – because it is empty and because he knows we will have no chance of recovering the monies paid for the damp villa.

We will always be grateful and always remember him and his huge sense of fun. The children will always remember the wonderful 'posy' of pressed wildflowers they left under the doormat at the Nissaki house in our hurried flit.

Corfu: Top: Village for an evening stroll. Centre: Michael Wegg and Costa demonstrate the art of Greek dancing. Bottom: Sidari beach with its amazing rock formations.

Yet it is the proximity of the sea and the atmospheric ambiance of The Pig & Whistle restaurant just up the road, and the magic of the evening walk to the restaurant encircled by the fireflies which the children call 'flylights'. It is what makes the Hotel Mega always the winner for perfect holidays with children and most years we end up there, yards from the sea, evening meals if required, all booked through Michael. It was Michael, of course, who named the hostelry The Pig & Whistle on Garnaby Street, not Carnaby! He was continually teasing Andreas, the owner, who of course gave as good as he got!

Costas the waiter with his nightly chant of "Cherries, Crème Caramel" always reduces the children to giggles at pudding time. Corfu has always been a place to indulge in luxury accommodation; small villas and houses set in olive groves on the north-east coast between Nissaki and Aghios Stephanos which are still basking in the glory of providing the film set for the TV serial "My Family and Other Animals." (this was first filmed in 1987, so history does repeat itself).

One of our favourite excursions during these family holidays is to the White House at Kalami which is a taverna where we enjoy tasty Greek dishes and imagine it as the house where Lawrence Durrell lived when he was writing on Corfu. Inland grand old mansions have turned into excellent holiday homes or perhaps more special in the 1960s *through to the 90s, the Lucciola Inn (now called the Lucciola Garden restaurant)* and since the early 1980s the nearby country estate of Casa Lucia, combine the welcome of a traditional country inn for comfort and food with superbly maintained country cottages in a large tended garden around a lovely swimming pool.

We find this magical location of Casa Lucia, centred on an old olive press which transforms the individual and architecturally beautiful cottages into a small estate. We learn that the young son of the establishment may be chosen to handle the animals as a stand-in for the child Gerald Durrell in the first filming of the book 'My Family and other Animals' because as he is a natural when it comes to actually holding the animals.

We owe a lot to Dennis and Val Androutsopoulos who throw a cocktail party and introduce us to many people including the British Consul, the vivacious Pippa Hughes, on Corfu.

CHAPTER 3

*Athens, Spetses and the
other Saronic islands*

April 1978

S everal more family orientated holidays
are not going to provide the thrills and
spills that will enliven a memoir, well not
the sort of thrills and spills that are worth re-
cording, so I will mostly spare our family's
blushes and relate these with a little less detail.
After the Corfu holidays over the mid-nineteen-
seventies, in 1978 early April, we fly to Athens
confident our nine and eleven years olds will
cope with a sea transfer to Spetses.

To be honest we had originally booked to
go to Andros but with the casual nonchalance of
tour operators at this time, days before our departure, we had been rung up to be told: "Andros
is shut, we have booked you into a good hotel in
Spetses. This island is open, you will like it very
much." …. Perhaps the casual way this information is relayed should have alerted us. There is

none of the professionalism of Michael's operation in this opening gambit.

None of us expect that it would also be difficult to reach Spetses and when we are met at the airport and taken to a hotel near Omonia Square in Athens, to be picked up next morning, we are confident that this will come to pass. We are tired and the Athenian hotel has a rather seedy air, but yay, it is only for one night but when our daughter drops her beautiful new camera into the toilet bowl, as it falls from her jeans pocket, it is not the best start.

We go out to eat and are not greatly impressed with this area of Athens and as soon as we can go back to the hotel retrieving a pack of cards from our case. Those in the family who are adult are suddenly aware this hotel is something far from a family hotel as the constant stream of soldiers trumping up the stairs to the bedrooms testifies.

John picks us up as promised around 7 am and our taxi heads to the Piraeus for the ferry to the Saronic islands. My Greek is not good, in fact, it is almost non-existent, but I can tell, from a news bulletin on the taxi's radio, that something is amiss.

I question John and wonder why he calls himself the English name, John.

"Yes," he admits, "the ferries are on strike. We can go down to the port and wait to see if it is fixed, or if you wish we can take you back to the hotel."

"No. Not that hotel, we must stay some-where more suitable for a family. We want to stay in the Plaka." I am so glad that I had stayed so many years ago in Athens and can be determined in our argument.

"We always use this hotel!" counteracts John.

"Then we will pay our own bill, but it must be a decent modest hotel." John, who also seems to answer to Yanni when addressed by the taxi driver, speaks to the driver, who takes us to the little Nireus Hotel in the Plaka, beautifully central and promises to keep in touch.

The hotel is perfect, and it is in an ideal location, allowing us to wander around the Plaka and take the children up the Acropolis to see the Parthenon.

The sun is shining and our youngest walks straight into a dustbin as we walk up a side street to the Acropolis! Cuts, snivels but fortunately we have a plaster in our hand-luggage, and we have to wonder if there is a hot-line to the gods in this country. We clamber up the steep ascent to the entrance to the Acropolis, filled with wonder at the achievements of Greeks, with none of the building equipment of today.

The ferry boat to Spetses is scheduled via Poros and Hydra. It is a new experience for us and the large bustling port of the Piraeus, even though the taxi takes us straight to the boat, is quite intimidating.

Struggling up the narrow steps with our luggage requires all our agility. An elegant lady speaking English takes our daughter's small bag and we begin to chat. She lives on Hydra; she says she was a secretary for Prime Minister MacMillan.

As each port of the Saronic islands is reached she points out the high points of each island.

"There is an ancient temple on Aegina, the sulphur springs on volcanic Methana are so smelly you will need to hold your nose the whole time while we dock," she tells the kids.

Poros is so close to the mainland that you feel you can touch both sides of the straits, but Hydra is wonderful. "Why not abandon your trip to Spetses?" she asks, "and stay here on Hydra?"

I ask her where are the beaches on Hydra and learning that there are none, I politely tell her for the children's sake we will continue with our itinerary. With hindsight, it turns out she may have been right. But we were not to know.

As the boat slows and pulls into the harbour of the mountainous island of Hydra, we can see what she meant about the beauty of Hydra. Mansions and stone-built houses climb up from the waterfront. Donkeys and their owners line up waiting to carry the luggage up the hillside. "Come and see me while you are on Spetses," says our new friend. "Just call at the kiosk over there, and they will ring me. I will come down and show you the island."

We are met in Spetses by a colourful character who is determined that we shall eat before we are taken to our hotel. He is fully aware that we are travelling as journalists, although it is a family holiday.

There are no motor vehicles on Spetses, and our luggage is to be taken to the hotel, we know not in what direction! Sadly, one of the colourful horse-drawn carriages is not employed for this task and we walk along to the Dapia, with its beautiful pebbled pavements, to a restaurant directly opposite the ferry jetty.

Our fixer accompanies us straddled across his idling motor scooter, allowed on Spetses, which when we arrive at the taverna he parks inside the restaurant.

It's early April, but as a family we might prefer to eat outside in the warm spring sunshine. But no, we are being looked after and with such a feast and wine as is presented to us, it is true we are being cared for in the tradition of philoxenia – friend of strangers. The cynical journalist among us is aware this royal treatment is because we are journalists.

The spring night has fallen as we are finally taken to our hotel. The children, and indeed we, are tired. But we are assured we are to be looked after for the duration of our holiday! Excepting... By breakfast the next morning we are demanding a full re-clean of our rooms or a move to another hotel!

Somehow the fact that we are here to write up our stay on Spetses as a glowing account of our family holiday seems to have escaped our 'hosts'. However, because we are assured that the maids will come avrio (tomorrow) and sweep up the dust from under the beds and in the bottoms of the wardrobes, in compensation we are taken up the hill to dine in style.

Best not mention how we get there, or how we are expected to get back! Two scooters, four adults and two children are a tall order.

Also, probably best to gloss over the number of toasts the adults make, including the superfluous ones to the pepper pot and the salt pot! But to be on the safe side as a family we walk back down to the port which puzzles our hosts.

We go to bed happy in the knowledge that even if the cleanliness of the hotel leaves something to be desired, they are trying to 'look after' us.

Even on Spetses Greeks do not walk if they can find some wheels to transport them. The only cars on the island allowed are those which are driven off the ferry straight to the owners' homes and there parked until such owners drive back on to the ferry and back to other roads of Greece. We are amused however to learn that Rupert, part of the duo of our hosts-cum-fixers, has driven his mustard coloured MG Roadster all the way from England to the island, just so he can parade it as he drives off the ferry and to his humble lodgings where he will spend the summer!

With our holiday on Spetses shortened to ten rather than fourteen days, because of the strike as we arrive, there will be plenty to do although the beaches are small.

We walk over the island, to Aghia Anagyri where there is a wonderful empty beach and wonder at the cavernous Bekiri's cave only accessible by crawling or swimming into the opening and then slowly allowing our eyes to adjust to the dim light coming only from this narrow low sea entrance. At the back is a large stalactite slowly dripping to form a bowl in the rock below. It is all rather special. The children make primitive shallow pots, moulding the silver speckled mud from the cave, and let them dry to harden.

In the elegant town with no shortage of beautiful neoclassical mansions, we are intrigued to see the house where Laskarina Bouboulina lived during the Greek War of Independence in the early nineteenth century. We imagine that from here she directed her not inconsiderable efforts to help defeat the Ottomans after 400 years of occupation. Killed in an argument, she never lived to appreciate the contribution of her four self-funded warships and her powerful naval skills made to the eventual victory by the Greeks.

Every morning we protest, with growing irritation, that the maids have yet to arrive although by this time we have taken a brush and cloth to clear some of the dust from our rooms. We realise that the delaying tactics on our first two days had been an inexpert attempt to divert our attention from a hotel that has not been opened up since it was closed for the winter season. Clearly, it is not just Andros which is still closed!

By the time the maids arrive, we have made ourselves at home. Our room and the lobby being the only rooms in the hotel where any attempt has been made to spring clean; and in our bedrooms only by the judicious purchase of a brush and pan in the supermarket!

Later, on our return to the UK, we had to write to the young entrepreneur who had offered us the trip, to say that in all conscience we did not think we could write an article that would do justice to the fledgling holiday company that we had travelled with and provided us with the accommodation for our holiday.

Many years later still, when our own travel business Greco-file began to collaborate with the tour operator Laskarina Holidays we heard that the hotel was no longer trading and had fallen into disrepair, eventually to be demolished. But the flamboy-

ant entrepreneur had 'gone-on' to become one of the big boys of the travel industry! Likewise, the young 'fixer' on Spetses also made something of a name for himself with his exploits as agent and hotelier on the island.

This book has taken many months, if not years to write. To begin we had to rely on our memories, but into the 1980s and beyond, there were countless diaries, notebooks, and brochure copy when we were running the companies Filoxenia and Greco-file/Abakos Worldwide.

There were videos, so deteriorated they are unwatchable, photographs too numerous to look through, because there are endless hotel rooms and uninteresting scenes taken to show to our staff in the travel businesses.

There are guidebooks relating to eras we enjoyed.

What we hadn't appreciated when I finished the first draft and we began editing that we would be working in a world we did not anticipate. As oldies we were concerned when we celebrated Simon's eightieth birthday in March 2020 with a visit to the Lake District, driving around Cumbria, delighting in the emerging spring scenery in Crummock Water, Buttermere (where we had to dodge a hailstorm on our walk down to the Lake). We lunched in The Bridge Inn in the delightful village recently made famous by Lord Bragg's true tale of The Maid of Buttermere. We drove over Honister Pass and up to

Watendlath, all in the pouring rain. We returned to our exceptionally comfortable lodgings at the Ravenstone Manor Hotel on Bassenthwaite and although the next day saw us travelling home via Great and Little Langdale, commemorating our engagement 55 years previously in an Easter hail storm on the Langdale Pikes we had little idea what a change in all our lives was about to occur.

Of course, something was alerting us to the Coronavirus problems ahead, every public place had a sign advising us to keep our distance and wash our hands thoroughly, but we were still only mildly alarmed although evening news alerted us to the fact that Cumbria had several cases, eight at this time, but rather more than most places. The news was just getting worse and there is a worry about President Trump's reaction with what appears to be instant statements to the disease which by 13 March 2020 was being recognised as extremely serious in the UK.

CHAPTER 4

*Nafplio, the Argolida
& Arcadia including
Tiryns, Epidavros, Tolo,
Porto Heli, Tyros, Livadi
& Plaka Leonidio*

July 1979

T he thunder of Zeus rolls in across the plain of Argos. We have just explored the ancient red and grey limestone citadel of Tiryns with its surprising galleries, but we must make haste back to Nafplio, while the curator of Tiryns waters his garden from buckets of cooling rain.

Today the mountains are the crowning glory, they are all around: first, our trip to Mycenae, awe-inspiring in its perfect construction and Clytemnestra's tomb, horrible in its history, lies in an oasis of sweet scents, great trees, oleander and tobacco plants. A climax of expectation. Each to kill each other: Agamemnon his daughter, Clytemnestra her husband and then Orestes his mother.

I have just embarked on a course within my studies with the Open University that embraces Classical and Ancient Greece in its history and its culture, I hope that my enthusiasm carries through to my family. The mainland of Greece is nothing like the islands!

Charming Nafplio, confusing to the new-comer, lies beneath its two castle crowned es-carpments, the Acro-Corinth and the Palamidi whilst the third castle on the tiny island Bourtzi watches all. The thunder has not been in vain, it is raining, plants are watered in plastic buckets under brown coloured modern awnings. There are grapes on the vines, and cars parked in glis-tening wet squares and we, in our hire car, are confused mostly by trying to find the right road to exit the town.

We experience the panic that driving rain and enraged crazy Greek drivers promote in hap-less foreign drivers. We promised ourselves we will come back another day when the sun re-turned but today, we will feel more comfortable in Tolo.

Tolo, Epidavros & Nafplio

We take our two children to the ancient theatre at Epidavros. The friendly owner of the Hotel Minoa in Tolo, Yannis, has been insistent that we will enjoy the performance and we leave clutching our picnic basket, wine, drinks for the kids and bread, cheese, tomatoes for sustenance. Sadly, nowadays picnics are no longer de rigueur, indeed probably forbidden.

The bus departs from the car park near the Hotel Minoa at seven. At Epidavros, the air is perfumed by the pine trees, and the huge stones silenced by its history and magnificence.

We find our places, settle on a tier of stone seats and eat our picnic. As dusk falls and the sun sets the amphitheatre fills up. Finally, late arriving Athenians are hissed by the audience as they access the front row reserved seats and as darkness falls the play finally begins.

The dialogue is entirely in Greek, towards the end of Euripides' play my ten years old son suddenly gasps with understanding and speaks softly: "Mummy, Mummy, look she's found her son, he's her son after all."

The entire audience up to this point has remained completely silent, but at this point, they have all murmured along with us. Greeks and foreigners alike, all fourteen-thousands of them for the theatre is nearly full, have silently followed every action, every nuance of the grisly story of the orphan Ion.

Although children under ten are not allowed, officially that is, in the great amphitheatre during a performance there is one other exception to the silence. At the point when a doll in a cradle is displayed from the stage a real baby cries, high in the gods.

Laughter and tears also punctuated this marvellous experience and one which we will remember forever. On the way back the coach stops at one of the many tavernas in Ligourio serving lamb on the spit.

We hire a car for a few days. Our drives on this trip are spectacular, released from the confines of the islands, the Peloponnese offered endless scope, north, south and west of the Argolida. Possibly the longest day for the children, but the most exciting is our trip around the Argolida peninsular itself, the thumb of the Peloponnese, when our route takes us up the slopes of Mt Didymo.

High mountains are crowned with juniper, tobacco fields, blue July flowers and groves of oranges, lemons, figs and maize in the fields below. In vegetable plots, there are tomato, courgette, cucumber plants and vines. A light haze over the mountains takes the heat out of the air; small farming villages clustered very occasionally in the plains or on the hillsides. Everywhere is pink oleander with touches of red and white and thus we come without much warning to the market town of Kranidi where when we come against a steep stepped street it seems too Greek to trespass.

A beautiful real place where apparently the Greek senate tried to put down roots in 1823, and which they did succeed in doing subsequently in Nafplio.

We are happy with our choice of a taverna in the square beside the great natural harbour which acts as the port of Porto Heli.

A local priest looking exactly like Peter Ustinov is seriously celebrating his saint's day! The octopus, fresh shrimps and swordfish steak are delicious. It is the sustenance we need for our continuing trip. It is clear from the map that we can consider the route back via Kosta, where we can look with fond memories to the island of Spetses, almost yards rather than miles across the water, and then towards Porto Hydra.

Once we are well on towards Porto Hydra the rough road deteriorates and we are driving literally along the beach, we know we are too far on to turn back and we plough on to Galatas and finally, we are on our way back via Epidavros. Many miles further we are tired when, again, with a flash of map inspiration, we cut off a corner to head down to the coast at Vivari.

A beautiful country road, a very narrow rough track off the mountain through a couple of hamlets, and yes, it brings us down to the coast, again the way being literally along the beach with the sea lapping the sand. There is no alternative, we are tired, the children are fractious but with light fading we take the last few miles, hugely relieved to see the conical mountain of Agia Paraskevi, backing the lagoon of Vivari, and finally, we seem to have arrived back to civilisation; and then the closing distance to Tolo and the welcoming Hotel Minoa.

"You look tired," says Yannis from behind the reception desk. "Where have you been?" "Epidavros and Porto Heli," I say not wanting to admit that we have driven such a huge distance, but adding, "and we found a short cut back, off the mountains, through Vivari!"

"Perhaps shorter, but not necessarily easier to drive, you had to come along the beach at Candia!" All knowing he replies.

"We took the car for a paddle!" say Oliver and Heidi simultaneously.

We spend many days lapping up the unique position of our hotel on the sand, no more than fifteen feet from the shallow seas, swimming to Romvi island, directly opposite, some of us taking the coward's way out by accompanying the serious swimmers on a pedalo, and even climbing up to the col on the island.

But it is hot and shade and long siestas are often on the programme.

Having mastered Nafplio traffic we decide

one evening to make a visit to this elegant old town and that, before we watch the sunset over the Bourtzi island castle, we will climb the 999 steps up to the top of the almost inaccessible Venetian Palamidi fort.

Indeed, it is thought at its completion that it would be impregnable, yet due to a traitor, the plans of the layout are leaked, and it falls to the Turks, three years after completion in 1715.

Many of the steps are in the shade, others covered in tunnels through the fortifications and slowly we make it to the summit and the impressive walls, buildings and turrets. Glad to be at the top we are somewhat piqued to find a large forecourt in front of the main gate and a taxi rank, with taxis!

The children, who would have preferred to have stayed at the beach with friends they have made, are less than enthusiastic to take a tour around this eighteenth-century architectural marvel, but if you want for happy contented children, high season school holidays are not the best time to travel, and it is far too hot for English skins to stay on the beach all day and the problem of keeping everyone occupied is intensified by the heat.

Future high-season holidays may involve beaches with high rocks which can be jumped off into the deep sea below to cool instantly, or drinking pint glasses of Robinson's Lime Juice Cordial (how did this arrive from Greek suppliers in the quantities needed to be consumed by Brits in Lindos), or choosing a shady taverna, misguidedly ordering a large seabream which the hornets at Pefkos devour before we could. But like every parent we are faced with the stark truth that holidays in May and June would be a better alternative but not a possibility and it is a choice, cope with the baking heat, the high prices and crowds in July and August or forego our Mediterranean trips. This is a possible reason why long car journeys, which kept us all out of the sun although not completely cool, in the days before air-conditioning, with all the car windows open, becomes a favoured pastime.

Arcadia

Memorable is the trip from Tolo south down the eastern coast of Arcadia as far as Plaka Leonidio. Our only map combined with our guide is our 1967 First Edition Blue Guide.

The road looks reasonable as far as Paralia Astros, which appears to be almost directly opposite Tolo and Romvi island on the eastern coast of the Argolis Gulf. We find as we leave Nafplio, with some discussion yet again as to how to find the road out of town, that it is hardly possible for a road to be nearer the sea. It is a hot day and local people are standing waist-deep in the sea, not swimming, simply standing. The views as we traverse the horse-shoe shape of the gulf are wonderful, right across the gulf back towards the town of Nafplio with its three great castle rocks, the immense Palamidi, the older fort of AcroNafplia and in the sea, the chunky Bourtzi islet with the Venetian fifteenth-century Castel Pasqualigo covering its entirety.

Only recently the Bourtzi was serving as a luxury hotel but in the nineteenth-century, and in utter contrast, it was the residence of the executioners.

A tiny Palamidi gaol, situated on the highest rock within the huge majestic fort, looming over the town, was where Kolokotronis, once the hero of the Greek War of Independence was imprisoned when his fortunes changed.

The massive bulk of the AcroNafplia as the second mountain within the town is only slightly less impressive in height but its length covers the width of the present town.

The shadow of the ancient citadel with its two castles, one Frankish, one so-called Greek is behind us as we turn right out of the town. In front are the mountains of Arkadia. Beautiful blue, green, grey mountains and completely menacing.

At Mili, after a small sign indicating the ancient site of Lerna, just before the paved road heads into the high hills for Tripolis we bear left, keeping to the coast. This is where the adventure begins as the road narrows, high steep-sided cliffs to the right, drops to the sea on the left. We make a mental note of the apparent superior status of the road on our right, winding upwards towards Tripolis, the capital city of Arcadia, (in Greek usually spelt Arkadia), a historic centre in the Peloponnese, which we have rejected as a destination.

From the town of Nafplio, we have been following the coast as far as Paralia Astros and curiously then turns to a larger town slightly inland named simply Astros before continuing our journey south, just away from the coast. Coming down into Paralia Astros we note an impressive castle on a headland overlooking the sea to our left, and we drive down to a small harbour settlement but find the road almost immediately veers to the right and inland towards a town which looks bigger, the road deteriorating to the left, into a narrow dirt road with marshy looking land and plenty of birdlife across a great plain.

The highest mountain of the area looms to our right, almost flat-topped it is impressive as we cross a wide dry riverbed and we pass by another village pressed against a hillside.

We are silenced by the grandeur as travelling slightly inland and upwards we come to a sudden col and below is a sight to take our breath away. Below us is a vast and surprising seascape, mountains across the sea from us and islands in the distance. Excitedly we realise we are facing Spetses where we holidayed the year before. As we travel along the road with more precipitous drops on the left and a high rocky cliff on the right, we come right down to the coast, with tiny beachside settlements until a larger village seems interesting.

Years later chance will allow us to stay longer in this area.

We drop down to the seaside, a magnificent large silver pebbled beach runs alongside the road through Tyros and its harbour with three windmills on a headland at the end where the road climbs up the cliff. No sooner back on the high road, where olive trees, myrtle, acacia, and pines change the landscape than we realise that we should have taken advantage of one of the small seaside tavernas in Paralia Tyros but time is pressing, the road not improving although there are signs to Leonidio and we find a tiny fisherman's taverna in Livadi, right on the sea, but not much of a beach with rocky boulders, rather than the inviting sea-kissed pebbles of Tyros.

The owner is washing out the wine barrels in the sea and he reluctantly stops this to come to ask what we want! The choice of food is limited but we choose some small fishes and enjoy what we are given with a generous plate of Greek salad dressed with a very tasty olive oil.

Because the narrow road is still signed to Leonidio and the Blue Guide is intriguing we perhaps don't engage our common sense and turn back to Tolo, but carry on driving up a narrow coastal road, old windmills on our left and a precipitous drop to the sea below. We pass old ladies – and men - dressed in black riding on donkeys. Our guide is ten years out of date, and it infers Leonidio, the chief town of Kynouria is best served by sea, with outlying and mountain villages reached only by mule. It says wolves roam in the game reserve on the mountains. As we are within a few miles, it is just too tempting not to visit.

Local people stare as we drive on, the windmills on a high edge above us to the right, huge pink coloured cliffs towering above us and finally we enter the stone-built town, gardens behind high walls entered by big closed wooden doors in arches. It is impressive architecture, but we are intimidated as our tiny hire car travels through the narrow streets; the children are frightened. After a couple of small squares, there is a road to the left taking us out of the town centre, which we take, ignoring the road ahead signed Sparta and the stares of the locals silently watching us.

We cross yet another wide dry riverbed and the road swings left back down to the sea, motoring along another sandy dirt road, through fruit fields, never leaving the mountains on our right. And then the sea with a most attractive small port, a tiny taverna with a low tile roof hanging over the deep blue-purple painted walls. A small inviting beach and we have to swim. It is then that we notice the great dark black clouds gathering over the mountains up beyond the riverbed.

The sun has been hot and beating down on us all day, and we are alarmed. Dressing quickly, we look at our inadequate map of the area, in the Blue Guide. The road towards Sparta, which is paved in the town centre is shown as positively on the map as the road that led us here and goes by a place named Kosmas and joins a wide main road to Tripolis which we know is a good road back to Nafplio.

We are quickly disabused of this.

Driving back into the town we find Leonidio consists of even narrower streets beyond the second square, shop windows are filled with dresses, suits, even wedding dresses, furniture, greengrocers with fruit and vegetables beautifully displayed under awnings. It is clear the town is thriving. Strange how images such as these stay with one over the years. Probably because our senses are so heightened.

Nobody stops us. Outside the town, the black clouds look even more ominous and we realise we are heading straight into the storm. We turn around on the narrow road which is rapidly gaining height and heading deep into the mountain gorge and we drive back through the glare of the townsfolk. The way back should have been one of the most scenic drives we have ever undertaken but we are only too aware that we are not racing ahead of the storm.

As we leave Leonidio and drive along the coast we can see the sea below where the waves are beginning to churn, fishing boats are making for the safety of a small harbour that we can see below, with a few small houses in a natural bowl, so outstanding in its photogenic pose. We had failed to notice tiny Sambatiki on the outward journey because we are driving on the other side of the road. Now we are overwhelmed by its beauty in its almost circular bay. But we hurry on... well, with the narrow dirt roads and the steep drops now to our right so very close we simply make our way as steadily as we can. Eventually, we reach the metalled roads of Astros, although with the potholes it is still no place for driving quickly. The first heavy drops of rain begin and increase and gather pace and intensity. This is like tropical rain, like a monsoon. By the time we meet the Tripolis road the tarmac is awash with water, we turn right and cross the railway line at Mili and start along the coast following an old worn sign to Nafplio.

Cars in front of us are hesitating, some turning round, but a few carry on. We carry on, in driving rain with a howling gale, the road now running along the seashore and realising that it is not just the rain which is causing the water along the road to rise in depth but the encroaching waves of the sea. It feels a long way, no views across the Gulf now just the wall of the grey a storm creates in the near distance, an awareness that the storm is driving even more of the sea itself across the road.

We can see four cars ahead of us, ploughing on and we follow. We reach a small town, the lights are on and we see it extends inland, but we can also see that at this point we are away at last from the coast and we know Nafplio is in the distance; we carry on as the rain, the lightning and thunder intensify.

We can scarcely make out the road in front of us but there is no hesitation when we come into the small city, our bearings home in and we head for the bulk of the Palamidi to turn left towards Tolo; urgency now as we drive past the army camp and then we see one of the Eucalyptus trees lining the road is halfway across the road. We just squeeze through, there is an enormous crash behind us, and we see through the rear-view mirrors that another whole tree has come down. The road is now completely blocked, and we are the last car to get through.

Amazingly the children are asleep in the back of the car. We say nothing and stay silent until we get to Tolo. *Not surprisingly when we come to run our travel company years later, and we are planning fly-drives, we recommend if our clients encounter storms, if they can, they stay put until it is over.*

When we get back to the Minoa, have parked the car and walked down to the hotel in the heavy rain, we are greeted by Yannis, the hotel owner. There are no lights on in the hotel, the town has been in complete darkness, but we have been too spooked to notice.

"Don't tell me! You've been on one of your long drives, but glad you are back safely," says Yannis and without waiting for an answer, "it's terrible, all the family's orange groves have been devastated by the hailstorms, next year's crop has been wiped out."

Hailstorms in August, we can hardly believe what we have driven through! We try to say we had driven as far Leonidio, but his thoughts are clearly on keeping his clients safe, on running his hotel and his own family's troubles and it is clear he has little understanding of how far we have travelled.

We begin to appreciate how miraculous it is that we have returned intact. The hotel, with no electricity, has somehow prepared a cold meal and it is welcome. We had wondered during our long drive if the Greek sweet cakes and Glyka (spoon jam) we had been given by the taverna owner, Michaelis and his daughter Margaret at the taverna in Plaka, near Leonidio before we left this tiny harbour would be all we would eat before we retired for the night.

The next day the sun comes out, it is as though the storm had never happened.

The world washed clean of the heat and dust. And then Michael arrives, Michael Wegg who had so kindly given us the use of a villa in Corfu during that disastrous holiday in 1974, rescuing us from the very damp villa in Nissaki, where we had left the pressed flowers which the children had gathered when we moved in a hurry. We can't believe that he is here in Tolo, but then we learn that as a tour operator he is using the Hotel Minoa for his clients – and then the party begins! We are beginning to get some understanding of how good travel businessmen operate.

The Hotel Minoa, Tolo

PART 2

*THYME FOR THE HEAVENLY
SCENT OF GREECE*

CHAPTER 5

The Winter Press Trip:
Athens, Rhodes, Crete
& Kamena Vourla.

November 1979

We arrive in Greece on the last day in November, the day that those named Andreas will be celebrating their name day: in the space of the six days we are here, six saints will have their name days. In England as we left on a mild day at the very end of November the English countryside is still marvellously beautiful.

Here in Greece, again as we walk through the aircraft door, down onto the tarmac and walk across to the arrivals hall I am aware of the scent of the herbs drifting down from Mt. Hymettus. The beautiful smell of thyme.

Strange thought though as we clear customs at Athens: from here, one can walk, if of course, one wants to do so, to India, China, Siberia or Northern Norway without ever being impeded by the need to cross the sea.

On Rhodes, our next airport of call - or from Crete for that matter – that would not be possible.

1 December: Curiously, to me, modern Athens can be construed as 'square'! I don't remember this from my first visit – nearly twenty years ago – but now we are becoming frequent visitors, and this is my fourth visit, three of them in so many years so I feel qualified to express an opinion, except I don't, not out loud.

So now there are white cube buildings, some are much larger than I remember, glass square windows, ladders, pylons and building sites. Winter Athens is a shock, a light blue sky but such a dusty place and such a contrast to beautiful exclusive Vouliagmeni where we had stayed last night. Or to put it more frankly, a superb setting for a rather inferior luxury hotel with an air of oppression.

We are an incongruent group of travel journalists, here to experience the excellence of a Greek holiday tour operator, a fast-growing company run by a flamboyant and savvy Northern Greek businessman, with a good business reputation and the fine quality of two of Greece's most prestigious hotel groups.

The road to the Piraeus is now lined with trees dug in, in a hurry, for the EEC summit meeting. Every moment of this trip is clearly going to be taken at speed and we have hardly had time to absorb the atmosphere we have been brought all this way to encounter.

The highlight no doubt is the Archaeological Museum which is fantastic. It is inspirational on the part of the organisers to include this in the itinerary. It is also fortunate there is a good lunch provided by the hotel on Singrou Avenue because waiting for a delayed flight to Rhodes with sixteen fractious, tired, and somewhat mellow passengers is not a task to be relished by our hosts. All of us are now becoming personalities and already rather regretting the pace of this trip.

Mandraki Harbour, Rhodes welcomes us, lined with the beautiful yachts of its cosmopolitan visitors but we are in little mood for sightseeing and appreciate the quick vista before we are whisked off to our hotel.

We learn that Rhodes, from the impromptu talk by our hosts while we wait for our delayed flight, is to be promoted for winter holidays: quiet and unspoilt Rhodes, winter-time Rhodes welcomes visitors and six thousand Japanese couples for a second wedding, who believe that by getting married on the island of Apollo they will be assured of happiness. Indeed, we are shown inside a beautiful church where there are women in veils and white dresses, just for this occasion.

Lindos is the obvious secret that has been lined up for us. The beautiful Greek village with its stunning horseshoe bay is obviously offered to us to captivate our hearts, as indeed it did on my first visit in 1960. Here in Lindos, under the might of the marvellous pink-tinged Acropolis where only a glimmer of winter sun can bring out fantastic light against the little white cube houses, with their mosaic pebble steps, this is that very special Greek ingredient which is so important to preserve.

This is history in a nutshell with ruins dating back to ancient times, the Dorian ages, 900-600 BC to the Classical period, and then the Byzantine era to the Knights of St. John and it is hard not to be humbled. We come away believing the Lindian Acropolis is unique, having been occupied from the time of the Myceneans and Minoans to the little Doric Temple of Athena Lindia dating from 300 BC, which is particularly evocative. But bringing us into the present economy, an impromptu visit to an orange grove is also memorable.

Again, we are blessed to eat a small meze, outside at the taverna, Mavrikos, which had so impressed me on that first visit, Greek salad, dolmades and Keftedakia, such a treat on a December lunchtime. Our coach takes us back to Rhodes Town, countryside drifting by, the rocky outcrops on the route can vary between the Corfiot type landscape and that which is so typically Aegean. The Aleppo pines seemingly with a bright green look to them is because, we gather, this is the time of year they put on growth. It is easy to be relaxed, and this island has the ability to brings its visitors back.

The fantastic lunch that started with the Mezes overlooking Lindos Bay is followed by a superb meal at the Xenia Hotel – which from the outside looks like a barracks, "Modernist" hisses a fellow traveller when I raised an eyebrow at the architecture, "they will tell us that we are here to understand the huge effort the Greek Government is making to boost tourism in Greece. We are here at the beginning of something big, mark my words!"

He is right, inside the hotel is very traditional, offering marvellous hospitality and food. Rhodes is full of hibiscus and bougainvillaea, the streets still reflecting the same sort of warmth one would expect on an English summer's day. We are strolling to the City of Knights, bringing back memories of my very first trip to Rhodes but for us as a herded group being given a flavour of the place and when the street with the shops has boarded up premises due to the siesta, of course, some of us are sorry.

We are not here on holiday, we remind ourselves, but tomorrow morning early, we will be back at the airport for a flight to Athens and there won't be other chances for shopping!

Back in Athens, our visit to the Acropolis is wholly successful except for the lack of sun! To see it again now, given that I am currently studying a course on ancient Greece with the Open University is wonderful, although I am reprimanded for imparting information to my fellow travellers as I am not a licenced guide! But the fact that five remaining Caryatids have been removed, in addition to the one Lord Elgin removed, now in the British Museum, is shattering. I have never approved of Lord Elgin's plunder.

I ask the guide when the five would be back to be told that they were removed this year and taken to the Acropolis Museum. "We will replace them with casts," she says. I look ruefully at the Parthenon, noting that a rope now prevents us from stepping inside its hallowed temple. Again, is this just for today, or is the shape of things to come?

"Four years ago, we started on restoration work," says another guide, "but what has been done only covers a fraction of what needs to be done. We have been told it could take thirty-forty years before it is finished."

We look out at the city, sprawling beneath us, at the sea beyond, the mountains with their coverage of thyme-scented vegetation. It might be overcast but few people are encroaching on our enjoyment of this ancient masterpiece.

"Wait until you see the views from the restaurant where we will have lunch," says Constantine. "Then you'll be really amazed."

The powers that be are concerned that we might be hungry, and we are whisked from the foot of the Acropolis by a smart mini-bus to the foot of another taller outcrop, Lycabettus. Here a funicular smoothly transports us three hundred feet up the sheer-sided limestone rock to a smart restaurant. Again, we can only rue the lack of blue sky, fortunately, as writers we have good imaginations and I can only marvel at how much the experience of the tourist has been improved in the last twenty years.

As a group, we have begun to bond, and perhaps it is tiredness, the generosity of the alcohol-fuelled banquets but there is a little rebellion as we pile onto yet another coach, this time a modern long-distance affair. At this stage, it is only muttering. Wisely most of us choose to sit alone, a notebook and guidebook on the adjacent seat.

It has started to rain and the road to Kamena Vourla starts badly through the vast ungainly suburbs of Athens; where once large expensive villas graced the land now new modern buildings vie for attention.

We cannot help but think back to the elegance of the buildings on the Acropolis and wonder if humankind ever improves upon its situation, Elizabethan, Renaissance, Georgian periods aside, there always seems to be the need to follow a period of outstanding architecture with one of utilitarianism.

Then suddenly all is changed and beyond Marathon, there are plains, mountains, woods and quite beautiful trees with soft sandy edges to the woods. Flocks of sheep can be seen herded in from the dells and scrubland. Add a few buildings, and signs of mountain dwellings loom through the winter gloom as the night descends. It is now raining hard, battering against the windows of the bus and it is like travelling in the English Lake District.

Another hour goes by, someone says "Thermopylae, can we stop?'

But it is pouring down and a mutinous voice says, "Stop at your peril, let's just get there!" It's Gavin speaking, large, affable and caring Gavin is beginning to crack in a tone which says: ignore me at your peril.

Constantine shrugs and sits down again near the driver and we don't stop, taking it that we are unanimous in our desire to get to this unheard-of place where we are heading. The coach drives on through the dark on the arterial road, I won't give it the benefit of motorway status.

The next morning, the view from the window of the mountain behind the hotel is quite unlike anything I had expected. A steep sided high-rise mountain densely-clad in almost black conifers is completely in our face. Last night we had both smelled and heard the sea, now the sun is coming out and we are also in the mountains!

Grumbling, we make it to the thermal baths by 8.00 am and really, they make us all feel good. There is a visit from the Mayor, and we take a quick look around the area and the Spa has possibilities! The colours from the contrast of forest and sea cut the winter air and the excellent food at the hotel, even the breakfast cake is so special it bucks up our spirits.

The food last night was fantastic: we started with excellent mezes, then veal, then a whole roast lamb! This morning, when they give us two boxes of mezes for the journey Constantine accepts them with effusive thanks, but we never see them again!

In many ways, it is a good trip. It is a curious psychological experience, not unexpected given the proximity we enjoy as a group but that it becomes the crux of the trip rather than our individual experience as travel professionals is probably not what has been intended. Ships that pass in the night. Just a random group of people thrown together, but we have relaxed and there is trust and much laughter.

It is a very long way for a very good meal, but it is also an introduction to a place which we would not otherwise know about. Of course, there are several meetings and talks during these travels, the NTOG, (The Greek National Tourist Organisation,) the directors of the hotels always keen to stress that Greek tourism is in its infancy, and I take copious notes.

We took on board that a new Athens airport, near Rafina, is planned and expected to be in operation in ten years – or so. A talk about Monemvasia alerts us to the possibility of investing in a Byzantine town, completely unspoilt but mostly ruined: it is just the place and the time to buy a property. Once back in Athens and on the basis that Greeks never travel on an empty stomach, we are down on the coast at Tourkolimano, (Microlimano), for another marathon affair! This is the haunt of the rich and famous, and from here in my youth twenty years ago, with the crazy pilots with whom we flew, we did hire a small yacht on which to sail - with a crew of course – into the Aegean Sea. Now I can recall that this said yacht had also been chartered by Elizabeth Taylor.

The magic of this trip rekindles the special feelings that this place generates and not difficult to do with a magnificent plate of garides (giant prawns) with tomato and charcoal-grilled sea-bass: one of the best meals so far!

Then a very rough landing into Crete, and thus we are driving to Elounda.

Elounda has great charm. It is a pretty place. One of the few places in Greece where the building of large white hotels has, if it has detracted from the natural landscape, added something else in terms of style. Most of these buildings are graceful, done very tastefully, and glistening in the sunshine, they do show the best of today's architecture. Agios Nikolaos with its sea-water lake (once it was a sweetwater lake, connected to the sea in the nineteenth-century) also comes across as a small charming place that looks as if it has a warm heart.

It is only driving west from Ag. Nik to Knossos that we realise that indeed this very eastern end of Crete is an oasis in what comes over as an otherwise fierce and fighting landscape, where survival is the first importance. In many ways, the drab development stretching along the coast road towards Heraklion is part of this survival. Modern day Crete is dependent on tourism. Our briefing tells us the fruit of the carob trees are fed to cattle and sheep and the olive trees can live for a thousand years, one at Vouves is maybe two thousand years old and perhaps older.

Knossos for me is always going to be a mixture of Dilys Powell in the Villa Ariadne and Sir Arthur Evans. It is a return visit, the first being made during a quick stopover during my flying career when it was considered interesting by the crew to see if they could fit me into a giant amphora! Fortunately, better sense prevails, and I am simply photographed standing meekly beside one!

Now we have the services of a top guide from the Cretan Archaeological Society and even aware of the artistic licence applied by Arthur Evans the restructured remains of Knossos, the tale of the Minotaur, and the legendary Theseus, are brought alive. As an eight years old child in primary school, I had been captivated by this story and now here I am able to immerse myself, completely enthralled.

Then suddenly we are homeward bound and our last meal near the airport at Vouliagmeni is out of this world, luxury sandwiches on the beach under the clear blue sky. Had we not packed, vacated our superior rooms and left them well behind in Crete we would have access to our swimsuits and surely would have gone for a swim, - 6 December: St. Nicholas Day!

We had woken to glorious sunshine in Crete, found ourselves escorted to a coach, to an aircraft and now away from that first destination of the day, Athens airport, we are on a Greek beach, enjoying the sunshine, a Greek beer and preparing – within sound but not a sight of Ellinikon Airport – to fly home. In the warmth of that sunny day we will take away the smell of the bushes, the box hedges, and the views not of a city but a seascape with the blue-grey mountains as a backdrop. It gives another meaning to 'in transit'.

We have had to confront several questions during our trip where we have been hosted with the utmost care and attention, every luxury available being at our disposal.

How do we think Greek tourism should develop? More accommodation, at what level, i.e luxury, modest or pension class?

Do we anticipate the opening up of airports in the Southern Peloponnese, such as Kalamata?

Can this possibly be justified given the inevitable damage to the unspoilt environment?

Does the same apply to other areas of Greece?

Will the EEC make a difference to tourism?

Will the regulations which worry British hoteliers and restauranteurs make the Greek hotelier as confused as they do in England?

Will the already increasing danger to the ancient ruins, particularly the popular ones, like the Acropolis and Mycenae be increased by mass tourism? In a nutshell is it possible to contain the ever-increasing tourist trade in areas where it already thrives, and should this be Greek policy?

I would like to report that it was a smooth flight home to our loved ones, but this is wintertime and there are solid clouds which pummel an elderly aircraft, sudden drops, fears, good memories relinquished, Gavin unable to maintain the bonhomie he has forced on himself all trip lets rip: the stewardess called repeatedly, repeatedly told this old aircraft is about to fall from the sky, to fix these old seats immediately, to fetch the captain. I have to admit I will be happy to land.

CHAPTER 6

Dodecanese islands

Rhodes

1980

But we do go back to Greece. And we choose to book with the holiday company who hosted my press trip the previous year, for a family holiday in Lindos, in the height of August season 1980.

Of course, we will remember most drinking pints of lime juice or better still lime juice and beer on the beach and watching the young bloods jumping and diving from the precipitous rocks into the sea below.

It is so hot with beach-combers swimming and sunbathing naked on the rocks, in this liberated hippy community. Two semi-detached apartment bungalows overlooking the small bay may be idyllic in their location but when our neighbours want to get our young family up to play charades at one in the morning it is not the holiday we have envisaged.

Yet wonderful rock music has hit town and it is romantic to wander the narrow ancient streets every evening, unaware that the music we are lapping up on the rooftop bars is to become so symbolic of our era. Boutique shops sell clothes which would be equally at home in Mykonos or Bond St London and this tiny majestic stone town has buried its fame within the walls of Mavrikos taverna, which has seen Onassis' yacht anchored in the bay below, Bridgitte Bardot and now Pink Floyd who will arguably bring even more fame to this stunningly beautiful place.

Kardamena & Kos

August 1981

Kos - the Asklepeion (top left & right and bottom right,) and the Nissiros caldera (centre right).

Doubling the number of young dependents on a holiday devoted to more than sandcastle building is not necessarily going to work. Kardamena might be a real kids' place, huge sandy beaches, a few shops and tavernas, a balcony with lapping sea directly beneath us, but it is not a pretty place.

This is an island famed for tranquillity and healing, but we need to keep a quartet of kids happy and free of headaches with no-one feeling 'off-colour' or on a different wave-length.

The Asklepeion, despite the beautiful perfumes in the pine woods, is not greeted with wild enthusiasm; a young teenager placing herself in the shade under a single tree in the centre of the site to declare "one ancient stone can look much like another", and there she stays.

There is more success with the younger boys who absorb the words of the Hippocratic oath and which we read aloud at the top of the site surrounding by the ancient monuments.

A convenient girly headache precludes us from returning to the site that evening, showered and changed for a re-enactment of the Hippocratic oath. But on the morrow, even though again a car journey is involved, a trip to Bubble Beach beyond Paradise Beach is much more successful!

In the August heat, the crystal-clear water is cooled by air bubbles rising from the sea-bed due to a volcanic phenomenon caused by the still-active volcano on the island of Nissiros. This we must see.

With Kos town, we fare better, and certainly the ancient plane tree can impress (somewhat farcically attributed to the era of Hippocrates but suitably supported by its own 'zimmer frame') and a tall minaret emphasises the proximity of old Ottoman lands.

If nothing else, we think the children may just remember this rather than endless beach-combing. Certainly, the Castle of Knights is impressive and somehow simply peaceful and un-sophisticated. A drink and toasted sandwich help reduce the growing appetites, with plants in pots hanging from the plaited bamboo and palm branches while a red and green hibiscus and purple and white geraniums frame the view out to sea.

It is with red faces we return to Kardamena with the underbelly of our Kos hire car covered in once wet but now dry tar. At the time of hiring we had persuaded the car hire firm to hire us a larger car for our large party. They had protested the only car of such size is not available, it is needed for a wedding.

On the way back from Bubble Beach we come across road workers resurfacing the road and are given no option but to drive through the wet surface, how they are going to clean the car before tomorrow's wedding we cannot imagine but surely this is something that happens frequently in Greece? Indeed, the hirers seem to take the mishap in their stride and not only that, they invite us to the wedding! We later learn, after another similar experience, that a liberal application of diesel does the trick.

We are offered honey cakes, wine, ouzo and

Metaxa brandy but we don't linger in the church; this is an occasion for the villagers.

Nissiros

The unmissable trip by caique to the almost perfectly symmetrical island of Nissiros brings us into the small harbour of Mandraki, the pier being outside the town. The tiny island, its topography dominated by its volcanic shape with the active caldera in the centre.

Less than a thousand souls inhabit the main town and three small villages, the only habitation on the island. Almost immediately we catch a small bus travelling up the volcano, past the terraced gardens and up to the edge of the crater and we disembark.

We can smell the sulphur and a white and yellow land beckons us as we start to descend cautiously. We have been warned the surface near the lowest part will be hot and the crater is larger than expected. It is also more exciting than we have anticipated. We are humbled by this unique access to this geological phenomenon, other volcanoes being far too dangerous to approach so closely. The pale volcanic rock is peppered with white and yellow crystals. Fumaroles, holes into the deep earth, bubble and hiss with hydrogen sulphide and the water under the surface is boiling, and Simon debates about trying to get some rock and mineral samples for his collection back home.

It is with some curious relief that the rest

of us are pleased to climb back to the rim and the bus to take us back down the hill. We stop at the small almost deserted village of Emborio, emptied of its larger population earlier in the century. One of the white cubist houses with its blue painted woodwork has opened its doors as a small bar where we have a drink and buy some dried herbs. We are still on the edge, in every way, slightly unnerved by the experience in the crater.

Lunch at the Three Brothers, chosen reluctantly, but of necessity, we wanted a typical village taverna, but hungry children decide the venue for us. The food is surprisingly good. Then we walk the short distance into the narrow quaint and clean streets of Mandraki village, the capital of Nissiros. The road in twists and turns with houses made of volcanic rock, smothered in plants. Here there is a wealth of white cubist architecture and pebble cobbled streets, Tiffany blue doors and shutters; it immediately makes up for the plain Jane feel to Kardamena.

The caique ride back to Kardamena takes us in front of the curious island of Gyali, one half pure white pumice, the other half obsidian lava domes, we can see white beaches, shallow seas but as we pass and turn north for Kardamena the swell gets up and it becomes rough, far, far too rough. Those sitting near the bow get soaked time after time, as the waves begin to break over the boat. The kids have another idea, rather than seek shelter they decide to get really wet moving right onto the bow, relishing it for the great adventure it is.

Back at our accommodation there is an electricity cut, no warm water for a shower.

CHAPTER 7

Karpathos & Symi

July 1982

We fly to Rhodes at the end of June, this is to be a two-island holiday, our young son accompanying us. It is a shock to the system to land at Rhodes airport and be transported to the port to await the Ferryboat Elli at midnight. It is a long wait in the waiting room, a cheese sandwich with a long drink hardly breaks the boredom. We are coming and going, in and out of the room with its dark brown leatherette chairs and filthy windows, looking out for the huge ferry boat, that may shake us from our cross-European jet-lag, but it shows no signs of arrival.

When the ferry eventually arrives, we immediately pick up our pieces of luggage and scramble along with all the others from the port-side café to the boat where the ship's bowels are about to open and disgorge its contents on to dry land.

As its massive ramp opens port handlers roughly push everyone to one side. Holding our son's hand, I find we are separated from his father. We gasp as the first huge lorry edges out onto the ramp, gathers some speed and eases onto the quay. Noise and exhaust make us gasp, most people stand firm but some like ourselves show alarm, my hand is grasped harder by the child.

Then another very large lorry spews forth, perhaps two or three more I think, but no, there are six more, and more and then endless vans and cars.

Finally, our son is reunited with his Dad and together we all climb up on deck. It is now 2 am and the ferry is two hours behind schedule; we had left Manchester airport at 8 am and it is safe to say we are all tired. Finding seats inside on the main deck we settle down to forego the Greek night air and perhaps sleep a little in the reclining chairs. Romantic and exciting as it is, it is nonetheless an experience that perhaps we would have been better to have scheduled differently.

A long hoot of the ship's siren and we are coming into port, the first of our three stops before we will disembark. Halki has been woken, in the dead of night, into some sort of life. The minute little port is scarcely discernible, but the bell tower of the church looms out of the black night and the excitement of this lifeline bringing weekly supplies does not go unnoticed on the quay although perhaps a lesser proportion of the population of 400 souls are there to help unload. Hanging over the ship's rail we can spot one man and his mule.

With little fuss, we are on our way and at daybreak, we are steaming in under the lee of the mountains of northern Karpathos off the coast at Diafani. Behaving like its own island this barren ancient land is totally reliant on sea transport. The shallow harbour does not allow the larger ships to dock and despite the large quantity of goods to be unloaded and uploaded, the residents of Olympos and Diafani are reliant on Manolis and his flat-bottomed boat to chug out to the ferry with all manner of chattels, load them onto the ship and reload with a new scooter, a new bedroom suite, all the food required, Coca Cola, beer, soap and chug it back into port.

We are tired, but it is fascinating to watch this Greek 'Pickfords' at work. Most Karpathians and the few tourists don't disembark here, and we all go on to Pighadia the main port and town.

We are booked into the modest Hotel Romantica by a small tour operator specialising in the Dodecanese islands. We are greeted at breakfast time, with a care for our comfort deserving of a family who had travelled through the night to stay with them.

Andreas who has brought us up from F/B

Elli in his taxi persuades us to take a trip around the island in two days' time. In the meantime, we can walk the short distance of about a kilometre into the little town of Pighadia, pass the day with coffee at one of the waterfront cafes, lunch in one of the tavernas or swim from the long sandy beach.

We intend to hire a car but are strongly advised to use Andreas' offer to explore the north of the island, back up into the mountain village of Olympos. Our hosts at the hotel tell us we should not miss this opportunity, "the village is famed for its industrious villagers who still bake bread in communal ovens, wearing traditional dress and worn out of choice by the inhabitants and not for tourist audiences."

Even so, we are not prepared for the beauty and isolation of Northern Karpathos.

"Here we do," says Andreas, as we set off on the long road journey, perhaps he meant to say go, "passing all the oliver trees,"

We laugh, Oliver is our son's name. We try to put him right, but he will have none of it! It is a slow journey taking nearly four hours, beginning through the groves of olive trees, the fields and orchards and then the forests. It is a rough, precipitous and very rutted road through the northern barren mountains, but it is worth it when we arrive.

Suddenly after miles without any sign of

habitation, there is a small immensely colourful town nestled into the grey barren mountainside. Squared mainly white houses, many decorated in pastel shades, seem to jostle for space. Behind them prominently built along the ridge is a line of working windmills, sails turning in the wind, and the wind is a feature of this town.

We know we are destined to come again. There is simply no time to dilly-dally for after the long journey there we have to remember also the fifty kilometre return journey.

We accept we will be unable to spend time to absorb the beauty and unique atmosphere of this vibrant ancient community. But the taster has been magnificent and the wonderful goat stew at a traditional taverna provides a lunch that we would certainly like to repeat. We take away images of the colourful black or white costumes, black aprons and kerchiefs embroidered with a profusion of red flowers, green leaves on black dresses and white or black kerchiefs on their heads. We gather this isolated place high in the mountains above the sea has been occupied for centuries but only recently with the rough twisting road we have travelled has it opened up to more visitors.

Sadly, Andreas does not have enough command of the English language to act as a guide and equally our knowledge of Greek is even more lacking. However, we do learn that if we wish to see the women making bread in the impressive outdoor ovens then we must come on a Saturday. Andreas seems to be poking fun at the locals: "Pah! These people, I no understand. They not speak Greek." We realise he is referring to their unique accent. Later, we were to learn that much of their speech is derived from the ancient Doric language which has been preserved from ancient times. But it is time to move on, although it is reluctantly.

Symi harbour

Symi is Greece's quint-
essential island!

With no airport, the visitor has to arrive by sea,
most usually from Rhodes where the two-hour
boat trip brings you within touching distance
of the Turkish coast, or so it seems. Once the
ship turns into the inlet and coasts into the deep
narrow bay any Turkish influence ceases. That's
not to say there are no Turkish stimuli and
smuggling especially – they say off the island of
Nimos at the dead of night – is not unusual. Few
of the ship's passengers are waiting patiently –
or impatiently - in the stern, ready to descend to
the bowels of the ship to rush off onto the quay,
the usual methodology for disembarking from a
Greek ferry. No, here almost all the passengers
are gathered at the prow of the boat, cameras at
the ready and on this beautiful sunny day, few
will be disappointed.

The villages of Symi are interconnected, a
town rising from the seaport of Yialos and clam-
bering up the cliffside, unabashed by the huge
number of steps, worn and ancient and often un-
even, to the Chorio.

In truth, you need to be young and nimble
here and on the Kali Strata (the four-hundred
steps) always to be negotiated when travelling
between the two, you are almost certain to meet
those you met two or three days ago, like ants

making their endless pilgrimages, but perhaps now travelling in the opposite direction. And talking of ants, what telepathy has warned them of the newly blue-painted crazy paving and forbidden them to cross from stone to stone.

Yialos is where most of the action is and because this is our second visit in two years we are remembered, welcomed by the taverna owners, at the Trawler, from Vassili and later from Stamatis! Then there is time to say hello at the Bakery, to browse in the wine shop and notice how green the green vegetables are at the greengrocer. The Pharmakion still has wonderful wooden glass-fronted shelves full of beautiful ceramic stoppered jars decorated with flowers with enamel ladles in the cupboards. On the great wooden counter, polished by age, jars of paste and powders for mixing with small amounts of medical spices and herbs.

Chances are in the evening you will be slowly making your way up to George's taverna, and if you are under twelve years old you could be rewarded with a free ice-cream for asking for it in perfect Greek; while adults will be treated to some of the best food and wine on the island. Our newly made friends, Lyn and Dominic almost certainly will have arrived before we do, for after swish cocktails on the rooftop bar of their hotel Aliki they will be more anxious to start on the serious business of the evening, the local krassi, 'doppia,' a pleasant enough light red wine and to have reserved one of the tables with a view down to the harbour.

For ourselves, I am more determined to finish the watercolour of the neo-classical mansions, in their sunset hues of pale pastels across from the harbour from our bedroom balcony, and to rely on Lyn and Dominic's choice of table.

Even on holiday, the most casual of plans can go awry and we arrive at George's, somewhat alerted by the sound of joyous music, each step upwards increasing its vibrancy and volume. It is clear as we approach that there is less than standing-room-only, not only inside the taverna but outside too! Excitement, colour and merriment, proclaim this is a wedding! Feeling a bit self-conscious we deduce we can only retrace our steps, back down to Yialos. But George has spotted us! He rushes across bearing Oliver's ice cream with entreaties by the villagers to join in and to drink and eat!

We never see Lynn or Dominic in the crush, but we are not to go hungry or thirsty and once again we are treated to genuine Greek hospitality – philoxenia. As the dancing becomes earnest, the bride encircled in white Greek lace, the groom in a shiny new suit we do retreat, warmed by generosity and happy to have been included in such a village occasion.

Next morning the lads are up early to swim across the bay to Nos (Nautical club of Symi). It is a long swim and the three-hundred-yard walk back is less taxying. The boys leave Dominic on the beach soaking up his suntan or perhaps trying to allay his hangover after his enthusiastic participation in the wedding. We are not to see Dominic and Lyn again, except for the once when we lend our 'after sun' suggesting that perhaps something more like Calamine lotion would be better to ease Dominic's red raw skin on his back.

Days on Symi are best soaked up by a general lack of a plan, although we don't forget to give the smiling waiter at the Paradiso the present, I had brought him from England.

However, to visit the Monastery of St. Michael Panormitis planning is probably necessary. We know we can stay the night in the simple accommodation but think better of such austerity. We board the boat trip in modest clothing that will let us into the monastery itself with its fine iconostasis, visit the museums and then allow us to soak up the atmosphere of this seaside village. The entire façade of the monastery is spread along the waterfront and we discover that its Venetian style bell tower is the highest Baroque tower in the world, let alone Greece.

The heavyweight of the silverware around the Archangel is padded up with as much bulk as an astronaut on the moon, Taxiarchis Michail's earnest face peering from his silver halo, simply emphasising his huge importance to all the Dodecanese sailors. We walk behind along the beautiful tree-lined street, with oleander, bougainvillea, carob trees, olive trees, tamarisk and eucalyptus. There is a veritable aviary with peacocks and a parrot in a cage with his friend the hen below who is just visiting! It is more impressive than we have been led to believe and we are sad when we depart; perhaps we should have foregone our sunset drinks on the Aliki roof. We arrive back after the sun has set and find that a late ferry is due to depart from the port.

An English woman accosts us as we place our feet on dry land. "I'm glad I've caught you," she says. "I am a nurse; your friends are on the ferry and I've come over from Rhodes and I'm going back with them this evening. He's not well at all, we've to get his temperature down and hospitalize him in Rhodes." So, Dominic should have heeded his wife's caution over his sunbathing.

Entrance to the beautiful garden of Mr. Angelo's Guesthouse with Pandeli fishing harbour below.

CHAPTER 8

*Greek Easter on
Leros & Patmos*

April/May 1983

Lolos Angelou has invited us to spend the Greek Easter at his guest house on Leros in the Dodecanese.

We start our stay on the tiny island of Leros in Mr. Angelou's Farmhouse, a traditional Greek guest house, a mixture of primitive comforts with aristocratic touches. The village of Lakka has been fasting for several days when we step off the ferry from Kos, indeed to hungry British tourists the Lenten Fast seems at its height and the weather late in April is not exactly summery. Finding food is something of a problem, most places are closed and shuttered, and bands of small boys roam the darkened streets staving off their hunger. The fact that all music and entertainment are forbidden turns their attention to the vicarious thrill of detonating lethal thunder flashes on street corners.

Inexplicably and perhaps foolishly we leave Leros on the Wednesday before Easter Saturday and this is partly due to the lack of hospitality available in the village of Lakka.

We are but a ferry ride from Patmos and it is easy to book tickets and travel to this island just north of Leros, well known to the Christian world, for its Easter celebrations. The Washing of the Feet ceremony at the Monastery of St. John the Divine on Patmos, on Maundy Thursday is just too tempting to miss. Mr. Angelou and his wife raise an eyebrow, which doesn't deter us when we promise we will go to Patmos and come back on Good Friday.

The Monastery of St. John the Divine, Patmos

Patmos

This is a strictly religious island, dominated by the Monastery of St. John the Divine where the monks will re-enact the ceremony of Christ washing the feet of the Disciples. It is the most important ceremony on an island famous for its celebrations and we expect that it will be the only one for us this Easter because we have been invited by the Angelou family to share their celebrations on Leros.

We make our way from the hotel to the Monastery of St. John the Divine, walking up the pilgrimage route early on the Thursday morning, halting at the Cave of the Apocalypse where John received the visions that he recorded in the Book of Revelation.

After our long walk, on paths strewn with lavender, we don't have time to appreciate the gaunt grey monastic buildings. We want to be close to the front of the crowd at the Washing of the Feet ceremony. Sitting on chairs about three rows back we have become the talking point! The women in front of us are curious that foreigners should be in their midst?

"Protestant?" they ask us. I have to think of the answer.

It seems our early morning start had been in vain, after a two-hour wait, we are all pushed back from the first three rows, as the police make way for three rows of influential locals, much to the hissing annoyance of a gaggle of devout ladies in black who had pushed and squeezed their way to the front only to have their view thwarted at the last minute by the Patmian worthies.

It must happen every year.

Even so, the music, the humble ceremony contrasting with the gold and red vestment robes of the priests, framed by arches of palm fronds, a blue and white Greek flag above, is imprinted on our memories.

Getting back to Leros in time
for the feast on Easter Day
proves quite an adventure!

On the Thursday evening, the large ferry boat pulls in along the quay in the port and turns off its engines. This is odd, we had understood that there wasn't a ferry due until Friday morning. A ferry that would go on to Leros, as usual. The crew walks off the boat.

Good Friday dawns and we go down to the port, the same ferry is parked in the same place. There are to be no boats today, or tomorrow. We have promised Mr. Angelou we will be back for the breaking of the fast on Saturday evening. We are British, we don't break promises with an old soldier who as we understand it fought with British in Kenya; no, for Mr. Angelou we had to keep our promise. If there were no ferries, we would hire a private boat.

We do just that and after an expensive and bumpy ride, in an old fishing caique, we are put down at the north end of Leros, the army camp of Partheni. This is not a village; it is a desolate encampment surrounded by a high wire netting fence. There is not a soul around, no taxi, no one to ask! We walk several hundred yards along the fencing. We are miles from anywhere, we know that. I am not far from tears when we see in the distance a public telephone.

With a hint of amusement, Mr. Angelou arranges to send a taxi.

Every region and island in Greece have a variant on the feast that breaks the Easter fast. On Alonissos for example, pies to celebrate Easter include many of the spring herbs including the young poppy plants before they flower, fennel and spring onions. These pies form the basic diet as Easter approaches, when fasting becomes stricter and stricter and even to eat eggs is considered a sacrilege. Just over the water to the south in Kalymnos, the young sponge fishermen try to prove their virility and valour by making their thunder flashes out of dynamite, often resulting in death, maiming, cratered roads and damage to property. In Crete, an effigy of Judas is burnt on a huge bonfire floated out into the centre of the lagoon in Aghios Nicholaos. A similar tradition is upheld in Tyros in the Eastern Peloponnese, while just a few kilometres down the coast in Leonidio hundreds of aerostats, (light paper lanterns) are lit and floated out over the sea towards Spetses.

Easter Saturday evening sees us in Lakki, down on the waterfront of the once proud exceptionally deep-water harbour of Leros, fiercely fought over by both sides in World War Two. The owner of the now dilapidated Hotel Leros, is reduced to a shell-shocked wreck as his arcaded terrace seems to be the focal point for incendiary and explosive experiments. But at least he is open, and we manage, guiltily, to extract from him toasted sandwiches and ice cream after an interminable lecture by this Anglophilic patriot, in excellent English, on his wartime exploits. A large portrait of Winston Churchill adorns his office walls.

Filling in time before the witching hour of midnight we go back to Angelou's farmhouse to change into our glad rags prior to the breaking of the fast. Then with topcoats on for it is chilly, we go down to the church in the village. It seems that the whole village is there and there is no space whatsoever inside the small church.

The arresting and sadly peeling Art Deco architecture of Lakki is not fashionable at this time, reminding the inhabitants of the occupation by Mussolini, but the Church of Aghios Nikolaos is particularly striking and despite needing a coat of white paint its handsome façade and dark brown doors are extraordinary for a Greek Orthodox Church. With only glimpses through a crack in the doorway of the white Bauhaus architecture the blue ceiling, the incessant chanting and the intoxicating smell of incense it is hard not to be restless but eventually, all the doors are thrown open, everyone pours out into the street, simultaneously the six bells in their ruler-straight tall white rationalist bell tower start pealing and people beg each other to share the flames to light their own candles.

It is the stroke of midnight when the Easter service of the Resurrection in churches across the island, across Greece, across the Orthodox world, reaches its climax with the Pappas calling "Christos Anesti" (Christ is risen) and the reply of the people, "Alithos Anesti" (truly he is risen). Every member of the congregation and those clustered around the doors of the packed churches had symbolised the sharing of Christ's love with the setting afire of their candles, taking light from the flame of the Priests' candles and sharing it one with another.

Then, guarding the guttering flames against the chill air, they scurry away through the town, hands cupped to keep the flame alive, so as to mark the sign of the Cross in sooty smoke on the crossbeam of their doorways, to keep away the evil of the year ahead. Time to walk back to foregather in the dining room of the guest house furnished in the English style with oak furniture and traditional table settings to match, in the Angelou family farm.

With the chill in the air, it is unsuitable to use the outdoor dining terrace which looks out over the groves of orange and lemon trees, that Angelou carefully tends each day, the scented blossom at its height in the spring season. Now, beyond the terrace in the groves of fruit trees fireworks explode in the night sky, silhouetting the ancient castle which stands on a col between Platanos and Aghia Marina.

We are a mixed bunch politically, the attractive lady editor of a Swedish newspaper, with strong liberal leanings; an American author with outspoken views about the Greek attitude to NATO and particularly American naval activity in the eastern Mediterranean, and a rather taciturn male relative of Mr. Angelou, who is a staunch supporter of the Greek socialist party, Pasok. Then there is Mr. Angelou's family, Marianna, Stavros, Lucy, Maria, Mr. Angelou himself, one of a dwindling breed of rural aristocratic Greek families whose fortunes have seen better times, yet who remains in all respects a perfect host and gentleman, and a champion of the New Democracy and the rights of Greek capitalism and the freedom of the individual. We are seated ready to break our fast with a meal as traditional to the Greeks as a Christmas feast is to the British. Eggs, hard-boiled and dyed red adorn the side plates. We crack them against our neighbours' egg. The egg that cracks first being surrendered to the owner of its tougher counterpart – a kind of ovarian conkers. There is much banter and also jollity, a light-hearted relief after the dull dark weeks of the Lenten fast. The highlight of the meal is Magiritsa soup made from the cleaned intestines of the young spring lamb, fried spring onions, dill and small pieces of liver. At the last minute, an egg and lemon sauce is added, and the hot soup is served. With the soup, Madame Angelou brings the traditional Lenten

Spanakopita, a deliciously cheesy, slightly minted, spinach pie, and Kourabiedes, the small shortbread cakes which have been made during the Easter week and sent to the village baker in huge flat shallow trays. Where there are children in the family, the cakes are specially baked in the shape of rabbits and the brightly dyed red eggs are stuck in the middle of their tummies.

For us the Easter Day feast begins early with calls of "Kalo Pascha" (happy Easter). Stavros, Mr. Angelou and Marianna set up the bed of hot charcoal and rack the Paschal lamb that has been so carefully husbanded over the past few weeks, onto the spit. Young Marianna sits turning the spit. Angelou from time to time anoints the lamb with a brush of fresh rosemary twigs dipped in olive oil and lemon juice while Stavros keeps the charcoal fanned to the correct temperature.

Meanwhile, Lucy and Maria bring out vast bowls of salads of lettuce, spring onions and dill, bottles of Retsina and the sweet Easter bread, Tsoureki made with butter, eggs sugar and little brandy, caraway seeds and decorated with almonds and a red egg in the middle. At last, the lamb is ready. Angelou stretches the feast on the carving block and with some kind of machete, swiftly dismembers it.

We fall to, tasting the sweet flavoured young lamb, sitting in the sunshine amidst the greenery and the flowers and the scents that only early season Greece can offer. It's kind of Nirvana and each year it is different.

We think back to other Easter days – on Skiathos at a huge gathering on the beach, six lambs on spits in a meadow filled with flowers; heroic dancing and singing from lunchtime to early hours of the following morning. To Kritsa in the eastern Cretan mountains and young children walking with their trays of Koulourakia through the village to the bakery. To Corfu way back in the sixties and the long religious procession winding down the hill village of Spartilia.

There will be others: all, especially those in the Peloponnese when once again we are smothered with the most magnificent examples of philoxenia and hospitality.

Footnote: By the twenty-first century, Lakki, still the main port on Leros, has had the necessary facelift: the rationalist architecture has been repainted, architectural students have sought the little town out and found it not to be the unimaginative rigid and even monotonous examples common in Mussolini's Italian conurbations but a small port offering a playful blend of appealing curves and straight lines in white with splashes of blue in paint or glass. Beautiful Marianna has taken over the 1895 family mansion in Alinda which she runs as a very special small hotel where breakfasts take on a vegetarian theme. The house was built for her grandmother and mostly used as a summer house by the Angelou family who lived in Egypt until after

WW2 when her father returned from East Africa and his guest house was established.

CHAPTER 9

Kastellorizo

1983

We sail to Kastellorizo on the good ship Panormitis. We leave Rhodes on a summer night as the sun starts to lower from its intense July heat.

Our doubts about setting off on this seriously elderly tub of a boat are not ill-founded. Yet the Panormitis and its Captain are legendary, and we have scarcely cleared the coast of Rhodes before we have confirmation that this is no ordinary trip with the jovial Captain going out of his way to meet his passengers on what will be at least a nine-hour trip. He singles out us, stopping to speak to our young son, asking if he would like to come up onto the bridge but suggests we might be more comfortable in the salon as the dusk turns to night.

We are no sooner buying coffee and Greek brandy from the snack bar and the lights go out throughout the ship except in the salon. In due course, we discover perhaps why as three Swedish blondes are being hosted to ouzo from the bottle, on the darkened bridge by the jolly Captain. And of course, why we had been gently encouraged to adjourn to the salon!

We are aware of the coast, of Turkey, dark and indistinguishable scarcely from the sea and the dark sky, for mile after nautical mile. Fortunately, it is a calm night but there is little except more cheese toasties to relieve the boredom. Eventually, we see a dark shape on our right and after what seems an interminable time, we edge into the perfect harbour of Megisti (which means the largest and given that it is only 4 miles long by 2 miles wide is something of a paradox). Megisti still the official name of the island of Kastellorizo (the red castle) and it is, in fact, the largest of the isolated archipelago just off the coast of Turkey.

This volume is being completed just as Turkey makes, yet again, ominous noises about an isolated Greek island so close to Turkey being under a Greek flag, but in late summer 2020 these are no idle threats and are being taken seriously by the watching world.

No-one is here to meet us but in the midnight gloom we can make out the neon hotel sign on the far side of the harbour directly opposite from where the ferry is moored. We are expected, this is not the place to arrive unannounced. An old man shows us up to the first floor, unlocks a door and shows us into a clean and fairly basic triple room.

Then he draws back the net curtains and opens the shutters and in front of us, on the other side of the bay is the ship we have just left, still lit and precisely framed by the lighthouse and above on top of the bluff the remains of the red castle of the Knights of St. John. The old mosque still with its minaret crowded into this magnificent view. It is worth the journey just for this romantic view from our balcony for the next five days.

Like Symi and Halki it is a handsome place, on first acquaintance, until you realise that Kastellorizo wears the frontispiece of a film set and one street back from the waterfront most of the houses are ruins. If their façade is intact, then inside is often a pile of stones, the result of WW2 bombing, earthquakes and burning.

We are shown around the island by the Australian, Mike – we are sure he said his name is – Karpouzi, Mr. Watermelon. Were we looking at these devastated ruins with yet another view to buying and restoring a classical seafront house?

"Hold your horses," says Mike, "this is our island, and if you see us Greeks swarming over it, camping out, grabbing every room that is going in July and August, you may change your mind. We might have only 200 permanent residents but another 30,000 are in Oz, the progeny of the many that emigrated from our shores. Since they rarely signal their intention to arrive, we are not always ready for this deluge every summer!" He adds, "we come back in such numbers to ensure that we are never accused of being underpopulated by the Turks, who look for every excuse imaginable to lay claim to this tiny bit of Greece!"

Here the layout is miniaturised but in keeping with other Dodecanese islands it is somewhat formulaic: a fine Crusader castle, this one sadly ruined, a Street of Knights and remains from Classical times dotted over land that is presently pretty much uninhabited. The island is still a sea-farers place, and its proximity to Kas just over the water on the Turkish mainland lends itself to smuggling.

We are walking up the steep path, off the Street of Knights, led by Mike, up to the Lycian Tomb with its rock-cut façade with Doric Columns. It is hard not to be impressed, and back to the Street of Knights, we have another treat in store with the handsome castle on its bluff atop the once classical fortress and its wonderful views across the ocean and back to the mountains of nearby Asia Minor.

The Blue Caves, known as Fokiala Cave, the 'refuge of seals', is both larger and more intense than its more famous counterpart in Capri. It feels a long way in the motorboat that chugs around the coast to the south of the island. After forty-five minutes we see the white cliffs and anxiously we wait to see if we have arrived in time to take the boat into its amazing blue interior.

It has been stressed since the moment we booked the tour that we must not delay our departure because as the sea rises in the morning, so it reduces our chances of entering the caves. We are in time!

Immediately we enter we are aware of how privileged we are to experience the intensity of the azure sea and its reflection on the walls and ceiling of the Grotto in all its many tones. The fact that there is an uncomfortable swell on the way back to the horseshoe shaped bay of Mandraki didn't spoil the excursion.

Mike finds the Churches are locked. We are not very bothered to find the modern church just back from the waterfront is inaccessible, but it is a pity to be excluded from the nearby Cathedral of Aghios Konstantinos and Aghia Eleni which is not open. Some of the Lycian granite pillars in the interior have travelled from Asia Minor from – they say – a temple of Apollo.

Everywhere we go we are very aware of our neighbours on the Turkish coast, so near but so removed from us, a strange feeling of being an outcast, a European excluded from the land of the genie with a lamp.

I decide to rest, but the boys decide to walk up the mountain to truly explore this small outcrop off the coast of Turkey. They report back rather sooner than I expected, once having scrambled up the hillside and reached an enormous plateau filled with scrub and thistle they are alerted by some curious inhabitants of the table-top. An unruly collection of wild and scrawny cows has passed the point of mere curiosity and is headed purposely towards them. The cattle are very frightening and mad. There is only one sensible option and that is to retreat, fast.

Back in the port, there is a very fine yacht in town! As a threesome, once again, we halt our perambulation to stand and stare, to admire this sleek expression of success! But we have been noticed, probably our English accents have attracted attention from the handsome young man on board.

"Welcome", said a cultured voice with a hint of Greek timbre. "Can I offer you a drink?"

The chaps, rather embarrassed at the dirt and scratches gathered from their foray up the hill, and even faster descent down, point at their boots and dirty shorts.

"I think we should clean up first," said Simon pointing over to the small hotel.

"Then I suggest, if I may, that you come back at cocktail hour, say about 6 pm, when you may feel more comfortable." It was thus that we meet Costas, son, and heir to one of the most prestigious group of hotels and tourist agency in Cyprus. Thus it is that we swop 'life stories' over a glass of fine Cypriot wine from the ancient Mavro grape and then promise to visit his offices in London when back in the UK to see if we can make some sort of co-operation, but never do, but probably sums up the shyness which is to dog my career and become filed under life's rich tapestry of events as 'missed opportunities.'

From 1982-1986 employment to keep one of us from the wolf's door has been with a small tour operator featuring the Eastern Mediterranean islands. We originally holidayed with this company when we first travelled to Symi and Karpathos and on our return learning that we were making our living as journalists, (one of us I must own, rather part-time as novel writing was the preferred occupation) the managing director rang us and asked if we could write their brochure.

Eagerly the part-timer agreed, the children are now into their teens and an Open University course can be slotted in between this less than arduous task. Of course, we will also have to travel to all their destinations, although Rhodes, Kos, Nissiros, Symi and Karpathos are already known. What hasn't been anticipated is turning part of our home into an office and actually selling these holidays to enthusiastic punters – a word I am forbidden to use by him-on-high. A jovial and charming boss who fluctuated between wonderful generosity and praise to sudden disapproval.

Working 'full-time' when not travelling once or twice a year is not something we have factored into our lives although when it becomes routine it is really quite pleasant. One thing is quite sure, our lives are going to change quite dramatically!

CHAPTER 10

Back to Karpathos

Another original painting: this time of musicians on Karpathos.

September 1984

We are very taken by Karpathos, so much so, that we are to return in 1984. The second visit is with a purpose, by now one of us is employed by the tour operator who first brought us to Karpathos, and we are lunching at a small taverna above the beach at Apella. We arrive by sea, the sensible way to arrive and given that there are a rowdy group of young Germans on the caique, we dive into the sea and swim to the shore making haste up the beach to arrive at the taverna to 'bag' a table and the best fish before the Germans are ferried ashore in the dinghy.

We have to impress: we have three eminent members of the travel press among us: Mark Ottaway, travel editor of the Sunday Times, a 'lovable maverick' (as he was described in the Sunday Times Obituary,) who despite his ferocious ability to pull a great story, is good company; Elisabeth de Stroumillo, reflected in her French name and aristocratic Russian heritage, the doyenne of female travel writers is as sweet and kind as she is fearsome, she is the Daily Telegraph's first full-time travel writer; Peter Chambers, of the Daily Express, is exceptionally laid back, perhaps his background on the William Hickey column or his previous wartime experience in the Navy in the intelligence branch gave him his a quick sense of repartee.

Meeting these august writers in the VIP lounge of Gatwick airport, prior to our outward flight, we have little trouble recognising them, veteran travel writers that they are.

One thing is certain we are regarded as youngsters! And as such we don't have the skills to forewarn Peter that trying to chat up a Customers Officer on landing at Rhodes airport is perhaps not the wisest move!

It is now obvious that they will search our baggage, isn't it? Even so, we can then transfer to the 'flying landrover' (a twelve-seater prop aircraft) for our flight to Karpathos, which travels so noisily and low we see as much as we would from a sea-liner; on past Kamiros, Monolithos on the left, Chalki on our right and so onto Karpathos.

Wanting to impress, we are not the least bit thrilled at the Hotel Romantica to literally bump into the parents of close friends back home. Denys and Doreen are recently retired and cannot believe that we should be on Karpathos, although they must have booked their holiday through the small operator for whom one of us is working, knowing full well that there is the chance we may be on the island.

They give us no choice but that they join us for an evening brandy, where they learn that after breakfast, we shall make an early start for a sail to a lovely beach. The next morning none of us know where we are heading, excepting Sotiris, the boatman, who has been anxious we shall set sail early so as to return before the afternoon winds whip up.

We are already four persons on the boat, and we see Doreen and Denys hurrying along the quayside, Doreen gamely hanging onto an unsuitable and wide-brimmed sunhat. It will be churlish to say they are not welcome on our trip, given the boat clearly has room. But there is no sign of Mark, who made no appearance at breakfast. Simon decides to sprint back to the hotel, and both reappear fifteen minutes later with Mark protesting that he must have something to eat! "Just a little tiropitta or two will do."

But even I, who have pulled this journalistic coup for our boss of the small tour operation, cannot 'magic' tiropittas from my bag. A rather sulky travel editor clambers onto the caique. It isn't a good start, for the first few minutes we wonder if we should ask Sotiris to turn back, one propeller only firing a very rolling boat, but eventually, the second kicks in and Sotiris smiles as though this is normal!

No one can stay downcast for long under the cobalt blue sky, the gentler waves, and keeping close to the shore we eventually coast into a small bay. Leaving ever so slightly drunken tourist friends and much more lubricated members of the press to make a more dignified landing we are swimming to shore to grab a table for seven before the Germans who joined the trip at the last minute take over the tiny taverna!

The formalities of the first-day meeting are dissipating and we find topics in common to inject into the conversations: Elisabeth worked with Airwork, a cousin to the small airline Tradair, I once flew with as an air hostess and is an acquaintance of Sir Freddie Laker who was in our crew-room bar from time to time.

Peter travelled by donkey along the Pennine Way and would endlessly tease us about our northern roots.

Mark who appreciated the way that we took to the highways and byways was endlessly seeking to get off the beaten track. After an amazingly good and impressive lunch, given we were not expected, we struggle down the cliff path and onto the beach. Sotiris pulls the caique towards the beach and we paddle to the boat, scrambling up a wobbly ladder with the boatman's help. Difficult for Denys and Doreen, who younger than Elisabeth and Peter, try to hold their end up!

Simon lifts a pair of men's red trunks from a tamarisk tree and wraps them in his towel with a wink towards me. We are halfway back to Karpathos port when a cry goes up from Peter: "my trunks! I've left them drying on the tree. We'll have to go back." Whereupon Simon pulls them with a flourish from his towel! We are clocking up brownie points, as they say.

Spoa & Olympos

The next day finds us on the Karpathos narrow roads, surfaced only in part. Spoa in central Karpathos is known as the stone-breakers' town. But we won't see the beauty, the history, or the interest in the town. Here the trees lie down and die.

It is not wind but fire which has felled them. It is not a pretty sight but the imagined smell of smoke, the reminder of forest fire and flames that leap from pine tree-top to carob, from olive to scrub is not a sight we want our important guests to see. And on Karpathos there are no more trees, a fertile island is green no more. We are looking at dusty clay soil, barren, dramatic and Titanic as Mark would say.

Then after several hours driving, around the only green corner of the northern island lies Olympos.

Olympos, made more dramatic by the lack of trees. Now the colours sparkle, pinks and blue, and blue and white and pale pastels colours, again outlined with white. A contrast to the greens of forest trees of most Greek islands but emphasised by the ultramarine of the deep, deep sea. Olympos on this second visit is where we first tasted delicious Katsiki (goat stew) and we aim to give our friends from the press the same culinary delight.

We sit at the restaurant, looking out to sea, the windmills on the skyline, a wonderful Mediterranean view with a bright sapphire blue sky and we are served by the lady of the house: an attractive Karpathian housewife dressed in traditional costume with a beautiful white dress, a black apron and headscarf embroidered with colourful flowers and almost certainly woven by her on her loom.

Mark and I walk to the windmills, needing every sinew to keep on our feet, in the brutal winds.

Mark Ottaway relaxes in the warmth of Olympos.

Olympos, despite clearly displaying a matriarchal atmosphere, still retains a Spartan air, and this in spite of all the beautiful decorations of carved balconies painted in soft colours, church domes in blue and white. From a distance, it has the look of a delicately iced wedding cake, all white with pale blue trimmings.

The most memorable moment of the day is the visit inside one of the mills which is actually grinding flour. The old lady clad in black is perfectly sweet and can explain in Greek how this is a perfect day for milling as the wonderful sails can be unfurled and the wind will drive them slowly, not too fast, not too slowly. The smells of the ground wheat and dusty but clean wholesome atmosphere brings back memories of my childhood. I am a cornmiller's daughter!

Sadly, most of the surviving windmills are now used for storage and in 2014 one of the still-working round fronted windmills was converted into a working museum.

It is a Saturday, the day that the women bake their bread in the communal ovens, from the flour milled in the windmills. It is a fascinating sight, the great round risen loaves are inserted into the cavernous fiercely hot ovens, clearly as hot as a furnace at the back; inserted on long flat trays with a long-extended handle, like a giant spatula. A custom which has prevailed since ancient times, continuing in villages where still the cost of fuel is prohibitive and wood kindling on this barren mountainside hard to garner. The taste of warm fresh bread will linger.

Bread makers in Karpathos

We explore the compact town where affixed just below the ridge there is a square with a church and Mark and Elisabeth who have enough Greek establish that the imposing church was built in Byzantine style but furnished with frescoes from the time of the Turkish invasion.

"These villagers are saying it is a very ancient village," Elisabeth says, "probably dating from the seventh century and for this reason, most of the people to whom we are talking are speaking a language close to Doric, that's derived from ancient Greek. It is hard to understand them, but they must be descended from the original ancient settlers to the country."

Other sights in the village include the cobblers where now the boots cost £100 a pair, a considerable hike from our first visit, a couple of years ago.

Our taxi takes us back down the road, back through barren inhospitable mountains which we had labouriously travelled up through on our way to Olympos just a few hours before, but on a road which is better surfaced two years after our first visit to Olympos and after a long drive we find ourselves on what could pass as a by-pass surrounding another of the hillside villages of Karpathos, Spoa.

Old men in Spoa

Ruined windmills with their curved pos-
teriors, as they are in Olympos, to blunt the
force of the wind, crown the ridges which deter-
mine this landscape and its wonderful views to
the coast and the tiny port of Aghios Nikolaos.

It is quicker to drive east around the mountains to Pighadia, the way Andreas, our faithful
taxi driver, drove us up to Olympos. However,
with his limited English he persuades us to let
him turn right and take the road with the wes-

tering sun, down to Mesochorio. Like Spoa the road stops just before it enters the village, just above it and we stop the car, get out our cameras and look down on grapes, figs, and currants laid out to dry. Church bells are ringing, Greek bells always sound like no other, melodious and undated by time, forever a constant. Customs in Greece go back to ancient life, weddings, baptisms, are often pre-Byzantine in their rituals.

The outstanding sea views as the September day prepares to bid farewell just become superlative as we get nearer to Lefkos, even from our height we can imagine the silver sands under the almost perfect semi-circular bay created by the small peninsula.

A vote is taken; we agree we have earned an evening swim in the magical waters. Magnificent rollers are tempting at one end of the beach, and we find them invigorating, like battling with great ocean rollers which are quite capable of undressing one!

They are quite frightening, particularly when Peter comes by to say he has lost Simon in the water! But as usual, he turns up, having got out of the water quite a long way down the beach. If we have to leave Karpathos tomorrow, then this is a satisfactory valediction. Then all of us drive back along the coast, dusty red soil, vivid green trees, and always the blue sea. Climbing up the road to Piles, along a bumpy track, we realise we have mislaid Manolis' taxi, containing half the party. This seems to upset our top journalist and we have to turn around and retrace our steps until we realise that the confusion might have been caused by a new road which doubled up the choice of route to Othos, the highest town in Karpathos with wonderful views out towards Kassos.

This is where we find Manolis and his taxi, and where we are inclined and do buy, some very primitive art: singers and percussionists serenading a woman on a balcony and I have to say a twin to the larger picture bought in Athens all those many years ago on my very first visit to Greece!

PART 3

GREECE UNCOVERED

CHAPTER 11

*The Cruise-ship Constel-
lation: Rhodes, Crete,
Santorini, Piraeus, Mykonos,
Kusadasi, Patmos*

4 July - 18 July 1984

R hodos, Crete, Santorini, Piraeus, Mykonos, Kusadasi, Patmos in the decades before the Millennium, these are the ports
of call that every Eastern Mediterranean cruise
ship worthy of its extortionate rates would have

on its itinerary.

We had never set foot on Mykonos or indeed Kusadasi for Ephesus in Turkey and when invited to go along to sample what our clients would enjoy it is impossible to refuse! To be honest we are curious whether such free spirits as ourselves will be able to settle to the routine of sumptuous banquet-style meals, evening cabarets, and most of all the strict tedium of being part of a group expedition. We soon find we have it under control.

We join the ship in Rhodes, wobbling up the shaky gangway and being delivered to a rather cramped cabin with uninspiring décor, although the Michelangelo shower suite is modern and curtains designed from line drawings are clever, even so it needs a second glance to be recognised as pictures of animals!

No time to unpack we scurry into first sitting dinner straight from the briefing. Clearly, we should be boarded earlier as this is a Gala dinner by the Captain's invitation. Caviar, hor d'oeuvres, swordfish and shrimp Kebab, fillet steak and finally Baked Alaska brought out flaming by fifty waiters simultaneously. And all served with champagne!

The Greek evening is surprisingly good! Dances by the crew capture the spirit of true Greek dancing, probably just because they are not professional dancers. Certainly, it is the first time I have seen dancers perform with a table between their teeth! We take to bed images of the sea rocking the boat, a small child dancing, only aged two, but with the showmanship of a professional and we sail into the night to Crete.

We could complain about the early start from the quayside at Heraklion. Going back for the fourth time to Knossos I do reflect on the fates that have brought me to this ancient and in many ways curious site. Each time my journey here has been paid for by others! The first two visits during my time as an air-stewardess in the 1960s, more recently in 1979, I came courtesy of a sponsored press trip as a journalist, and now with K-Lines as a travel designer.

We feel blessed. But the images from Heraklion are the same: a great sprawling city with some interesting Venetian relief but in the main modern and ugly.

Then at Knossos, so close to Heraklion, the beauty and peace of the site are overwhelming. I cannot fail to be impressed by the work of Sir Arthur Evans, even if it is criticised for inaccuracy, it portrays a living palace. Columns are reconstructed with smaller bases than their full diameter at the top. Some cisterns still work, drains are still in existence and there is evidence of flushing loos. There are lively frescoes although we are told the real ones are in the museum which we visit next.

Officially the museum is closed but we are

taken quickly to the important exhibits: the two golden bees on a brooch from Malia, the double-headed axe, the anointing vessel and to my mind the most magnificent of the treasures, the ivory figurine of the boy jumping over the horns of the man-bull monster, the Minotaur.

Back on board, we eat a leisurely buffet lunch around the swimming pool. Our minds scarcely cleared we are approaching the amazing cliffs of Santorini. Whether one knows how this island in its present form was created or not, approaching it from the sea is very impressive.

 Our small ship, by now it is 'ours', draws into the harbour and we are transferred to the wide-bottomed blue and orange tenders and then step onto the small quay furnished by two tiny Greek tavernas, a donkey station which we rightly shun and incongruously an Austrian built cable car. Probably there are few more exciting and beautiful views in the world than this as we rise up the cliff and the speed that launches itself forward before steadying is probably similar to the sensation of hang-gliding. This is Cycladian drama at its best! Black volcanic cliffs rise sheer from the sea, rocks that are upset by Neapolitan splashes of red and yellow bands of obtrusive strata and everywhere on the rim of the caldera the crazy frenetic atmosphere you would expect from living on a volcano! Every corner displays white cubist houses, some with rounded roofs like caves, and there are real caves, churches, all packed tightly, steps making dizzy progress down the cliffs between shops, hotels and apartments.

Once in the Santorini village of Thira, we feast our eyes on the gold bee jewellery, a replica of the very item we had seen in the Crete museum just that morning. How can we be travelling at this speed? But it is expensive, very expensive! We pause in our sight-seeing for a drink in obviously *the* bar on Santorini. A beautiful African hippie with skin the colour of black ebony is running the show. It is hard to leave such a magnificent island and we have really just had a post-card view.

Back on board, we partake in the Greek Taverna evening and find the food is excellent and the carafe of wine good. The floorshow is vivid, musical and amateur, straight out of the northern City of Varieties in Leeds.

Mikrolimano or if you prefer Tourkolimano is not in an area of the Piraeus where you would expect to find fishermen filling little boats, on the shore of a big city, with crushed ice. Around the little port there are geraniums and tubs of pale blue flowers, marigolds and what at first glance we mistook as wisteria – wrong season – are they Judas trees? Again, wrong season, no they must be Jacaranda. We take in the colours of the fishing boats, blue and white, and some vividly striped awnings as well as red cabins for the wheelhouse. Behind, the buildings seem little altered from the twenty years previously, my first visit to Tourkolimano when we hired out, in 1960, another swanky yacht to go to Aegina.

There is still no way you can imagine there is the huge complex of the Piraeus so close unless it is the noise of the traffic which even so can cease to give way to the island atmosphere. And, of course, this precious area and all the Piraeus was once on an island. To me it epitomises the famous film, "Never on a Sunday" with Melina Mercouri – "and everyone was happy, and they all go to the seashore." Perhaps this is the very spot where it is filmed in 1960?

Bouzouki music plays over other sounds, generated by the cassette player of a fisherman mending his nets. It is so peaceful here and such a change from the never-ending clatter of the "souper douper" boat, where one is continually summoned over the tannoy. Even this morning on the one occasion when we could sleep in while most of the passengers got off to career off to the Acropolis, it is impossible to sleep because from six-thirty onwards we have been regaled with the information that "you are now in

Athens, this is your chance to see the world-famous Acropolis!"

It feels slightly wicked to forego a trip to the Acropolis, but it also feels wise. When you have encountered this great monument without the crowds and restrictions it attracts nowadays you know you will not be able to improve upon the experience.

So, for a brief morning we have broken free and now caught up in a traffic jam it has taken the taxi half an hour to drive back to the Constellation although we are back on board in time for lunch. And so on to Mykonos.

Sailing over a clear blue sea and after fine views of Vouliagmeni and Sounion in the distance, Kea is on our left, then Tinos with Andros to the north and Syros to the right, finally Mykonos. The light is fading, but there is still enough bright sunlight to highlight the windmills, white churches and cubist houses for which the island is renowned.

We adopt a fast cruise ship excursion pace to catch the surrealist church in the right light and skip through the houses to also capture the wooden houses on film. We then need to decide where to eat, slowing down considerably, parading up and down the street to choose the most inviting taverna. We approach a likely choice but are rebuffed when we are curtly told we couldn't have a drink unless we also eat as well, but we are intending to eat, but of course moved on, when treated so discourteously.

We are rewarded further up the street, with a view overlooking the harbour in a tiny restaurant and it was quite a lot of fun although we are paying UK prices! Afterwards, I succumb to temptation and pop into one of the fine sophisticated boutiques to buy a skimpy black sun top, which lasts for years, proving expensive clothes are still the best buy. Given more time, I would have bought more but, as ever, time is a premium.

Back on board, we are too tired to watch the moon rise over Mykonos and we sail out for Kusadasi. I am so tired when we wake this morning, I just wonder if Ephesus will be just another tourist site, not worth struggling out of bed for at six a.m. Should we have another lazy day like we did yesterday in Athens? However, we make it to breakfast in the blue and green metallic walled dining room.

Once we disembark at Kusadasi it becomes apparent this is another world, another country! It is hardly after first light, but eager local businessmen are here and we are in no doubt that we are in Turkey; an army of salesmen promising us the earth if we would just take time to visit their carpet shop, their ceramics, their jewellery, the best in the whole bazaar!

I love bazaars, each I have visited over the

years, Cairo, Tangier, Jerusalem even, have filled me with expectation and excitement and always I seem to acquire a small exceptional souvenir!

Our guide is firm, the bus will stop at the shopping promenade on the harbour front on the way back. All so different and yet Samos, another beautiful Aegean Greek island is lying just offshore. Kusadasi seems more oriental, more Eastern, and with more palm trees than Greece. And it isn't just the mosques, also the streets are cleaner and there is none of the 'avrio' litter which the Greeks always mean to clear up 'tomorrow' but never do. Also, the land is extensively farmed with crops and there are many fruit trees, apricots, oranges, lemons, plums and peaches in particular.

The ride along the coast to Ephesus is not as scenically beautiful as Greece but it is surprisingly different. Houses are built in the square Turkish style without any of the spontaneity of Greece. The hotels look more functional, more European, like Germany or Austria.

The road goes inland from the coast to Ephesus, up the silted valley which had once formed the harbour of Ephesus. As the bus passes the outskirts of the village of Selcuk we are shown the remains of a fort and possible evidence of St. John's domicile in the area, with a ruined Basilica where the saint is believed to be buried. Then the bus passes through the village into the hills

169

just beyond.

Here begins our  long walk (about one and a half miles, down the valley which had formed the main street of Ancient Ephesus). Only about twenty per-cent has been excavated of this huge site and of this, we saw only twenty percent. We started at the gymnasium, moved down to where Roman columns show evidence of a hos-pital with the sign of Asclepius.

Further down this ancient street, we are shown rooms where Romans chatted, gambled and drank, then through the main gate to see the marbled street after which chariots could not proceed further, but where there are coffee shops, a rest house and evidence of a set of flush toilet facilities.

Men met communally to perform their daily functions here but more to gossip and do business. Their slaves are sent ahead to warm the marble seats in winter, little privacy here. The Roman Library of Celsus is a fine building but does not compare in my mind with the delicacy of Grecian remains.

Opposite our attention is drawn to the brothel or house of love. Here men would donate the taxes for one hour's pleasure to the city, running out on the hour – or to feed the meter – if their time ran out! The expression 'by the hour' is one with historical roots! The ladies of the house were said, in one year, to earn enough to pay six years of taxes to Rome.

We walk on to the amphitheatre but although it is crudely restored it is nothing like as impressive as Epidaurus, although it is larger and the view over the harbour, before it silted up would have been magnificent.

Back to the bus, and as promised back in Kusadasi we are treated to a demonstration of the finery of Turkish carpets. They certainly are very beautiful, and we are assured that this shop is controlled by the Turkish state. Even if we believe the articles are handwoven, and we do, it is still offered as a fixed tourist attraction as much as the camels which we had photographed a few minutes before arriving at the market.

Simon tries his hand at a bit of bartering without much success but after much persuasion, we do end up with a finely crafted knotted silk mat in the style of a prayer mat. *We love it to this day!*

We don't forget the Turkish Delight and we are on board again for lunch heading for Patmos, the penultimate stop. The ship passes through the narrow strait between Turkey and Samos, and we arrive in Patmos where we are greeted by June and Yiannis, our agents on the island.

As with Athens, where we have seen the historic attraction several times before, this is too good an opportunity for working travel business-people not to do business! And we even manage a swim in the sea at Skala.

It is our last evening on board, and we delay changing to our dinner clothes to see the boat cast off from the stunningly beautiful island of Patmos. The great grey monastery castle crowns its hill and our minds are taken back to the perfect archways and magnificent architecture in the castle, the gentle monks, and the evocative Maundy Thursday service for the Washing of the Disciples' feet, just a few years ago.

We pause to think how fortunate we are to have had this opportunity to visit this island twice in a short space of time. We have made friends on board, although there is only one other English couple and after a final lavish dinner, we go through to the Leo lounge for the floor show, where we are entertained to another amateur and splendidly costumed Can-Can, followed by American deep south music.

When we leave the next morning, it is tinged with sadness. Have we always played fair? Sometimes teasing the hostesses with shouts of "Consternation", mocking their placards of "Constellation" as they tried to muster the passengers on the quayside. Should we have walked in the heat up to the Monastery of St. John the Divine or were we right to take the opportunity to increase business and spend an hour inspecting the hotels on the seafront.

There is a sense that this travelling as a travel professional is a life of luxury, but the reality is that mostly it is a grind of early starts, counting of hangers in wardrobes, picking up on substandard mattresses, inspections of bathrooms and in these days of the early 1980s there is often a need to draw the hotelier or apartment owner to the basic standards of hygiene or fire safety regulations, not easy to do in a foreign language. Evenings are often spent writing up notes and yes, it is always fun but mostly travel for business is hard work and tiring!

CHAPTER 12

*Another Dodecanese
island: Astipalea*

May 1985

We don't know it on our first visit; but we are to make several visits to Astipalea because when finally, we manage to get there we are smitten, and the first visit could have become life-changing.

An expedition has been arranged to Aghios Ioannis for tomorrow morning. We are to meet young Kostas the taxi driver, as opposed to old Kostas the taxi driver, there being only two on the island.

We are down at Dimitri's for an early drink of mountain sage tea before setting off. Dimitri, apart from being in charge of the docking of the ferries, runs the little ouzerie on the tamarisk tree-lined harbour wall. He is usually the first and last port of call for visitors to Astipalea, that displaced landmass isolated between the Cyclades and the Dodecanese, although officially belonging to the latter.

It is usually to Dimitri that jaded travellers turn after their long-haul overnight ferry from the Piraeus, or the shorter but often more turbulent boat trip from Kalymnos. *Until the opening of the little airport around the time of the Millennium these are the only choices for travel to the island of our dreams.* So, it is not surprising that visitors receive a true welcome and much-needed refreshment.

Likewise, for those departing, the cognoscenti sit on the harbour wall or at Dimitri's little rickety tables, drinking a last ouzo, nibbling a last meze, waiting until Dimitri puts on his harbour master's hat before rushing to the jetty as the big ferry rounds the headland, filling the little harbour with its towering mass, surging water, noise and the seemingly uncoordinated activity of crew, islanders, traders, tourists, lorries and motorbikes, that is only a hair's breadth from chaos.

Above it all, the cubist white high town of Astipalea, crowned with its ruined Venetian fortress and wedding cake churches sits aloof, waiting for the turmoil to subside and the island to return to its settled way of life.

We have rented the Frenchman's house in the high town from Louisa, the English girl who has an agency on the island, distinctive by the red motorbike she rides up and down the steep hill to Chora.

The house has been restored to its original style, but there is electricity now and a cold-water tap. For hot-water, we heat a pan on the gas ring, while the shower relies on its warmth from the water tank situated on the roof. There is a simple living room with a wide-planked wooden floor and iconostasis on the walls, a minute kitchen, a tall ceilinged cool bedroom with a stupendous view through the white linen shaded window. The view is shared by the loo, which sits in a little wooden hut on the wooden balcony. Below the land drops steeply to the cliffs and one can sit in contemplative peace, like a ship's captain in the crow's nest, looking directly across the headland to the bay of Livadia and beyond, to the little secluded pebble coves, where the young people swim and sunbathe in the nude.

It is the day of the expedition and we leave the house early to avoid the heat of the day, slipping down the stepped streets from the high town to the harbour. The air is full of swooping swallows and the sound of crowing cocks. As we sit supping the sweet aromatic sage tea waiting for young Kostas who has had to take some passengers to the north of the island, Dimitri hustles us into his cupboard of a kitchen to show us some lobster and a kakavia (an exotic fish stew cum soup) he is preparing.

"Tonight," he whispers, "special for you."

We nod, knowing he will tell the same tale to all his favoured customers. We decline the lobster but put in an order for the kakavia. Dimitri grins – we have made a wise choice. A good choice on a day that may possibly become life-changing.

Young Kostas arrives and we set off, up behind the harbour and then high onto the narrow saddle. From here you can see the sea to both sides of the island and get a fine view of the whole town as it snakes its way from the harbour up the hillside to the Venetian fortress. At one time the two settlements were quite separate but new house building has linked the two together.

It is a tedious journey through the centre of the island, barren, bare and stony land, a grey army camp hidden in a shallow valley and the road beyond it the object of a stream of Kostas curses. "A man should not have to drive his new taxi (it must be all of ten years old) over such roads," he complains.

After about an hour the track enters the head of the ravine that leads to Aghios Ioannis. Suddenly, round a bend, there it is; the tiny domed church, not spectacular in itself, although it is striking but spectacular in its isolation. Three shepherds and their dogs are enjoying the shade cast by the shadow of the church wall; they are at once curious as to our presence and resentful towards the disturbance of their world of peace and solitude.

Kostas goes to reassure them of our bona fides, while we set off to explore.

Above: Aghios Ioannis and the 'loo with a view' on the balcony of our simple accommodation!

Below the church, the land falls steeply to the narrow confines of the ravine. A white rocky, heat-reflecting funnel leading eventually to the sea and a hidden pebble beach. But the most remarkable aspect of this bleached bit of landscape is the sound of running water, a waterfall, and as our eyes swivel from the funnel of the ravine towards the sound, we see a total contrast, a green and verdant garden, an Eden in the wilderness, overgrown now, but lush and fertile, sustained by the underground springs whose water has been harnessed in a series of ancient sternas, lagoons and irrigation channels.

There are olives, apples, pears, oranges and pomegranate, walnut and lemon, carob and kumquat, and in between the trees some signs of more recent cultivation, a patch of tomatoes, sweetcorn, struggling against the inroads of brambles and the rushes. Someone, please love me it shouts!

It is a magic place, warm, green, fecund, full of the hum of insects, the colour and movement of butterflies, the murmur of water. What work must have gone into its creation, the discovery and the harnessing of the water and the painstaking cultivation by the priests and shepherds living so far from the rest of civilisation, secure in their own self-sufficiency?

Just above the church, there is another building, a ruin. Does it have potential, is it for sale? Young Kostas is anxious to be on his way. We bump our way back over the dusty, rocky excuse for a road, living with the memory of that green oasis and its white pearl of a church.

Suddenly back from the tranquillity of a place, as remote as any we know, to the mod.

cons of our tiny rented accommodation with its loo on the balcony and with a view! To be honest all Astipalea is deliciously away from the modern world.

In the evening, we have arranged to meet Nikolas in the kafenion run by the deaf-mute. Ordering food and drink here is by a complicated form of sign language and the result is often haphazard and quite often different from the comestibles one had hoped to receive. Nevertheless, he is a cheerful man and one gets used to accepting discrepancies. Besides the unexpected always adds to the spice of life.

Nikolas is at the back of the bar drinking whisky with his friends. Is this wise we ask? Surely it is tomorrow that he is due to sail to Kalymnos for his driving test?

He is a great brigand of a man, a veritable Zorba and the Mr. Fixit of Astipalea, greeting one with many a slap, grin and a roar. A builder by trade, he is gradually restoring many of the high town's ruined houses, as well as being the official custodian of any archaeological finds and remains on the island.

"Does he know who owns the house at Aghios Ioannis?" we ask. "Does he know if it is for sale, what it will cost?"

With five daughters, each of whom will require a house as a dowry when they marry Nikolas' building skills are well employed. At least,' he says, the girls will now have the chance to grow up. Not so long ago, girls, in this part of the Dodecanese, were married off as young as ten or twelve at the onset of puberty."

Nikolas says he will see us later and we head for Dimitri's and the promised kakavia, to end the day as it was begun, at a little rickety table, under the tamarisk trees on the harbour wall in Astipalea. The talk is of old ruins and the wisdom of trying to buy such a house!

CHAPTER 13

Greco-File is conceived!

I n 1986 fate took charge and we change to another well-respected Greek specialist when we are asked to do much the same sort of work and then quite suddenly this company goes into liquidation.

Much gnashing of teeth throughout the industry as this company is very highly regarded. It seems that investing too heavily in large cumbersome computer systems – a machine that had to be housed in its own dust-free temperature-controlled room – had been an expensive mistake and only months after the company folded, smaller more compact computers were appearing on individual worker's desks.

Embarrassed that Suzi had been employed at this unfortunate time we are given a massive bonus which allowed us to travel around Greece for five weeks, visiting areas not covered by our previous employment. Together with our exploration in the early years of our married life, after this trip, we felt we had the expertise and knowledge to set up our own travel company and in 1986 GRECO-FILE LTD is born.

The Sporades & NE Aegean

Skiathos and Skopelos

We spend much of 1986 researching areas we don't know, and this leads us to Skiathos for Greek Easter on 1 May 1986 using the Timsway accommodation kindly given to us.

By chance, we meet up with a friend of mine from college. Deidre is something of a live-wire and her stylish Greek dancing is a show-stopper. Her Greek partner, a local soldier is much taken by her.

We fit in what we are becoming expert at: inspecting hotels and apartments as well as finding time to explore Banana Beach (which is shockingly nudist!) But what we will take away is the magnificent fields and dells of wildflowers, after the heavy rain which had greeted us when we arrived, as we landed. We have never seen rain of such intensity and the aircraft captain kindly suggests that we remain in our seats, parked on the apron until it ceases. This is kind, but what he hasn't organised is the baggage handlers to be alert to the change of plan, and we watch aghast as the luggage is unloaded from the hold and stacked on the tarmac as we wait in the dry!

When we do arrive at our accommodation it is to find that the suitcases are wet throughout their contents. However back to the wildflowers, over the years we have become accustomed to the glorious colours and scents of the wildflowers of Greece. On Skiathos, red and yellow poppies, anemones, green and golden euphorbia, purple and pink-tinged orchids, white and yellow centred camomile, tassel hyacinth and grape hyacinth and wild gladioli all meld in the breeze and create a true feast for the eyes.

We even make an excursion to Skopelos. Now Skiathos is gentle with low lying hills and tree-fringed sandy beaches but Skopelos is clearly master of the seas, a more rugged island with sharp white edges to its architecture, stony beaches, cliffs, and narrow roads linking places which are more at home being reached by sea. Whereas Skiathos is all bright green, deep blue, red roofs and white houses, Skopelos is a much darker, more muted green and silver slate roofs, (although there is talk of replacing these traditional slate tiles because the red clay tiles are much safer in earthquakes, heaven forbid!) Its beauty is more intense but its presence calmer, probably because there is no airport.

We don't have long to explore but we walk up the steep streets of the main town and failing to get as far as the Venetian Castle we chose a small café with picture-postcard harbour views.

We are not to know on our next visit to Skopelos that we are to witness an extraordinary event: quietly sitting just above the quayside, one autumn evening we see the ferry boat fast approaching at a vast rate of knots. It dawns on us simultaneously that the ship is not going to stop, it is heading bow on straight for the harbour wall.

"Move, now!" says Simon, grabbing my arm, "it's going to run into the harbour wall!" There is an enormous crash and the boat with only a few passengers aboard deliberately wrecks its bow against the concrete quay. A small flotilla of sailing yachts moored alongside the quayside is inundated by the huge wash and completely swamped as the innocent occupants are trying to cook their supper. We hear first the clatter of pots and pans and then much cursing and swearing ensue.

We are only about twenty feet away, not hurt; indeed, no-one was hurt or damaged except the fabric of the vessel and the pride of the yachts. "Why would anyone do that? Did he have no brakes?" I ask, innocently.

"Malacca," cries a local from his café table, uttering a very rude Greek word.

"The insurance isn't going to fall for this one, everyone knows it is the end of the season and he doesn't want to pay for the crew when the boat is not working," says our waiter calmly removing our coffee cups.

"Sorry mate, it just doesn't look like an accident," says a British bystander.

LESVOS

Later in 1986 we fly to Lesvos and drive across to Sigri. I had asked to go somewhere remote and the long drive from the airport at the island's capital, Mytilene to Sigri confirms it is remote!

We can see we have arrived, long before we reach our destination. A westering sun is beginning to sink, and the horizon seems to draw across the sea to the long thin island that protects a natural harbour and gathers in across land which would be as at home on Yorkshire's tufted moorland as here in Greece. The rock here is called Tuff, created from volcanic ash from past eruptions from the volcano the area is situated on. There is a river which attracts migrating birds and the tall grasses are beautifully green.

It was Simon's good friend Anthony who recommended the place to us. It is late July and blisteringly hot and very windy when we arrive. We can see the beaches are wonderful, just right for kids and we have chosen the place because we have been told that the rather uninspiring village backing a magnificent natural harbour has some good tavernas.

The village has its own imposing mid-eighteenth-century castle, Turkish and reasonably intact and probably because it is Turkish it doesn't appear much appreciated by the locals.

It is so hot when we arrive! Later, as dusk falls and the brittle heat cools rapidly, we discover it is windy, very windy in Sigri almost every day, and we are told we should take a light sweater out with us when we go to eat.

It is sound advice, except coming to Greece in high season we have not packed sweaters. We even need the blankets thoughtfully put out on our beds, by our landlady, Sophia. We decide we don't want to spend each day on the beach, although it is beautifully situated near the village. The whole of this area is famed for its wonderful beaches and we begin to explore.

There is a dirt road to Eressos which has more character and Faneromeni beach is beautiful and again uncrowded. We go further afield to historic Molyvos and Petra. Molyvos, officially called Mythymna, is a fortress town, with a hilltop crowned with a Byzantine and Genoese castle, the stone dwellings are clustered all around. The main drag with its cobble-stoned paving leads you uphill but we are not deterred from the walk given that it is mostly shaded by wisteria, and amazingly some blooms on this spring vine are still flowering. It's a memory which endures although it is a very long drive and perhaps too much to tackle on one day!

And when we venture south to Plomari we can smell that this is the heartland of Ouzo production long before we reach it. If you can cope with the smell it is an attractive town with pleasing architecture which bows to the Turkish style. It is the second largest on Lesvos so more of a city and for ouzo drinkers a fascinating place to visit. The distilleries appear to be open to visitors and the shops and tavernas have bottles of the different brands on display.

Nearer to Sigri, the hill village of Antissa is almost completely undeveloped. It has a beautiful and traditional village square and it is a cool place to sit under one of the three plane trees that shade the cafes and tavernas.

The petrified forest, near Sigri, again highlighted in the brochure and guidebooks is another main excursion. "Only this isn't a terrified forest," says a youngster. "It's just bits of wood which have turned to rock. Another load of old stones, you just can't get away from them in Greece, either in the old ruins or the old woods!" We are clearly not going to inspire archaeologists or naturalists. We return by ferry to Kos, for our long flight home. This gives us the chance to glance at Mytilene and we know from this glance that we should have had a full day's excursion here.

CHAPTER 14

Easter time on Eastern Crete

Agios Nikolaos

April 1987

In Greece, the palest, pinkest white fluted marble is brushed by dark green palm tree fronds but on Crete, white belongs to the snow on the massive mountain tops and pink is brown and beige and pale orange, the colours of Knossos, straight lines, corners and strength.

Crete is another country, sea encircled, its virile faces etched with poverty and wind, blistered by the sun and polished by the dust from Africa.

It rains: rains when we land, rains when we unpack the hire car outside our accommodation, rains when we leave the taverna, that first evening, and rains when we drive into Agios Nikolaos to find a zacharoplasteion where we enjoy a sticky cake! It is still raining next morning and at breakfast in our apartment we are pretty ragged, having spent a less than comfort-able night.

It is so urgent that after a hurried break-fast we go to the 'welcome meeting' provided by our tour company. This isn't the best beginning to an Easter holiday we have had with young people. The charming rep Annabel tells us, as we along with all yesterday's arrivals, foregather in a nearby hotel, that it hasn't been her best day either.

This isn't what we want to hear, we want a private meeting with her. Not happy to speak to us before her meeting and not catching on to our urgency.

"It's due to the rain, very unexpected," she explains. "So, let's have a bit of hush," she laughs with a self-conscious smile "and I will tell you how you can have a wonderful holiday even in this weather. And if you don't mind, I'll have a bit of a rollcall and then if anyone is missing, I can go round to the rooms and apartments and see if they are alright." She begins reading out the names of the passengers, checking out we are all gathered together in the pretty hotel over-looking the sea. "Smith x 2, Stembridge x 5," until she gets to "Balls x 2," when one of the two girls in our party who is old enough to know better starts to giggle, sadly encouraging others. How embarrassing.

We have a very urgent matter to discuss with her and hope she has a solution. We don't hold out a lot of hope, it is Easter and the resort looks busy.

"Annabel," I begin when the meeting is over, edging myself to the front of the queue. "We have a bit of a problem in our apartment. My daughter suffered a very rude awakening last night. I must insist that we are found alternative accommodation before this evening."

"Oh, what is wrong?" asks Annabel showing concerned, "it must be serious?"

"Well, my daughter had to spend the night sharing our bed. It wasn't just a single mouse in her room, which at first we thought it was, but a whole nest of mice and their babies have come out of her mattress."

I don't have to labour the point. It is easy enough for Annabel to visualise our petrified daughter rushing into our room half an hour after we had gone to bed. Her father at first thought Heidi was exaggerating and told her it would just be a mouse.

Whereupon Heidi spelt out in great detail how she had been woken by something running across her face, and when she and Sarah put on the light and pulled back the covers and under the lower sheet, there they found many little mice.

All night long we could hear the patter of tiny feet and by breakfast time we had all re-packed our luggage and had the car loaded up ready to move.

"We will go anywhere if the company cannot help us. We will just move into a hotel, wherever we can find three rooms. But I'm not paying extra," I say.

"I am sure they will be accommodating. This villa will have been shut up all winter, and although they clearly haven't cleaned it thoroughly enough, to be honest, if the nest was within the mattress, maybe it was not easy to spot that an octet of mice was about to be born, if they had not been born by the time the sheets were put on." Simon tries to look on the positive side.

"Stop making excuses for bad housekeeping,"

I am rattled with a night without sleep and a Greek holiday starting on a rainswept morning. But the company do find a solution within hours and we are moved to a lovely new expensive four bedroomed villa, so the girls even had a room each.

The next morning is fine and warm enough for a swim after lunch. Well, it is for Heidi and Sarah. The rest of us do not feel tempted. The following day we feel like an excursion and drive inland to Kritsa.

Kritsa

Panaghia Kera, Kritsa is one of the most geometrically styled churches in Greece, three perfect triangles span across the roof; the three naves are perfectly positioned, and the central nave is domed. Looking at the 13th-century Byzantine monument as you approach it just off the road, we are very struck by the symmetry of the architecture against the mountain background and sturdy pine trees gracing its features. Fortunate indeed that we can explore this ancient church without crowds for when we go back to the village of Kritsa we are upset how touristy it all is.

Although there are tempting breads and cakes on display for Easter in "O Fournos", the local bakery, plaited or woven into shapes with red eggs placed with the plaits.

Above: Cookies for Easter celebrations.

Ierapetra, Makriyialos, Sitia & Vai

Good Friday comes and the weather worsens,

we drive to Ierapetra on the south coast and I dive into a clothes shop leaping over the puddles the size of flash floods where I triumphantly purchase a pair of pale blue jeans, (these remain a favourite in my wardrobe for many years to come, Greek trousers have always suited my figure best!)

Our half-hour visit only scratches the surface of this interesting town and our journey then takes us along the sandy alluvial plain to Makriyialos which with Analipsis is very different to what we expected.

Our route is dominated by the vast hectares of polythene greenhouses. Crucial research for our travel agency as there are many holiday villas and apartments linked to the sandy beaches of the area. The slightly peaky hills here are definitely interesting, set back from the plain but it needs the sun to come out; we make a decision to eat at one of two tiny tavernas open on the waterfront protected by huge tamarisk trees. We feel protected from the huge hotel complex, a monstrosity just up the road. What had been a tiny harbour with glorious long sandy beaches, (the name of Makriyialos means long beaches) is growing fast. It is not beach weather and we motor on back to the north coast of Eastern Crete, to visit Vai.

On the map, Crete looks very narrow in the east, but the roads are twisty. It is a good slightly mountainous road peppered with small villages but not with the dramatic beauty of other Greek islands. As the clouds shifted there are good views out across to the Libyan Sea and then we are looking out again to the Aegean. Sitia is disappointing on the approach and although the sun is now out it definitely still has its winter coat out. The beach is sandy and long, probably magnificent in summer, but it is full of flotsam and we wend our way up towards Vai. It is further than we imagined. Not unusual on our journeys where we often underestimate distances! The coast is now barren and the scenery bleak with the odd palm tree to show us what is in store. Still, in the last of the sunshine, we arrive, startled by the formal entrance of the long impressive grove of palms leading to the lagoon and sea. Dark tunnels of jungle vegetation lead from the fence to the beach, a golden sandy and wide beach.

We go through a gate and up some man-made steps on to one of the impressive rock formations and we can see yet another beach beyond, completely deserted and well worthy of exploration. This is the largest natural palm forest in Europe. But we have to hurry back from this magnificent location.

We have an appointment with a hotel owner in Sitia. The town, like Makriyialos, grows on one, here is bustle and a truly Greek feel but it is more sophisticated than Ierapetra. In time we will develop an association with this town. After a magnificent drive through the mountains which are mostly under heavy cloud, we catch glimpses of sunlight and then the setting sun sifting through the cloud with a dramatic effect, highlighting churches on the mountain peaks and sombre scenes in the villages as bells toll for Good Friday. Old men with big moustaches sit on benches, young men stand underemployed in groups, it is a day of reflection and waiting.

Easter Celebrations in
Agios Nikolaos & Elounda

Amazingly we arrive back in time to change and eat, after which with perfect timing we find somewhere to park in Agios Nikolaos just as the procession with its dignitaries and military band passes by.

On Saturday evening we are back in Agios Nikolaos.

Our daughter Heidi and her friend Sarah have yet to witness the magic of a Greek Orthodox Easter, and here the local celebration centres around the burning of an effigy of Judas on the Lake Voulismeni at Agios Nikolaos where a large wooden raft has been constructed for the purpose, with 'Judas' placed upon a yet-to-be-lit bonfire in the middle of the raft. As the midnight hour draws closer, we take up the expectant atmosphere and we foregather at the Bottomless

Lake Café awaiting the Easter night tradition of lighting of the bonfire on the lake.

People come and go but the dark grotto-like background gives an unusual balance to the place: white light on the black lake makes great yellow and silver seersucker lines across the water. There is a tamarisk tree above a blue awning which in turn is covered with naked light bulbs and we need to adjust our eye-line if we are to see the expected action.

Suddenly everyone stirs as a flying arrow lights the bonfire and all the fireworks discharge their brilliance and the echo from the grotto is superb for sound effects. As the locals watch in sombre appreciation of the just punishment and effigy now reduced to a ball of flames falls off the raft. Then before the fireworks finish, we make a speedy departure to claim our table at a restaurant where we have booked our place to break 'the fast'. We are old hands now at this festival, especially after our experience in Leros but Heidi and Sarah are not as skilled with the practice of cracking opponents red hard-boiled eggs.

On Easter Sunday the sun looks more promising, but it is still cold. At least the wisteria is at its height and the scents are almost overpowering.

We regret that we feel we have to drive to Malia, but reports are so bad that we feel we have to know why we would recommend that clients should not go near the place. However, with our eye on the Pension Grammatikakis which had always attracted such good attention and we can certainly see why, because it remains a lovely hotel, we accept that good management can make the most of an outstanding location.

These family-run hotels are all over Greece, in coastal villages that are being absorbed into a fast-developing resort but survive by offering excellence. We thank the hotelier for their time given to show us the hotel and then we have a good lunch at a taverna recommended by the hotel near the beach before we drive on through the town. Malia has lost all its dignity. Had we seen the mile upon mile of bars, cheaper tourist retail shops, half devoted to rental-cars, amusement arcades and other depressing outlets, as we saw on the way out, we might not have even driven down to the beach. But we are glad we did, and we take away the good spirit from the Hotel Grammatikakis.

The little church lapped by the waves is very evocative, but oh, how you have changed Malia!

The local excursion from the Elounda region is a boat trip to the islet of Spinalonga.

This won't become de rigueur until after Victoria Hislop publishes her book "The Island", (in 2005) based on the true events around living on the island which suddenly makes everyone aware of the horrendous situation of quarantining those in the

population tragically afflicted, and who would suffer from leprosy, forever. No ifs, no buts.

Therefore, it is with curiosity that we gaze at the island, with its Venetian fort, from the vantage point of our taverna table.

I notice Heidi has gone very white, she says she feels faint and we decide to return to the villa, leaving our visit perhaps until another day, another year, another decade.

The weather so disappointing, not just wet but freezing cold, the girls' health worrying and the state of the villa when we arrive leaving much to be desired, it feels that Crete has not become a priority destination for the time being. I am sorry this holiday has had its fair share of lows, particularly for the young people, the girls returning to the UK.

Western Crete

Gerani, Paleochora, Kastelli Kissamou

We drive along the vast northern coast of Western Crete, to base ourselves in the Anthi, attractive apartments, west of Chania and set in an extensive bamboo grove, at Gerani, near Platanias.

Our arrival, tired from our long drive with the sun in our eyes the whole way from Agios Nikolaos via Heraklion, is somewhat spooky. We find we have to negotiate our way through the tall stalks of bamboo, like driving through a maze.

Then suddenly through the mist and rain, a huge mass appears in the middle of the undergrowth through which we are tunnelling, along the lane, and the driver jams on the brakes. The obstruction is a very wet and bedraggled donkey. We don't know whether to laugh or scream!

Good with animals, Simon gentle persuades it back into the bamboo where there is a gap leading to a field and I edge the car forward. "Close shave," I say. "Literally," says Oliver, "we could have taken his whiskers off."

"Well at least, that's a polite way of putting it," adds his father.

However, our abiding memory of this place is the owner who has a large fierce dog called Dick who he says it "would be best not to confront".

Therefore, whenever we see the dog out of its kennel or off its chain, the chant will go out: "Ey up, be careful Dick's Out!" And one that will go down in the family annals.

We spend a wonderful week in Western

Crete. On most days the sun comes out through the clouds, wild-flowers are everywhere and the sky and sea increasingly are blue, we walk down through the bamboos to the beach nearest to the apartment, but it is still in its winter scruffs, a few pedaloes have been pulled up to the back of the beach and they are dirty. In any case, it is not beach weather, a pity because this rural area much neglected over the centuries could, in general, become an area to develop just because of its magnificent sandy beaches.

Sadly, in the not very distant future, this is exactly what did happen and far too many apartment blocks and hotels grow up jostling for space along this coast, each trying to be nearest the beach.

Anxious as we are to see as much of the island to enhance our selling skills, we would have liked to have had a day to rest. Totally different topographically to Eastern Crete which is dominated by Mt. Dikti on the Lassithi Plain and massively independent Mt. Ida in Central Crete, this area is always overshadowed by the magnificent White Mountains (the Lefka Ori). Fractionally less high than Mt. Ida, the White Mountains are hugely impressive, still snow ensconced, true to their name as this is April.

We drive to Paleochora in the extreme west of the coast with its two-faced outlook over the Libyan Sea, a peninsula which forms a long village with a long pebble beach as you arrive to the left and a sandy beach to the right, away from the village where cedar trees and juniper grow wild.

The weather is not co-operating and although we find a convivial taverna where the wine barrels outside have attracted our attention we are focused on the waves dashing against the large harbour rocks, although there are signs that the weather is improving.

There are fine views from the crumbling Venetian Castle of Selinos, (named after the celery plant) mostly rebuilt by the Turks in the seventeenth century but we are not tempted to hang around and nor could we find evidence of the Pelican who is rumoured to have lived here, although we spot a café named after the bird.

We drive back via Kastelli Kissamou and are struck by a limestone gorge we pass through and we are tired when we get back. We had passed through superb little villages with pantile roofed houses, which became smarter as we approach Kastelli Kissamou. Perhaps Chania has a stockbroker belt!

It is an intriguing place with character, set in a plain with two peninsulas enclosing the Gulf of Kissamou and from the port mostly the beaches look to be of pebble. There is a small harbour in the old port with brightly coloured caiques creating a very traditional scene. The new port itself is out of the town. We understand that the ferries dock here from Kythera, and perhaps from Gythio and Athens.

We make a note to check this when we get back to the office. Exploring towards the long pebble beach where two tiny tavernas offer hospitality down a little road we spot a sign marked "to private area, free parking"! A little bit contradictory!

All in all, it is a miniature city with the business and bustle confined to the esplanade and the tiny streets in the centre leading to a pleasant main square, the bell tower of Ag. Spiridon and very conveniently the wide main road sweeping by which had allowed us to visit easily.

Chania, Rethymno, Akrotiri monasteries and more villages

Each time we visit one of the southern villages we come down from Rethymno via Hora Sfakion or from Chania, making each excursion as a separate full day trip a necessity. The whole coast is stripped by deep gorges, with very few roads running east-west along the sea so the small seaports and beach villages in the south are more connected to Rethymno or Chania than they are to each other.

The geology highlights the problems the Resistance would have had in World War 2 and so although these ravines are in view, uppermost in our minds are the stories of the brave Britons and Allies such as Patrick Leigh Fermor who joined with the Cretans to take on the Germans. The famous film "Ill Met by Moonlight" was based on Paddy Leigh Fermor's account, "Abducting a General" the audacious kidnapping of the German General Kreipe and George Psychoundakis's book about the crucial work of a war-time runner, The Cretan Runner translated by Paddy.

With full days spent in Chania and Rethymno exploring their characterful harbours and narrow charming back streets packed with Venetian architecture the days speed by. There are castles, ornate fountains and some of the once ramshackle buildings lining the cobbled streets have been converted into small luxury hotels, those which are now called Boutique Hotels.

We spend our days mostly driving south and when the destination is Plakias in central Crete, there is a certain frustration to driving through Hora Sfakion, which is a surprise. We would have liked to stay longer, it is a lovely little village huddled at the end of a ravine, and the port for the excursion boats for Loutro can only be reached by sea, and for Agia Roumeli, also not connected to the road network, which is one of the nearest places to the seaward end of the famous Samaria Gorge.

Besides the long drives, the days are packed with meeting agents and visiting numerous hotels and apartments, mainly in the early morning or the evening. Yannis is particularly accommodating, taking us out for supper on at least two occasions. Particularly memorable is the evening meal on the Akrotiri peninsula, near the airport, at Nikterida, outside Chania, where the affable Babis was the owner. He impresses us with traditional Cretan dishes, and we are treated to a superb Mezes, spinach pie, fried cheese and cheese and meat pancakes. It is superb food including a goat casserole served in a lovely old restaurant and we are introduced to Babis' father, an old man of 87 years.

"I don't think you will believe him," says Babis translating as his father earnestly breaks into our conversation in Greek: "but he does still frequent discos!"

We have to be convinced! We feel honoured to be treated to an evening in a restaurant obviously loved by the Greeks.

Finally, we cannot contain our interest in the city of Chania any longer. Down on the waterfront great waves are crashing against the seafront and flotsam and seaweed smells of fish, but not pleasantly. It is far too windy and cold to sit here so we walk back into the town where the leather shops are very tempting. We order some magnificent traditional leather boots which take two days to make. They look so genuine and indeed they are, but the leather does not seem to give so will they become the life-time investment we hope they will be?

We walk up to the Agora with its profusion of fruit and vegetables, fish, meat and gaily coloured bunches of balloons, fascinating stalls selling fresh and dried herbs. "I wish now we had a villa with a big kitchen, I would love to do some shopping and make a wonderful banquet," I say.

"Think, what you are saying," laughs Simon. "Be honest, would you swop the magnificent restaurant meals we are enjoying, to be sweating over a hot stove?"

"Well, I will dream on!" say I. One day we have our own home in Greece, I am sure!

We drive out in the daylight to the Akrotiri Peninsula as the first rays of sun break through the gloom, to see the area we visited in the dark last night.

"These are beautiful villas in this area," I say. "It's a pity some parts are very spoilt. But I can see how the beach here was chosen for the filming of Zorba the Greek."

"The mountain is very dominating, very bleak," concurs Simon as we stare at the beach lying beneath its bulk.

"I don't like it," says Oliver firmly. "Well, shall we move on? Let's go on to the Monastery, it might lift our spirits. There are two, which one shall we visit it first?"

Gouverneto is one of the oldest monasteries in Crete. We approach it through a marvellous limestone gorge coming to the monastery walls which hide a building with almost Doric columns, a beautiful façade and a traditional three bell tower and a lovely interior. Simon and Oliver then take a cliff path and find the cave with stalactites and stalagmites which come together to form pillars and one stalagmite which has formed a bear-like structure which in time had been covered by more flowstone.

Goats are gathered in a herd, when we reach Agia Triada, Tzaragaroli. The yoke of history clearly weighs heavily here. Although well preserved and active it is crumbling a little and hens are clucking around in the forecourt. The museum is well worth seeing with historic silver and wooden crucifixes and lovely robes together with some impressive icons.

Plakias, Agia Gallini, Matala

By Saturday there is a cold wind but as finally we set off for Plakias on an increasingly beautiful drive we are treated to a sunny day. With the ever present White Mountains still snow-covered, we traverse through Alpine scenery and across the plain of Rethymno dominated by the Venetian fort and begin to climb through rolling countryside, similar to the Yorkshire Dales, immediately changing to deciduous woods and more open mountain scenery and then finally entering a wonderful limestone gorge with sharp sides as though the earth has opened up we descend to a small village overlooking Plakias Bay.

Excited we hurry down to the coast to park, to discover there is a reason why everyone is wearing winter trousers and anoraks: it is very cold and windy, and the sunshine has been deceptive. But even this doesn't take away from the extraordinarily long beach backed with massive dunes and the impressive mountain scenery. It is a fine-looking harbour scene, blue, white and red caiques with yellow nets. It has a more genuine atmosphere than any other place we have found on Crete and we begin our quest for suitable accommodation for our programme.

After looking at several establishments we halt to take lunch at the taverna at the far end of the beach, the Paligremnos, which has been recommended by the friends we are meeting. The dish of artichokes and snails is delicious and most unusual. Here we have found what we had been searching for! With our friends, Peter and Penny and their children Catherine and Francis we wax lyrical. One of the pluses of travelling around as we do is we also seem to make many friends, and even chance acquaintances after two or three meals together can become firm friends and were it not for Peter and Penny perhaps we would never have been persuaded to come to this delightful eatery in Plakias.

There are studios here and the newly built Hotel Plakias Bay is even more appealing. We decide to stay, enjoying the thoughtfully positioned writing desk where I can catch up with my notes, the blue painted wooden window framing the golden beach, the blue sea and sky with a backdrop of table-topped mountains sliced into sections.

Here to explore Crete the next morning the penultimate day to our departure we go further east, to sum up Agia Galini and then Matala. These are places of unusual character clearly with their own devotees.

Agia Galini with its steep main street leading to the harbour has a lot of charm, mixed with the ugliness brought by modern tourist infrastructure.

Perhaps in time, the new concrete buildings will blend in, but it seems to have taken away the historic allure of the old fishing village, timber and olive oil port. There are plenty of shops and facilities and with houses built up the steep cliffs, it reminded us of the fishing villages on the east coast of Yorkshire.

We knew we would raise our eyebrows at Matala. In the 1960s the caves towering over the beach had been the hideout of hippies who had been driven out a decade or so ago by the Junta and disapproval from the Orthodox Church. Thought to be artificial constructions made in Neolithic times they certainly had their uses and perhaps were used in Roman times as tombs.

Now the small beachside place sports a large beach and a chance to stare from afar at where those liberated people of the flower-power era had lived rent-free. They say these free-spirited souls included Janice Joplin, Joan Baez and Bob Dylan. We don't have the time or the inclination to climb up to inspect the caves which may have had so many uses, although Simon, a caver in his youth had expressed enough interest to drive all the way to down the south coast to see them and then daunted by the distance we are from Chania with our departure flight in the morrow we stay only half an hour!

It is around 17 April 2020 that the awful thought dawns on the Sagittarian involved in this account and the inveterate traveller in the family, that the Coronavirus lockdown imposed on the population might not be lifted on the older members of the U.K's population, or worse it such a reducing of restrictions may not be considered until a vaccine is found. Nor is there any escaping the fact, however much I try to deny it, that a birthdate in 1938 will not allow me to escape under the net.

PART 4

*HEADING INTO THE
HILLS & BEYOND*

CHAPTER 15

*Mainland touring plus
the odd island or two*

July – August 1987

S imon has been granted a Sabbatical holiday by the Yorkshire Post to 'Research the
Effects of Package Holidays in the South-
eastern Mediterranean.'

Suzi puts it to good use to research for her
newly created travel business: Greco-file.

This is the itinerary of our Sabbatical Route: just to
put it into context we leave our friends, Ant & Dee, whose
house in West Sussex is a convenient stop-over before we fly
out of Gatwick to Corfu on 7/7/87.

We overnight Hotel Xenia, Ioannina, (approx.
130Kms) have lunch the following day in Metsovo (56kms)
and come to rest at the Hotel Divani in Kalambaka for our
second night. (56Kms)

(PLEASE NOTE ALL DISTANCES ARE APPROXIMATE,
AND CORRESPOND MORE TO MODERN MOTORWAYS AND
A ROADS RATHER THAN THE OLD MOUNTAIN AND
COASTAL ROADS OF THE 1980s)

The next day we drive via Trikala & Lamia to Delphi
where we stay at the Hotel Acropole. (242kms)

On the 10/7 explore the site of Delphi and the

Hosios Loukas monastery, Nafpaktos, Anti-Rio/Rio ferry boat, (Delphi-Rio 115kms) Zachora (Hotel Rea) supper near Kaiafas. (Rio-Zachora (153kms)

It is then back to the hills to visit Andritsena, (65kms) onto Ancient Bassae, and down the coast to Kiparissia, (65kms) and on to Pylos. (48kms)

Curiously this town disappoints us, and we press onto Methoni, (11kms) where after a very long day's drive the Methoni Beach Hotel suits us very well.

On our first day 'at leisure,' an excursion to Koroni goes awry and we find ourselves stuck in a sand dune near Finikounda, getting to Koroni very late.

So, we stay put on 13/7 in Methoni and sensibly explore the castle.

Back on the road on 14/7 we drive east via Pylos and Kalamata, (66kms) over Taygetos mountains, for Sparta and Mistra, (53kms) drive south back down to Gythio crossing over the Mani Peninsula and go back north for Stoupa, (90kms) where we settle at Hotel Lefktron

On 15/7 back to Kalamata and area Kitries, where we meet an agent and putting on our tour operators' hat, we look at lots of property before returning to Stoupa. (112kms)

Then we drive south again 16/7 and move down the coast back to Hotel Itilo, drive right around Mani and lunch at Gerolimenas (113kms)

17/7 Leave Itilo for Caves of Pyrgos Dirou and drive east to Monemvasia (144kms) and north to Tolo to stay. (209kms).

18/7 Another day on the road, drive to catch a ferry to Spetses for a day where we meet Kate Murdoch, founder of the renowned. tour operator Laskarina. and then back to Tolo. (160kms.)

The next day we leave Tolo for Palea Epidavros where we lunch, before driving to Athens airport to meet one of our oldest friends, Max. We all stay at the Hotel Emmentina under the airport flight path at Glyfada. (170kms)

On the 20/7 we have another very long drive to Kalamos in Pelion, where we holiday for seven nights! (375kms)

27/7 Leave Pelion and undertake a very, very hot drive, and because it is so very hot, after Lamia we take the high road to Karpenissi, Agrinion, and finally Astakos. (395kms)

Here we have an enforced two nights stay waiting for a ferry and on 29/7 reach Ithaca.

By 30/7 we are in Fiskardo on Cephalonia. (local mileage)

We are not thrilled with the accommodation we have been allocated by a tour operator on 31/7 and on 1/8 move to better accommodation in Vigla.

We spend 2/8 looking at property and explore Cephalonia and on 3/8 catch the ferry boat to Corfu ending up in the northeast of the island on 4/8 at Aghios Stephanos, (Corfu town to Ag, Stephanos 35kms) looking at another tour operator's accommodation.

A chance meeting with one of the directors of one of the tour operator, Greek Islands Club, whose island property we had been inspecting, on the night ferry going north to Corfu from Cephalonia results in us being upgraded to a very welcome first-class cabin. We don't forget the way that Rick, the tour operator, wearing a purser's hat sprung from behind the purser's desk, surprising us with the upgrade!

On 7/8 we explore Corfu, Sidari – Aghios Georgios, Bellavista, Corfu town, the Lucciola Inn at Sgombou and introduce ourselves to the owners of the nearby Casa Lucia. (local mileage approx. 120kms.)

A trip south10/8 to Kavos and cross the tip of Corfu to stay overnight in Maltas with Sunvil Holidays. (161kms).

Echoing the beginning of our Sabbatical, on the 11/8 we take the ferry from Corfu to Igoumenitsa and Parga Hotel Bacoli, again with Sunvil Holidays. (48kms.)

We cross the Ionian Sea again, to visit 13/8 Paxos and Anti Paxos for a day trip.

On 14/8 we are back in Parga for the last four nights.

On 15/8 drive to Preveza, simply because driving has become a habit. (135kms)

Finally, on 18/8 leave Parga and Igoumenitsa for Corfu and flight home. (48kms.) Total kilometres driven:

3,309.

Some of our journeys take in huge areas of Greece. It is what we do! Other people take walking holidays, trekking or climbing mountains, some sail boats across choppy seas or around turbulent capes dreaming of the calmer waters they know they will enjoy. We explore the byroads, driving way off the beaten track!

In the more worrying times of the early twenty-first-century, we may not be so keen to jump into a petrol driven car and drive many, many miles.

Indeed, as I write this in mid-April 2020 it is not at all clear how we will travel after the Coronavirus pandemic comes to a close. It is not even clear that it will come to a close. But in the mid twentieth-century touring holidays are the backbone of our tourist business and a way of life for us and our clients appreciate the detailed itineraries we provide and the wonderful unspoilt places we help them discover. If nowadays endless touring in a motor car is not considered environmentally friendly it is worth remembering that our main excursions in Greece are at a time when Greece desperately needed visitors and sustainable tourism.

Furthermore, some of the isolated mountain villages and remote coastal communities from the 1960s through to the year 2000 are still suffering from the poverty engendered by 400 years of Ottoman occupation to be followed by two world wars, then civil war and finally a Financial Crisis which is hard for Greece to endure as it comes into the twenty-first century.

It takes a long time for a country to climb out of such deprivation and so we feel our life-time of curiosity and the little we contributed to individual places in terms of financial reward is justified even if our travelling is helped by the combustion engine! What follows is a more detailed account of this wonderful Sabbatical tour in 1987 where we covered the majority of the mainland of Greece and some of her islands. However, be aware to write a full account would be a full-length book in itself!

Corfu to Igoumenitsa

8 July 1987

Putting some flesh on the bones of this account, we head into the hills. When we look over the sea from Corfu, even in the early days of our travels we always knew that one day we will head to the hills, even Mt. Pandokrator, the highest mountain on Corfu, is not enough to stand in as an adventure and today July 8 is that day.

We land in Corfu and pick up a brand-new hire car, the hire car representative driving us to the port to save time, luggage on the backseat passenger's knee. One of us is an editor and journalist and the new car is the way our car-hire agent expresses his appreciation of our interest in Corfu and the mountains of Epirus.

As we reach the port, and having dropped off the representative, the ferry from Corfu to Igoumenitsa is showing signs of departure. We wind down the window of our brand-new red hire car and shout 'stop' 'wait'. We wave our official letter from the Greek National Tourist Organisation at them, with its distinctive logo.

We do not have the Greek words, and an argument ensues, but they stop raising the ramp and with Simon now driving they hasten us forward.

The ferry is full, there isn't an inch to spare,

well maybe a foot can be found! But how can they put our little car on the boat? It is the last ferry of the day. But they continue to beckon us forward, one of us now out of the car watching with apprehension, the other concentrating on the impossible task of driving a car up the ramp onto a boat with absolutely no room for it!

It's so easy when you know how. We discover you simply throw a few ropes over the sparkling new car, secure it after a fashion and then let it travel suspended gently on the ramp to its destination. "Phew!" And we look at each other as we take the gangway up to the deck, and smiling, nod with a knowing look of misplaced confidence!

Driving the car off the ramp is more difficult, Simon having to climb into the car through the window because the doors are packed against the next-door vehicle. He is greatly encouraged by the gang of Greek sailors who need us off and away so they could start unloading their cargo of lorries and cars. As we are driving backwards, we need to swing round now we are safely away from the boat and turn on the quay.

Seconds later there is a loud crunch as we back into a newly painted anchor bollard. Cheers from the sailors and gales of loud laughter!

We don't stop to inspect the damage to our shiny new hire car but drive onto the waterfront, park on the street and take a cautionary look. It is no better or worse than we expected but we walk in silence to a café well along the waterfront. This will be the first sustenance we have had since we left Gatwick early this morning. We have a long drive ahead and we are both very shaken.

Apart from ordering a comforting coffee and a nourishing ice cream we don't say much, indeed we don't speak at all as we drive up into the mountains, glorious mountain scenery, blues, greens, rounded hills, blue skies – the very views we had dreamt of during all our coastal holidays. Occasionally a soothing hand is stroked over the driver's leg.

Then the passenger speaks, "well if that is the worst thing to happen on our six-week tour of Greece, then I'll be content with that."

"I just can't think what we will say to Spiro in Corfu. How could I have been so careless?"

We are on our Sabbatical trip, the journalist among us being on leave from the Yorkshire Post. We have six glorious weeks and we have not yet spent one night of these weeks in Greece: Ioannina, Metsovo, the daunting Katara Pass to Kalambaka for the Meteora is all we have planned so far.

Ioannina

Heading north-east one reaches Ioannina, beautifully sited on the shores of one of the largest lakes in the Epirus region, Lake Pamvotida, and the island home of infamous Ali Pasha with the striking Fethiye Mosque.

To add to our stress, we have difficulty locating the Hotel Xenia in the centre of the city, so once found we park the car, repair to the bar for a drink and then for a well-earned meal. Unable to contain our curiosity we take a post-dinner amble and find wooden buildings in a narrow street with shuttered windows, undoubtedly concealing the famous silversmiths.

We take a coffee and eat a very sticky cake in an elegant coffee shop, with a wonderful lattice wooden ceiling and an ornate balcony. We decide we like Ioannina and the comfortable hotel is very quiet for a town hotel.

Breakfast features the ubiquitous cold boiled eggs but the red ladderback country style Greek chairs set the unfamiliar tone. We begin our sightseeing on this glorious morning on foot in hot sunshine; a lizard is climbing over the pavement bushes which are round and clipped with Michaelmas daisies and gladioli in the bed below and we move into the old town, below the citadel.

The Silversmiths Street is now open which tempts us to buy a ridiculously cheap filigree bracelet but with time pressing we don't start early Christmas shopping. Moving through the castle walls the buildings are so architecturally foreign with Turkish influence that is easy to remember that as recently as 1913 this important city was under Ottoman jurisdiction.

There is a pervading sense of evil. The flamboyant reign of Ali Pasha is not forgotten, his influence so strong that in the late eighteenth, early nineteenth century those who would carve out their places in history, but should have known better, were drawn to accept his hospitality, including Lord Byron or Markos Botsaris, key players in the Greek War of Independence.

We shudder as we look at the Lake and remember the women who were sewn into sacks, alive, and tossed into the still waters, drowned by the tyrant. Was the Mansion we see, with its overhanging upper floor, the place where Byron and Hobhouse stayed during their visit?

There is evidence of archaeological digging – have they found new classical ruins on this ancient acropolis.

There is always the backdrop of the Pindus mountains.

Time is pressing and we don't think we should honour this man, the evil Pasha by inspecting his tomb in the foreground of the famous Fethiye Mosque but have to admire its elegance from afar. Even scheming and evil men wish to be well remembered for posterity.

Metsovo

We drive around the lake and we are soon ascending the broad backed, heavily rounded slopes of the Pindus mountains, a challenging mountain drive, pre the motorway, on the Via Egnatia, but a convenient drive of ninety minutes for lunch in the mountain resort of Metsovo with Tyrolean style main street, embryonic skiing developments.

Rewarded by an excellent mountain goat casserole with a Greek salad we round the meal off with a delicious baklava. We appreciate the air here, noticeably thinner and cooler, the red pantile roofs taking over from the traditional grey stone slate contrasting with the green of the conical forested mountains and the very clear blue of the sky. We walk to the bottom of the village captivated by the old-fashioned shops, the old cobblers and the carpenter's workshop, fashioning kitchen spoons and vessels. Two women sit outside a shop with woollen carpets on display, plucking and sorting the wool and a third is spinning it into thread.

We are told by a shopkeeper with amazingly good English that the size of the village has quadrupled in five years.

The village is obviously earmarked for big development and I recall that the press trip I did a decade ago spoke of this. There are plans to bring the ancient highway, where necessary via a tunnel through the highest mountains. The old Via Egnatia, from Thessaloniki to Igoumenitsa, was originally carved out in the time of the Caesars when they were visiting Cleopatra in Egypt, and before that as a trading route. It is still used today by heavy trucks from the Middle East to Europe, and in time it will be brought up to the modern standards, keeping it open in winter.

Now as we leave Metsovo and take this beautiful old road rising up the challenging Katara Pass we consider these plans for a modern motorway.

Occasionally a heavy long-distance lorry, possibly making the trip from Europe to Syria or elsewhere in the Middle East slows our progress down to a crawl until we can find a safe place to pass.

It becomes annoying when just past one there are another two or three ahead, and it is clear there is a need for a motorway! The countryside immediately becomes more Alpine, with bovine comfortable pastoral creatures, the cows, adding to the scene. It is a very impressive route and once over the pass the route downhill becomes very twisty all the way to Kalambaka, with the inevitable caravan of lorries and tractors.

Passing through the wooded lower slopes the extraordinary bulk of the Meteora is suddenly visible in the distance. Too obvious to be ignored for they are weirdly untidy, strangely out of place! Huge pinnacles of rock rising out of the earth. Creations of the god of nature indeed! But we get closer and when finally, the monasteries atop these rocks, some of a thousand feet or more, come into view these are some of the most spiritual buildings we will ever see.

Kalambaka & Meteora

The night is to be spent in uninspiring Kalambaka which allows time on the morrow to explore the strange pinnacle perched monasteries of the Meteora.

To be honest our senses are still singing with the sheer wonder of a second mountain drive in one day.

We book into the Hotel Divani, on the edge of town, which frankly is lovely and very reasonably priced given the quality. Cool marble floors, air-conditioned and very quiet, an oasis at this time, in an otherwise boring town.

The magic is rekindled by a visit to the rocks at midnight, lit by a full moon. Total silence, peace and tranquillity, the monasteries on their rock towers in black silhouette against the moon, the few lights from the windows stars in the darkness; an unforgettable experience. One by one the lights are extinguished as the monks complete their prayers and retire for the night.

Some of the mystique has been dissipated – we know the monks no long ascend and descend by way of winch and basket – and large numbers of visitors tend to destroy the aura of remoteness and isolation; but the juxtaposition of the individual monasteries, each on their own rock tower, makes for a remarkable bit of scenic romanticism. We retire, relaxed and overawed.

Arising in good time we are driving back through Kalambaka and beyond the little town of Kastraki, dominated by the huge Meteora rocks. As we turn into the valley these colossal key pillars loom upwards and there perched upon some of them, we can begin to discern the shape of beautiful monasteries.

There seem to be one or two hermitages in unexpected places – and then what appears to be a line of washing hanging on a precipitous rock in front of a cave! It is a few visits over time that make us realise these are flags of devotion marking the original hermitages which were created two or three centuries before most of the monasteries.

We don't wait long for our first close view of an actual monastery. First to our left is Aghios Nikolaos and then immediately around the next corner Roussanou to the right and across from this Varlaam and behind it the Great Meteoron.

(overleaf) Rousannou, the beautiful nunnery at the heart of the Meteora

We know we will not have time to visit inside all six surviving monasteries (of the original twenty-four).

We drive to the crest of the hill and turn right and then beyond to Agia Triada, the most precipitous of all the rocks crowned by buildings with a very strenuous long climb up from the valley and difficult access (although in the twenty-first-century an elevated bridging causeway was constructed from the road almost to the height of the monastery).

Finally, we come to Aghios Stephanos with the easiest access. We stop and take photographs before going back towards Varlaam, stopping again to admire Agia Triada, the Holy Trinity, very taken by its position 400 metres above its valley and knowing that it has been used as the location for films, including the James Bond movie, For Your Eyes Only.

It seems that the monks can cheat and by-pass the precipitous climb up to the monastery from the valley below by using a kind of 'monk-in-a-basket' whisking a passenger and goods from the outside world to their scared eyrie atop the slender pinnacle.

Sometimes the monks prefer an easier way than the long climb from the valley!

There are considerably more people here at Varlaam, but it is definitely the best place to start given that here of our choices for this morning there are the most steps. In the heat, we slowly start to ascend the narrow steep pathway. As we climb slowly, thoughtfully, we contemplate how the young ascetic in the four-teenth-century managed not only to climb this vast flat-faced grey rock but how he and his mates managed to do so time and again, hauling up building materials to found and create this amazing place. Apparently, at first it was all achieved with wooden ladders pegged into the rock face and probably each time the ladders were scaled their lives were at risk. Certainly, in future whenever we are faced with a daunting task, perhaps we will consider these heroic masonic achievements!

Varlaam is very beautiful and the monks so welcoming despite all the hordes of people. It is very impressive and almost simple in its monastic beauty. We are taken by the refectory and the kitchen with a vaulted ceiling as well as the breathtaking Katholikon, one of the most striking monastery churches we have seen. But it isn't until later in the day driving to Delphi when we see the storks nesting, in the craziest, narrowest, highest point of a church dome or building that we realise the similarity. Nature climbs high to display and isolate itself, man imitates to profess his loyalty to God or escape persecution.

After we have seen the Grand Meteoron, which is bigger, better, more beautiful, but more tourists, we begin to leave from the sacred aura of Meteora as we drive down to Roussanu – St. Barbara which with its delightful, feminine, charming nuns is much more peaceful. It all seems so wonderful, so exquisite that it is hard to tear ourselves away. But go we must because our scheduled has marked tomorrow for Delphi and thereafter the Peloponnese. How could we ever have considered these stelae as cumbersome as we did when we first arrived!

Our decision to stay a night in Kalambaka had given us time to study each monastery and the nearby base also allows us to visit at a time when coachloads do not overwhelm the place; it has paid off. Nowadays there are a host of beautiful small hotels, some classed as boutique, from which to choose but at the time of our visit Kalambaka received relatively few overnight visitors.

We are hooked, this is an area to which we know we will be back, at least we hope we will! Heading south through Karditsa, and beyond, is where we are fascinated by the populations of storks nesting on church domes, chimney pots and telegraph poles, again and again, we are to be reminded of the monks of Meteora.

These birds at Artesiano find the highest point and build something there.

Delphi & Hosios Lucas

We arrive at Delphi, by way of Lamia and Amfissa through the thousands of acres of shimmering silver-green leafed olive trees. Delphi is perhaps the best known of Greece's classical sites after the Parthenon. We are happy to draw breath although we have avoided the national road by turning near Thermopylae towards Amfissa and heading to our first visit to Delphi – 'the centre of the earth'.

We rave and wonder at our luck when we find a small hotel, overlooking the Gorge, (they all do!) But the hotel is very clean and cheap, and we rush out expecting the site to be shut. But it isn't. The splendour of Delphi on a beautiful smmer's evening after the amazing glory of the Meteora and a long drive, falls a little flat. Perhaps the anticipation has all been too much! Or like Byron, we feel nothing much is still standing, but the situation and atmosphere do have much to commend it.

Delphi is set in a mountain bowl with steep limestone and pink sandstone flanks with tough grass and herbs clinging to sheer granite limestone rising above. A leafy walk brings us to the theatre, a real natural amphitheatre which is wired off. A few tall Cypresses and mainly deciduous trees like almonds are an attraction and there are still a lot of wildflowers, wild hollyhocks and pale blue campanula and many weeds in the ruins, particularly in the theatre.

But it is not so easy to avoid the tourists of which there are hoards. There are fewer ruins than expected which are not in my case easy to make head or tail of in an hour's climb to the top of the site. The temple of Apollo is a great disappointment. Again, we are rushing; is this to be the normal schedule of a travel consultant?

When the sun goes down, we walk along the esplanade outside the ancient site to the Castalian Fountain. The ever-present dark and forbidding gorge invites no guests and we walk back into town for supper. Although the view over the Gorge is again magnificent, the conversation of an American at the next-door table monopolises the meal to the extent that it overwhelms the whole experience. He is clearly overtired or not enjoying his brush with Greek culture.

Outside on the veranda of the Hotel Acropole there is a mingling of woodsmoke, Gauloises, crickets, the full moon and Greek music, we have chosen a very simple and romantic hotel.

Next day, straight after breakfast, we visit the museum before the coaches arrive. We begin to absorb the splendid atmosphere of the remains. The small museum, manageable to the casual historian, in its thirteen-room layout, is particularly rich in Archaic and other sculptures of all periods and if you are only going to visit one museum in Greece, Delphi will not disappoint.

The twin representatives of the transition from Daedalic style to early Archaic, style, the two statues Cleobis and Biton are prominent among the exhibits. The Ionic winged Sphinx of Naxos sentinel on his plinth stops us in our tracks but it is the fifth century Classical masterpiece, the life-size bronze statue of the Charioteer in his long, pleated tunic, reins in his hand, which of course is the abiding image we take away.

We are captivated by the composed look of the onyx eyes, the copper eyelashes and lips. Three pieces taking us through the ages.

Our visit to the site of the Tholos of the Athena Pronaia is to another world. Charming peaceful and quiet, the charabancs of tourists have been disgorged at the main site and are ignoring this little paradise. Here all is relatively silent. Only three columns remain with Doric proportions that for us make the whole trip to the site of Ancient Delphi more than worthwhile. We can see the four surviving metopes above these columns, with fragments of a centaur and the woman he is abducting and a warrior mounting a horse, (badly damaged in antiquity). From the remains of the treasuries and temples, we can immerse ourselves in the magic of Delphi in a way not possible at the main site. Here birds chirp and can be heard, and here we can take photographs to our hearts' content.

Footnote: We shall come back to Delphi, and each time we do we shall become more enchanted, the secret of Delphi is to plan a visit so you can be there before the crowds, to arrive before the buses converge from all other parts of Greece, chose the season, and the time. Each time we shall also be captivated with the view across the gorge, from the hotel balconies or the restaurants on the main street; right down to the sea and the Gulf of Corinth with the hills of the Peloponnese beyond.

We press on to the impressively huge monastery Hosios Loukas, its dazzling gold mosaics bringing tears to one's eyes – this is one of the 'big three' Byzantine churches in Greece, the others being Daphni in Attica and Nea Moni in Chios. It is of course, equally over-run with visitors but not to the extent that on this first visit we could not enjoy the beauty and peace of this place. It is time to say goodbye to mainland Greece for this leg of our journey. We know we will be back.

CHAPTER 16

The Peloponnese:

*Rio-Antirio to Zachora,
Andritsena, Bassae,
Kiparissia and Pylos*

July 1987

After lunch in historic and lovely Nafpaktos, its fort reaching high up into the pinewoods we drive along the coast to Rion, and thence by small car ferry – The Rio-Antirio suspension bridge yet to be built – we reach the Peloponnese, that huge almost-island part of the Greek mainland.

With an essential night at Zachora, we draw breath and begin to relax in a genuine and non-tourist town with a drink in the square among the paper pamphlets thrown from a taxi by a lottery ticket seller! For supper, we make enquiries from the hotel reception and are directed inland to a garden restaurant with tables under what has to be described as a tholos of tree-leaves where the trees have white painted trunks and blue spots. Polythene transparent sheets cover a beautifully embroidered table-cloth. Crickets are chattering competing with the Greek music. And strange how a simple taverna in a remote area can conjure up a scene where superlatives would not be enough!

Later we realise that we have stumbled on the magical area of the thermal springs at Kaiafas, an area of great beauty where the spa is still active, and the lake and its beautiful coast backed by pine forests.

Next morning, we take to the hills again, by-passing Ancient Olympia. Somehow, we know we will come back to visit this most prestigious site at a later time, even so it is a curious omission from our programme.

Heading for Andritsena and the Temple of Apollo at Bassae.

This is a particularly picturesque route through glades and meadows rising through woodland to the mountains enhanced by white and pink oleander, cypress trees and many flowers and herbs, a particularly thorny blue thistle being most attractive.

At Andritsena, a very attractive little town literally perched around the mountainside the road climbs again and on the crest below us, hidden from view initially is the Temple of Apollon Epicurus.

Furthermore, the temple is shrouded in scaffolding and the guide in broken English gives us to understand that the ancient monument is to be covered and roofed over to prevent damage in the future; the recent earthquake in December having severely shaken this unique and well-preserved edifice.

It doesn't strike us at the time that we are among some of the last people to see this awe-inspiring temple as it should be seen, albeit through the steel scaffolding but without its 'tent' for decades to come. Nor do we know that the journey we have enjoyed so much that morning will be almost destroyed by the fires of the early twenty-first-century. We never know what life has in store for us, which is probably just as well but as I write (the end of April 2020) there are now indications that the lockdown imposed in March will not be fully lifted until a vaccine or drug is found to combat this horrendous virus of Covid 19.

This will have huge implications for travel and hospitality and for the older members of society who may be asked to stay in their homes perhaps for a year or more, unfathomable distress. Is this one rare instance of having an insight into our future which we cannot tolerate? And how will history see the decisions made by a government whose leader is recuperating himself from the disease?

The route down the mountain is clearly one we should not have chosen. It may have looked shorter and obvious on the map, but it is hair-raising and on a dirt track, but possibly saves us about fifty or sixty kilometres in distance and an hour in travelling time.

Even so, we inch our way down, steep ravines fall from the road on either side and the landscape is not as lush as it has been on our earlier journey. Bit by bit we come down through the valley, through small villages where we feel self-conscious and again, we are in a beautiful wooded landscape.

Eventually we reach the coast, turn left and in a few minutes arrive at Kiparissia, an attractive town where from the headland we can look down on magnificent sandy beach stretching for miles. Here is a quiet harbour with a few boats moored and we are ready for a lovely lunch of red mullet and keftedes, only a smell of sewage later spoils the effect.

Years later we discover the old town and castle on the hill above the town.

Navarino Bay to Pylos

We drive on to Pylos taking the inland road with great expectations of coming down to the coast at the celebrated Navarino Bay.

The reality is disappointing, a heavy agricultural smell hangs in the air, possibly olive oil or soap factories and in Navarino Bay at least six massive oil tankers are sheltering. Pylos itself is very attractive with a French influence pervading the small town, with wrought-iron balconies and colonnades shading the shops, along three sides of the square. But still the strong smell persists.

Forty years on Pylos is a home-from-home, a much- loved destination to which we are drawn almost every year. The smell of oil in those days is unaccountable and the wine refineries and raisin stores on the shores of the bay at Gialova have either been demolished or converted to modern usages for the tourist infrastructure.

Methoni

So, we don't stay in Pylos and 11 kms further we reach Methoni to rest for a few days. It is only the fifth night of our adventure and we feel we are at the beginning of our explorations of the Peloponnesian mainland.

We consider many of the hotels in Methoni, but it is the Methoni Beach Hotel which screams "No contest! Stay here!" High ceilinged rooms, the height of the rooms, literally the height of two staircases (and there is no lift!) which lead to the upper floor with old fashioned furniture, comfortable beds, a deep old bath and bidet in the bathroom and an outlook on the huge and wonderful old port, the acres of sandy beach and the sea with the Venetian Bourtzi tower on the harbour wall.

Dinner served on the terrace confirms this is a wonderful place. Melizanosalata, (aubergine dip) with an interesting batter style topping like Yorkshire Pudding, is followed by Hare, Stephanos' stiffado kouneli, with bay, sweet shallots and juniper which is excellent.

We walk around the town, admiring the balconied buildings along two long parallel streets with shops and amazingly British style of window display, quite unlike the jumble of Greek shops generally.

The attractive hexagonal Bourtzi at Methoni Castle has a grim history.

The hotel is covered with creepers and we awake suddenly after a good night to the heavenly smell from the blossoms of the fragrant creeper (is it ampelopsis?) and swallows flying in and out from the eves. It is Sunday and our first day 'off' and it nearly turns into a complete disaster.

Approaching Finikounda the road appears to go along the beach. Except there are numerous tracks and stopping to ask, a friendly Greek woman and her daughter give us directions and we offer them a lift for a short distance. Then we set off on a track in the wrong direction and get hideously stuck in the sand dunes. But for the help of a French couple, the loan of a spade and a tow from their camper van we would have been stuck for how long? Except a tractor comes down sometime after we are free and went back without stopping to see what had grounded us! Obviously, they are used to rescuing stupid holidaymakers!

But we do notice that immediately our little red car is free our tracks are covered. All that remains in the sand are my sandals which had come off as I pushed the car free, with the young French girl.

We couldn't come all this way without visiting the tiny harbour of Finikounda. It's a charming spot with a cluster of pretty houses around a coarse sand bay and the little colourful harbour but because we are so dirty, covered in sand we simply lunch in the first taverna.

This evening back at the hotel, as we sit in the dusk, a ballet of bats and swallows begin their performance without waiting for their audience. Five bats and two swallows vying for the available midges. A sixth bat joins them above the forest of young tamarisk trees, and behind the beach the carpobrotus plants still display their colours in the dying light. Pulled up on the beach, bright orange pedaloes creak as a child bounces from one to another. A few people are still swimming, and the yachts turn on their cabin lights, one by one as inhabitants volta to the end of the beach.

Methoni, together with the neighbouring equally ancient ports, of Koroni and Pylos on the Peloponnesian peninsula of Messenia, form ideal touring bases. All have wonderful sandy beaches, the one at Methoni is remarkably shallow with hard sand, perfect for children. Each is dominated by a huge fort, of Venetian, Frankish and Turkish origins. The visually stunning early sixteenth century Bourtzi tower guarding the seaward side at Methoni is exceptionally photogenic, its octagonal shape perched on a long causeway most holidaymakers ignoring its sinister purpose as a jail during the Turkish occupation.

The castle site is usually approached over the fourteen arched bridge, over the now dry moat and through the battlements and on into a domed road that leads through two more gates into the interior of the castle. The immediate impression in this vast space is one of emptiness.

With a lack of ruined buildings, it is hard to imagine that only two centuries ago this was a thriving historic fortified settlement, one that had represented an important seat of power at various times in history but particularly during the time of the Greek War of Independence 1821-1827/32.

At this point, it is worth pointing out that apart from monasteries, churches and castles, and some surviving Venetian public buildings that there is very little architecture that predates the end of the Greek War of Independence.

At the Methoni Beach Hotel, the owner,

Stephanos Manoleas, is a wonderful cook and goes on to run the highly praised Klimataria restaurant in the village. At the hotel in the late eighties, we aren't offered a menu, but each meal is freshly cooked and balanced to satisfy. To sit on the outside restaurant terrace eating Stephanos' fish cooked to order, a wonderful treat -, while the swallows and bats sweep back and forth above the Tamarisk trees in an aerial ballet between you and the setting sun over the sea is the epitome of what Greek touring is all about. The hotel still functions today (2018) run by Stephanos relatives.

We have touched only briefly on the spell that Messenia will cast over us. So different to Methoni is the almost perfectly preserved Niokastro above Pylos, sometimes referred to as Navarino Castle to which we return many times in future visits to Messenia. Here atop the rocky escarpment, this Turkish/Venetian hexagonal monument is well worth a visit but in 1987 we passed it by together with its colonnaded town square, one side open to the harbour!

From Methoni we go on to the sad 1986 earthquake-shaken city of Kalamata, now mostly devoid of its elegant neoclassical buildings, with the homeless, a year on, still living in tents or metal cargo containers. Great gaps exist on the streets where buildings once stood, few old buildings remain and those that do, most of them propped and shored up, show they were beloved old houses. The area around the New Agora is awash with hundreds of beige tents for the homeless but it seems removed from us and we are due to meet the local tourist agents Nick and Maria Kirtsakis the next day when we may find out more. In the meantime, it is a sobering place to visit.

Especially now as I write in 2020, we are beginning to relate to shattered dreams, when they are saying travel to Greece may not be possible until mid-summer 2021, particularly if you are classed as being in the vulnerable group. Perhaps if our prime minister, Boris Johnson returns to work on Monday after his extended convalescence after contracting Covid 19, things may look more positive. We know we have to take the warnings seriously, this week two of our close friends have succumbed to the disease. One of these friends I had known since we were both babies, friendships don't come closer than this.

The Taygetos and Sparta

So today we pass through Kalamata, knowing we will return in a day or so. Our trip today is intended to put the towering mountains of the Taygetos into perspective. They frame Kalamata City and beckon as we begin the long climb up and on towards Sparta. This tour de force of highway-engineering winds its way up the mountains, passing large villages, shaded by huge pine trees.

The Taygetos is a vast range separating the remote Mani region and plains of Messenia from the eastern side of the Peloponnese and the road to Sparta is a succession of forested ridges to be crossed, deep dramatic gorges and tumbling hairpin bends to rival any found in the Alps.

Sadly, some of the forest has succumbed to fire in recent decades but nothing will diminish the colossal engineering employed in its reconstruction in 1940, a road which has been used since antiquity connecting Ancient Sparta to Messene, to allow it to become useable by motorised vehicles.

Mystras

Sparta is a fine base to explore Mystras, the once vast Byzantine city with some of its monasteries and churches, still intact and with its fortress and mansions deserving more time than the flocks of coach trippers can devote to it on their brief visits.

Founded in the thirteenth century, Mystras is dominated by a castle, below which is the famous Palace of Despots, a rare example of a Byzantine civic building and a host of churches, houses and monasteries spread over a large area. In the heat, we are fortunate to know that there are two entrances to the site, one leading up from the village and the other at the top giving access to the castle and the path back downhill to the Lower Town. We work out it is best to park twice, once at the top and once at the bottom.

The Pantanassa is considered to be the most beautiful of the buildings in Mystras, and we have left time to explore its treasures including the paintings in the upper galleries which are outstanding. Moreover, we have our binoculars with which to view them! The Church has unusual pointed Gothic arches, which may be a sign of Western influence, as it is the last church built by the Despotate. The nuns who reside here at the time of our visit welcome visitors, and the flower-filled narrow courtyards beg us to linger. As I write six nuns and a small community of cats are the only residents of this beguiling place.

Sparta

We are tempted to dismiss Sparta itself, and glad we don't! With its spectacular location between the jagged sheer Taygetos peaks and the softer Parnonas mountain range we realise this is a city with completely natural fortification!

For some years the history of Troy and the story of the Trojan war with Menelaus supported by his Mycenaean brother Agamemnon when his wife Helen absconded with Paris from Troy, has captured my imagination.

This is regardless of few artefacts to back up the tale, and it is a place upon which to ponder history. Did Helen miss this spectacular scenery when transported to the besieged city of Troy? Or perhaps Thucydides was correct, in surmising that a mere collection of villages was at the heart of this battle thirsty city-state. Even so, the visitor is rewarded with an Acropolis, the Sanctuary of Artemis and the Menelaion, a vast space in a place known for massiveness, where a dedication has been found to the ill-fated couple. Surely it is fitting that the Spartan, Leonidas, the hero of fifth century who fell at Thermopylae in 480BC as he attempted to halt the Persian invasion should be Sparta's best-known son.

The town is constructed on a grid pattern following the Greek War of Independence (1821-1827) which creates a legacy of Neo-Classical buildings and broad streets lined with orange trees, reflecting that modern Sparta is an agricultural town in the heart of the citrus growing area.

The Mani: Gythio, Neo Itilo and Stoupa

Taking the road south, beyond Sparta, away from the mountains and travelling to the sea we reach Gythio, the seaport from where it is claimed Paris and Helene made their getaway.

Here both the central and eastern prongs of the southern Peloponnese beckon with a variety of choices of exploration.

The central Peninsula comprises the bare-rock wilderness of the Mani, famous for its independent people and populated mainly by goat and sheep herdsmen and their families.

In August 1987 taking the road out of Gythio towards the Deep Mani, we come over the crown of a hill, one of the few lower passes over the Taygetos range and stop where two young boys stand under a tree with a horse tethered in the shade.

A Maniot tower stands by the side of the road.

This monument is a symbol of the gateway to the Mani, although nowadays the hillside shares a monument to the brave fire-fighter Konstandinos Dounias, who lost his life in the devastating fires of 2007.

We move on a few yards anticipating a great view and we are not disappointed. Beyond and below us is a magnificent vista, the almost circular vivid blue bay of Neo Itilo, framed by the white shingle beach and rich parched lands of the Mani.

We are captivated and scarcely looking left to the magnificent looming mountains or the unwelcoming entrance to the small town of Areopolis, not knowing what we are missing by not venturing into this historic town, we wind slowly down the steep hillside almost certainly following an old track as it meanders, with huge zigzags, down to the coast. We never even notice the massive Ottoman castle of Kelafa (1670) but then shadows so often hide this historic fortress, so important in safeguarding the area, whether its occupants were Turkish or Venetian.

Our guidebook is still the first edition of THE BLUE GUIDE 1967, the collectable Stuart Rossiter edition, which warns us that the road is in varying stages of improvement, in parts very bad.

The reason we had not considered a stop in Areopolis is that far below us we had spotted what looks like a new modern building, perhaps a hotel, and time and our stomachs suggest we should find somewhere to spend the night. Also mesmerised by the vivid aquamarines and blue of the sea we want to explore the smaller bay within the Bay of Itilon, that of Limeni and its enticing little harbour.

We drive along the seashore with fishermen's houses crowding either side of the narrow road and our first glimpse of a tower house, which we find out, is a historic abode of Petrobey Mavromichalis, the nineteenth-century leader of the Maniots during the Greek War of Independence. But Limeni is a pretty but desolate sort of a place. Eyes seem to be on us, clearly this area does not see many visitors and we press on confident that we have spied a welcoming venue in the large building along the coast.

Out of Limeni Bay once again we have a commanding view of the vast Neo Itilo bay and another semi-ruined tiny seaside village in which to run the gauntlet. The houses in Neo Itilo are in an even poorer state of repair than Limeni, not even a cat prowls, although a single dog barks and at the far end of the bay the 'hotel' itself is taking on a proud, somewhat intimidating, mantle. We lose our nerve despite the modern façade and the hotel's look of a 'classy' establishment. Tired and hungry we drive on.

The road now climbing up again and along the narrowing road up the northern side of the bay until running along an escarpment high above the sea on an increasingly rough road we begin to pass numerous Byzantine churches. At a later date, I will variously count up to thirty-five churches, some in clusters or in tiny villages and some isolated or almost built onto the road! Then the road again winds down to a large coastal plain where in desperation we turn left following signs saying Stoupa and the Lefktron Hotel.

The Lefktron Hotel incidentally became one of the properties to feature in our first brochure when we launch Filoxenia Holidays a few years later. It is not the first: that is reserved for a small seaside villa near Kitries.

We had first visited the Outer Mani in 1986 but did not get beyond earthquake rattled villages down the gulf near Avia and it was the Sunflower villa at Kitries featured in another operator's brochure that encouraged us to explore further down the peninsula eventually and expand the programme, not just in the Peloponnese but in many unusual and interesting places in Greece.

When we first visit Stoupa in 1987 it is a very small and truly unspoilt village with a magical, sandy, empty beach and within short walking distance of another fabulous sandy cove at Kalogria, where you can definitely feel the cool springs in the sea. In those days there are not a huge choice of tavernas although every year more and more will be established. There is always Ilias' near the rocky harbour wall, which is wonderful, but as the 1990s brings more visitors to the Mani, the taverna of Ilias' sister Rena and her husband Costas at Kalogria, backed by tamarisk, is frankly idyllic and in time this becomes a small pension growing in size over the years.

Kalamata

Now blissfully happy in unspoilt Stoupa, we know we have to drive back to Kalamata, (taking the more direct route) to meet the new agents who will show us some accommodation for our programme. Although everywhere we have been, we have seen a great deal of accommodation which is always time-consuming since it is not, by any means, all suitable for British tourists. We meet Aris and Sophia on the main thoroughfare through the city, outside their office. Sophia is to show around a huge number of properties, and in one of them there is the sad realisation that the people living there are refugees from the earthquake. In another, Greek philoxenia is shown by the owner, with peaches, and cake and café frappe and the owner and Sophia talk about the impact of the earthquake when Sophia admits that she had been thrown down from the second floor of the apartment block and cracked her head, "it was the worst night of my life" is not an understatement.

We are thankful when we are shown a pretty villa which is an outstanding property and perfect for the programme, being almost on the beach and with a lovely garden. Nearby in the little port of Kitries it is clear that they had felt no tremors at all.

Back in Kalamata, Sophia goes on to show us the full horror of the disaster with demolished and derelict sites, in spite of the enormous effort to clean up much of the damage.

On our return it is clear that we have been away from their office a long time and Aris, who has been left with his paperwork the whole time Sophia has been away is insistent that we share a glass of ouzo with him. We give him feed-back on our tour.

It is then that we realise that they are living in a room above 'the shop' since the earthquake in 1986, and with no water, no toilet. I decide that everyone is too emotional; we promise to go back to our office in the UK to seal our co-operation with them. Right now, doesn't seem to be the fitting time.

It will be a year before our programme will be up and running and initially, we will continue to offer the villas under the umbrella of another tour operator, through our travel agency. It is a first step, but it is a big one, not just for them but for us as well.

Back in Stoupa, we can enjoy a refreshing cool evening swim and a pleasant evening dinner in the taverna. Nothing will divert our thoughts from the horrors we have seen that day, but we are confident that in another year Kalamata will be returning to normal.

Kardamili

A day later we explore a few miles further north to reach Kardamili, a most attractive main street with substantial old houses on both sides of the street, which is, and still is the main road.

In addition, picturesque, old Kardamili is set back off the road where walking up to the small acropolis we discover a medieval castle which at the time of the Greek War of Independence was the home of the Mourtzino family and turned into Kolokotronis' headquarters, who along with Petrobey Mavromichalis, from Limeni, played an enormous part in creating a successful outcome for Greek independence.

The Church of Aghios Spiridon with its beautiful pointed spire is a landmark for visitors as they approach the town, particularly from Kalamata.

Just outside Kardamili going south is the handsome home of Patrick and Joan Leigh Fermor, knowing this, I am such a fan, I can do nothing more than gaze in awe at its beautiful location just above the sea, the island beyond and when years later we discover there are new buildings that had encroached on this place of peace we are sad.

Although we never meet them, many do. We love to eat at Lela's tavern, welcomed by her lovely smile, on a rocky plateau above the sea near the old soap factory. Meals have rarely been as romantic and as tasty than at Lela's with her home-cooking, honed when she was Leigh Fermor's housekeeper.

You would think that we would never want to move from this stunning area, perfect and quiet beaches even in August, beautiful architecture, mountains coming down to the sea, but something is nagging at us.

"I'm told that it is even more wild and remote in the lower part of this peninsular, the area south of Itilo. I think we should go back."

"I've heard that too," says my husband, "the area is called the Exo or Outer Mani and the southern bit is called the Mesa Mani or Inner Mani."

"It's calling to us, it sounds very wild. They didn't even have roads until 1956, or thereabouts and the people are still very cautious with strangers."

"Do you actually mean downright unwelcoming? Do they still live in the tower houses? Surely the vendettas are over, and they've ceased lobbing off rocks from the top of their towers, intentionally aiming at their neighbours?"

"There's only one way to find out. Let's go! There're numerous barrel-vaulted churches dating from the ninth century, more I gather than we saw on our journey up here in Platsa and Nomitsi."

"And they may have frescoes worth seeing. And anyway, I felt bad driving up to that hotel on the seashore at Itilo and driving off again, in and out of their parking area without even looking inside. I feel less spooked by the area, now I have seen Stoupa and Kardamili, and knowing that Kalamata is within reach."

We retrace our steps, taking time to stop and photograph the little churches on route and wonder at the magnificence and height of the mountains of the southern Taygetos and to notice the peninsula of Messinia across the gulf.

Oitylo & Neo Itilo

We stop as we begin our descent to look down on the ancient village of Oitylo, the original capital of the Mani, although we don't spare the time to wander through its narrow streets. The name was used at the time of Homer and it is said that Napoleon 1 sailed into the bay on the way to Egypt.

Still a little apprehensive we drive down

to the little plain and pull into the yard in front of the Hotel Itilo. Its golden stones shining in the sunlight and we are very taken by its pleasing architecture. We remark how quaint to be greeted by hens, little knowing that hens will run under our feet at breakfast time and that their eggs, and then the honey and toast will be as delicious as it is possible to be.

Sophia and her husband Nicos, without a word of English, greet us with the sweetest of smiles and show us to a luxurious room on the second floor under the eaves with a magnificent sea-facing balcony. The rooms even have a bath. Their family, Evangelina and Theodoros, are being trained to help run the hotel. Furthermore, we eat like kings and when we demolish a huge fish on a platter, Nico tries to persuade us to sample the eye, insisting it is the main delicacy, by scooping it out of the fish head and popping it into my husband's mouth!

We visit the Alevras family very many times over the years and when Sophia retires her daughter-in-law, Panayiota, joins son Theodoros in running the hotel and the cooking is as home-made and good as ever.

After the tragic fires of 2007, when Theodoros is instrumental in stopping the fires by allowing the use of his private water-supply, hoses and pumps (just one of his ecological systems,) he is awarded a grant. With this he has the funds to begin a huge renovation to the hotel, which to all intents and pur-poses means that he can pull the old hotel down, and a few years later we return yet again to a com-pletely new hotel, rebuilt on the original footprint by Theodoros in Maniot stone to a traditional design after he pulled down his parents' pride and joy, Nicos and Sophia's handsome hotel and rebuilt it in stone. This must have taken both courage and vision, but the resulting boutique hotel is a finished result which has paid off.

Now with a stone-built swimming pool, the often-adventurous sea swimming against the bra-cing rollers of the bay, where Napoleon is rumoured to have landed, can be avoided. On our last visit So-phia is visiting from her home in Athens and her grandson young Nicos is taking on more and more of his grandparents' and father's roles.

The shore, never the highlight of the bay, with its grey rocks and ecologically positive seaweed, has been transformed with thatched sun-umbrellas and sunbeds, and the shallow waters and sandy bottom under the huge rolling waves are as wonderful as they have always been.

In 1987 being the proud owner of the book called THE MANI PENINSULA (Treasures & Austerity) by Aurelie and Jean Ioannou, we agree that we have come here to see as many of the churches and chapels of the Inner Mani as we can. Besides, we want to explore the villages, the fantastic caves of Pyrgos Dirou discovered at the end of the nineteenth-century, and the area's oddities such as the Emporium at Stavri, a shop so out of the way, but stocked with everything you would expect to find in a modern supermarket. It may no longer exist.

Areopolis, Vathia & Gerolimenas in the Deep Mani

Climbing up the hill from Limeni, about 5km, but not as far if you are a crow, and parking on the narrow street which leads into Areopolis we decide that to explore the narrow streets and push open the doors of the fine Taxiarchis church (1798) would probably deflect from our wider tour, in any case apart from gazing at the fine statue of Petrobey in the main modern square we are seriously inhibited from exploring the slippery shiny paved narrow streets with ridges across the path every few yards.

In 1987 visitors venturing into the beautiful grey gaunt old town feel overshadowed by the dominating tower houses as though every unseen eye is upon them. *A few years later we are able to overcome our fears and seek out the new cafes and look at the new sophisticated pensions without feeling self-conscious.*

We find the best way to spot the churches on our route to the tip of Mani and the village of Gerolimenas is to drive straight there, enjoy a superb fish lunch with Yiannis and Giorgos Theodorakakis at the Hotel Akrogiali and amble back and with the sun behind us, some of the churches will be visible through the waving golden grasses. On our outward journey because of the angle of the sun, we have simply not noticed them!

And we don't leave the tip of the central peninsula of the Laconia before we make a diversion to the amazing tower village of Vathia, from a distance the presence of these towering building looming above us intimidate us, as our little car makes it way hesitantly up the mountain where these eighteenth and nineteenth century buildings are perched.

Once we arrive, we hesitate before leaving the safety of our car to photograph the phenomenon and to look out to Cape Matapan. *(In years to come, we do discover that some of the properties are still occupied, and in time by immigrants from Western European countries who restore a few as holiday homes.)*

Clearly, in a few days, it will not be possible to visit all the churches but those we find are not locked: Episkopi, Aghia Varvara, Gardenitsa and more allow us to simply open the door and enter. *(Sadly, nowadays they all are locked.)* In some beautiful frescoes remain and the marble sculptures make us gasp but the church which takes to our heart is the fourteenth-century neglected Trissakia with the roof open to the elements which has walls covered with frescoes; some in such good condition that we take photographs and create a postcard to send out to our clients and more importantly to the Greek National Tourist Office. Coming back a year or so later we are delighted to find that some attempt has been made to shore up the building and protect the treasures with a sort of corrugated roof-shelter, but it is an effort probably too late to save it.

The Last Supper: a fading fresco from the ruined church of Trissakia, Mani & view from the church, probably ruined beyond repair as it was in 1987.

As the churches over the years have been smartened up and access often improved so the tower villages, once so intimidating are now being restored, with the houses used as second homes. But when we first visited barking dogs and stony and thistle filled paths would deter us from exploring on foot. Nowadays their stark beauty contrasting against the prickly pears, pitched against the dark peaked mountains and the brutal heat of the sun is one of Greece's wonders.

CHAPTER 17

*Pyrgos Dirou, Monemvasia,
Tolo, Spetses, Gly-
fada, Athens*

July 1987

We are leaving the Southern Peloponnese to meet a friend in Athens off his flight and then driving up together, for a week's rest in Pelion. We have booked a small house right on the seashore in South-Western Pelion. It sounds idyllic and we hope to make a co-operation with the agency offering this house and other properties for our Greco-file programme. Our friend Max is 'good news', a man of high intellect and a huge sense of fun. I have known him all my life.

We leave our base in Itilo, imprinted on our memories as we drive away are the two faces of the Mani, the hard, unyielding mountains and seashore, the uncompromising climate, the fierce inhospitable reputation of the

Maniots and the truth that we have been really welcomed.

Before we start our journey, we make a well worth short detour to what at first appears an incongruous experience in this hot sun-baked spot – the Caves of Pyrgos Dirou – which rank as one of the world's major subterranean attractions. We park and book our seat in the small boat which will take us into the caves.

We are to be treated to formations from another world, there is always a formation whichever way we turn, tastefully illuminated; they are endless. Stalagmites and stalactites formed millions of years ago are gently lit: pink, green, brown, copper and lignite streaked. It is an amazing experience. If we are told that they are the entrance to the Underworld, we will have every reason to believe it. Certainly, there seems to be some evidence, through the bones brought out of the lake that prehistoric man lived here and most certainly worshipped here with some of the bones belonging to large animals including a hippopotamus.

The caves are thought to be about 14kms long and some think they may extend under the Taygetos as far as Sparta, with numerous waterways.

We are shown evidence that the Southern Peloponnese may have sunk, and a river flowed through or the seawater filled up the cave creating a lake. Visitors are transported through this vast cave lake, said to equal in beauty the Zeita cave near Beirut and the Padirac cave in France, in flat bottomed boats for about 1,200 metres with a further 600 metres negotiable on foot. Once inside the caves much is as it was, and has been for – possibly –millennia, certainly thousands of years with the remains of fossilised of animals alive two million years ago.

The whole trip takes about an hour – a cool otherworldly timeless experience with an unbelievable concentration of very finely coloured stalactite and stalagmite formations, curtains, pillars, screens and bosses, which just seem to go on and on. All the while there is the strangely calming, echoing lapping of the waters of the underground lake as the boats are paddled through narrow passages linking chamber after intricate chamber – a veritable labyrinth. *In the 1980s the caves had been noted but the many tourists brought by coach had yet to descend. In those days, the roads are simply not wide enough...and in any case, Stoupa is yet to become a large enough beach resort for travel agencies to take up residence.*

It is time to move on, Monemvasia is on our itinerary and it is an even longer detour. But I wanted to visit this fortified citadel which had attracted my interest when it was highlighted, during the tourist lecture on the Press trip I did with a party of journalists to Athens and Rhodes.

Pristine ruins and remains are being restored to preserve the buildings as a medieval citadel. It is a long drive of two hours, and others would say "It was a long way for a very poor lunch."

The amazing beauty of historic Monemvasia outweighed the fact that we think we have been lured into a tourist hotspot. The expensive meal might have disappointed but the great citadel of Monemvasia did not.

After the long walk up the causeway from where we park our car to come face to face with the great grey wall of the citadel where the Z-shaped entranceway into the town is not immediately apparent, we can draw breath to admire the whole stronghold, hidden inside this huge Gibraltar-like rock promontory, still appearing almost complete.

This is a preliminary visit but nothing about it gives any indication that we should not come back to explore the city in a more leisurely way. We walk hesitatingly on the shiny slippery street paved in polished limestone, worn by years of donkey's feet and warrior's boots. It is narrow with shops and cafes now filling the houses once inhabited by merchants and captains from the time when it was a Medieval trading centre. It has been a commercial port perhaps since Minoan times and known certainly for the locally produced Malmsey wine.

The street, the width of a donkey-with-a-pannier-either-side leads down to the beautiful church in the square of Christos Elkemenos, its stones almost golden in the sunlight. Venetian and Byzantine buildings jostle for attention in the Kastro and they only scratch of the history of this miraculous town below the gigantic rock.

There is no time to climb the steep path up to the Church of Aghia Sophia in the ancient citadel on top of the rock. Our heads are full of the amazing sights we have seen, a town which is to be perfectly preserved on a volcanic precipitous rock surrounded by sea, the only access nowadays being the man-made causeway and then through the single entrance in the ancient walls – highlighted by its name, Monemvasia. This Greek name means single passage derived from the narrow entrance through the walls with its almost Z-shaped design to disallow any person arriving unannounced from seeing who or what is waiting to greet them as they negotiate the dark and forbidding entrance. As far as we could ascertain there is only one other breach in the seawalls, an ancient gateway, used by those who wish to board boats or leap off the rocks into the sea.

It is a rock-bound city guarding the eastern peninsula of the Peloponnese. Even today it is forbidding to arrive on foot after the long hot trek along the narrow causeway separating the massive rock headland from the rest of the coast. The original settlement was founded by the Lacedaemonians in the sixth century when they abandoned Sparta. Through seafaring, the settlement prospered, became rich and developed into a fine cultured and artistic settlement.

Monemvasia still retains much of its former Medieval character and is being systematically and very sympathetically restored to its former glory and is now, as then popular with those connected with the arts and culture. By day we know of nowhere where the china blue of the sky is so complimented by the ochre pink of the sandy ground, the stone and roofs and white of the plasterwork of the settlement, along with splashes of bougainvillaea. Everywhere there is the weight of the outcrop, curiously shaped like a Safari hat as you start approaching it from Gefira.

Its overwhelming presence invites the climb up to Aghia Sofia the church at the top of the flat-topped bluff; in the summer this is probably only possible to do in the early morning or late evening.

One of our subsequent visits to the historic citadel occurred when we escort our clients, Michael Frayn and his wife Claire Tomalin, the well-known writers, to the tiny walled city. Using the tried and tested "do you know who they are" we are able to get our celebrities moved from a tiny pokey cell, one of the 'unique' rooms offered to guests in the Malvasia hotel to the much more salubrious and deluxe room which had been ordered by our tour operation Filoxenia. What would have happened had we not been on hand to make sure our guests were accorded what was theirs by right I don't know. Always with the travel company, a phone call out of the blue was answered in the knowledge it could be a client in distress who rather than communicating with our agents preferred us to deal from afar, and thus making our task of fixing a problem that much more difficult. At least, in this case, we are able to haul up the management for their misdemeanour and soothe over what could have been an embarrassing moment.

Many of the restored houses now form part of the hotel complexes – possibly one of the most romantic situations in which to stay in the whole of Europe. Add to this the evening walk back from the hotel room to the paved square, overshadowed by the immense bulk of the rock on the rear side, and the beautiful Greek Orthodox church of Elkomenos Christos in perfect symmetry on the left side with the ink-black sea and sky in front of you.

Walk to the right, climb the steps and be shown a table, covered with a red and white check cloth, lit only by candle-light and prepare for an unbelievable quixotic experience, and it has to be said a memorable meal.

Leaving Monemvasia we look at the map and decide that the easiest way to Tolo where we hope to spend a night is via Sparta and Tripolis. It's a beautiful run and the views to the mountain ranges of Taygetos on the left and Parnon on the right are breathtaking, the road is good and quiet, and we make good time.

We haven't been back to Tolo since our holiday with the children in 1979 and we are surprised that we are recognised immediately with a wonderful welcome both at the Hotel Minoa and the Taverna Goodheart where we eat.

Both establishments are unparalleled with their beach location, the sea is feet away. Sadly, we are not staying at either, it is high season and the only availability we are offered is a small studio which is pretty basic, (we are getting used to better!)

This is not a trip for relaxation. We intend to see and develop as many places and properties as possible and develop the business of Greco-file as one which truly knows Greece.

As such we have an appointment to meet Kate Murdoch of Laskarina Holidays on Spetses and on the morrow we are up early to depart for a day trip to Spetses.

There is a boat excursion to Spetses, but we need to be more flexible and to enjoy the luxury of a day-long boat trip is not for us and of course Spetses and to some extent the road there is an old haunt for us.

Compared to our route down to Argos

from Tripolis yesterday the route is tame, and Porto Heli looks smart, white almost gleaming. Kosta on the mainland directly opposite the island of Spetses has got busier but not much has changed. We have to park the car and catch the little water taxi to Spetses, which takes about fifteen minutes.

Spetses is just as colourful as it was a decade ago, bobbing boats and the blue and yellow Flying Dolphin hydrofoil in the harbour, blue and white tables, blue and white painted houses. Our first impression is of a busy and relaxed harbour front. The familiar pebble mosaic pavements and the streets are lined with cafés instead of Yannis-in-the-square and the place is shaded. Café owners vie for custom and turn their radios up high. A complete mixture of people is totally at home, eating or drinking coffee: cosmopolitan, smart, elderly, Greek-speaking and then a predominance of English conversation wafts through the air as we wander up to the Dapia and clearly, we are expected.

Are we strangers looking for our Laskarina contact!? A young man, dark-haired and obviously Greek comes towards us. "Suzi and Simon?" he greets us in faultless English. "Kate has asked me to take you to the beach for lunch. Let's take this water taxi to somewhere a bit more peaceful."

If we had been expecting to see Kate, herself, we don't show our disappointment. A tour operator who has many clients staying on what is known to be their prime island in high summer obviously will be much in demand.

The water taxi takes us round past the harbour and the town to a beach with a wonderful pine-clad backdrop with a taverna serving chicken in sauce with spaghetti which is excellent as is the bottle of wine chosen by Costas. We warm to Costas and it is an enjoyable lunch and hopefully a profitable meeting for our co-operation next year.

But it's time to see the accommodation and boating back to the Dapia where after our tour we thank Costas and sneak off to see how our disappointing habitation from our first visit is fairing, the old Hotel Myrtoon.

We are sad to see that it still looks dilapidated and filthy.

Meeting up with Kate we can be genuinely enthusiastic about the quality of her accommodation on offer. She is disappointed that we can't stay overnight but how can we, tomorrow we are due in Athens but leave gratified that after the sour experience nine years ago we have been hosted and welcomed as we would expect to be!

We assure Kate that we know the island well from our first visit and we have been impressed by what we have seen today. We take the water taxi back to Kosta and then it is the long drive back to Tolo, with the traffic heading for the Epidavros drama festival slowing us a little.

We wonder what classical performance will be staged tonight, grateful that we have had that experience when we did.

Perhaps the rare quality of that play should remain as our only special enjoyment, for now it seems unlikely we could sit comfortably on the ancient stones for another production of Euripides "Ion". Memories are sometimes better left untainted.

A very quick change and again we go down to Babis' taverna, the Goodheart so close to the sea guarded by its large pine tree, unusual, as a windbreak, the dark silent calm sea about ten feet away, where children paddle and we find this harbour end of Tolo as magical as ever.

I am happy we feel like this because when we arrive and are shown to the small studio, we feel Tolo is very busy, noisy and fretful, not as we remember it from our first visit.

We leave Tolo next morning making ourselves known to the Georgidakis family at the Hotel Minoa, we explain that we are running our travel business, Greco-file, specialising in up-market holidays by specialised tour operators featuring Greece. Yannis is very interested and offers us a drink while we discuss the company's potential, making us promise to send many more English!

Pretty little Palea Epidavros is a wonderful stop for lunch, a virtually enclosed sea bay with a little church and the fish taverna is quite lovely. A group of Tyneside builders is at an adjoining table. We liken to them to the popular TV series "Auf Wiedersehen Pet" characters, and true to form they are bewailing the distressing unemployment situation they are experiencing whilst tucking into pints of lager and platefuls of moussaka.

In future years we rarely make one of our numerous visits to the Argolida without visiting the Poseidon hotel's fish restaurant. Now as I write my heart is heavy because with the constant news of the world in quarantine, and no let-up in the seriousness of it we wonder if we will ever get back to Greece, because this dreadful disease is attacking the whole world, Covid-19.

We pick up the highway to Athens, through the city and arrive comfortably at the airport before the plane lands bringing our friends from the U.K. Max, always larger than life, and wearing a huge Panama hat which makes him look more like Peter Ustinov than usual, introduces us to his friends, Nick and Jane.

En route to the Hotel where we will spend the night in Glyfada (on the Athenian Riveria), we get lost on a new motorway, which we cannot get off! Uniquely the Hotel Emmentina, under the flight path, literally, is very comfortable!

Choosing it in later years as our airport

hotel of choice we would land from the UK we would rush into our rooms pull out our swimming costumes, jump into the swimming pool on the hotel roof and wave to the pilots feet above us, who, ten to one, would wave back as they guided their huge planes down to the end of the runway!

At supper time we stroll down to the main square. Already part of the sprawling city of Athens, Glyfada remains a fishing village at heart with the huge almost circular glistening orthodox cathedral of St. Constantine and Helen rising like a wedding cake from the main square. We choose what will surely be the original taverna with traditional red and white checked tablecloths for our meal and we are not disappointed. Max pushes the boat out and we order a very large and tasty fish.

It is good that we eat well because our drive the next day is long, with no time to dally over lunch, even though Kamena Vourla, which I remember – again from the press trip – looks tempting as the main road north sweeps straight through the town, waiters risking life and limb carrying food and drinks across the busy road to the diners at the many tavernas on the sea-side. We make do with a drink and a snack.

Besides our unsatisfied hunger pangs, the road to Volos is long and dull and we stop again for a much-needed drink on the quayside where the ferries dock.

The countryside changes again, wooded and mountainous to our left, rocky coves and promontories to our right. Then around the inland hill town of Argalasti where the countryside becomes almost English with mown hay and wheat fields, there are many woods of myrtle and shrub, but many plantations of olives damaged or destroyed by the late snow of March 1987.

Behind us, the car bearing our friends honks its horn. Max is waving the map around from the comfort of his front seat as if he was waving a flag of distress! So, I get out and see if I can help.

"Where is this God-forsaken place?" he demands. "We have come up all this side of the Gulf, just to go down the other!"

"Nearly there!" I reply with the patience of a parent to a restless child traveller. On the map, I point down the coast to a place called Kalamos. It seems to satisfy him, and in a few minutes, we do indeed turn right heading down to the coast. Our spirits rise, as we drop down on the long sandy pot-holed track and Kalamos all looks so wonderful and peaceful.

We park by the kafenion, as we had been instructed by the tour operator and Max eases his large frame from the small car seat and we follow the rest of the directions on foot, to the last house in the little bay.

Sadly, I am initially disappointed by the

siting of Magda's House, our patio is narrow much of it taken up by a huge tree and almost non-existent the beach is just a stony stretch from the house with the sea lapping slippery pebbles on the shoreline.

Magda greets us with her husband by her side, almost overbearing, tired as we are by our long journey. We need to rest.

For ourselves we have driven almost the length of Greece from the bottom of the Mani and the Taygetos mountains to the foothills of the Mt. Ossa, and thereby Mt. Olympos in less than four days!

CHAPTER 18

*So, this is The Pelion
cocooned in a brittle heat*

July 1987

There is a heatwave. It is too hot even for the Greeks. "Poli zesti" (very hot) they add to their morning greet of "Kalimera" (good morning) and "ti kanete" (how are you). In Athens, they tell us, they are fleeing like lemmings for the seaside. Costa, the owner of the local store and coffee shop, and our link with the outside world, keeps us up to date. We understand what he is trying to say, after an Anglo/Greek conversation of phrase and sign language – "118 degrees Fahrenheit yesterday," that's 47 degrees Celsius if he is to be believed! In the rustic house we have rented on the water's edge at the end of the village, our friends who have recently joined us from England including Max have imposed a 75-metre rule, banning travel beyond this on pain of sunstroke. Fortunately, the coffee shop falls within its confines.

The house itself relaxes in the shade of a massive pine; the courtyard screened by olives. Languor launches each day as one by one we slip from our beds across the courtyard and into the lead crystal stillness of the sea. "Good morning." "Good morning, Kalimera," drifts over the Gulf of Volos, fracturing the silence. Even the cicadas start the day late here. It is nearly too hot to fish, but one old man wades his way to his red caique, rippling through the glazed, heat-hazed gulf. Siga, siga, (slowly, slowly), is the name of the boat. It sits in the gulf as if upon a sheet of glass.

Pelion is an appendix-shaped peninsula on the eastern coast of the Greek mainland, as Max had so rightly pointed out as we neared the end of our journey. It is opposite the islands of Skiathos and Skopelos. The village where we are staying is reached by a half-hour drive down a rattling potholed, steep road, ending suddenly at the water's edge. A sand track runs between the sea and the dozen or so houses, bends inland, crosses a narrow creek and meanders among the olives before ending abruptly at the coffee shop and general store. Thereafter it is a walk along the shoreline to reach the house. Everyone is living out of doors. Life centres around the coffee shop, where a freshwater fountain, one of three serving the village, spills a constant flow into a trough giving an illusion of coolness. People augment the chairs and tables with their own furniture, naked children toddle between fountain and beach, absorbed in water games; gossip eddies to and fro. Strangers are assessed and judged. The one public telephone in the village sits outside on the coffee shop window ledge. Nothing is private. Max is playing the tycoon – wondering why he hasn't had a telex yet.

Up on the promontory at the far end of the village, sits the more attractive of the two tavernas. Not that it advertises its presence, except for an elderly, rusting, ice-cream advertisement nailed to a tree on the roadside opposite the tiny church. Reached by a sandy path through the backyard of a smallholding. It perches on the rocks above the sea, striped awning shading a gravel terrace.

The owner's caique is moored below, blue, white and Pasok green, with a white awning against the heat. Cooking has been reduced to three dishes, keftedes, (meatballs) pork chops and ropa, the little sardine-sized fish. Even so, the heat in the kitchen has invested in the taverna owner a new understanding, previously unknown in Greece, for the phrase 'fast food'. Anything taking longer to prepare will undoubtedly lead to his expiry through heat exhaustion. Having ordered, we descend to the rocks to swim, to cool, before eating.

Things are getting serious though, all the Coca-Cola, orange and lemon drinks have been consumed. We are reduced to Gazoza –the Greek version of lemonade –to quench our thirst. To think of retsina or ouzo in this heat would be a big mistake! We spin out the lunchtime, making full use of the shade against the mid-day heat. The landmass on the opposite side of the Gulf of Volos appears and disappears like a mirage in the shimmering haze. Another Gazoza or time to move? Perhaps to purchase a watermelon for the beach, bury it up to its neck at the water's edge.

Beyond the taverna, a narrow track between orchards leads to a cliff path descending to a brace of coves. Passing through the orchards bemused cicadas cannon into us, droning off as soon as they discover we are not olive trees. Overripe artichokes bursting with blue thistle-like flowers line the path; lemons, figs and oranges droop on their branches; tomatoes and grapes stalk in red and purple rows. From the shingle of the beach the sun strikes back. The sea becomes our solace, a refuge when the beach mats are unbearable and the factor 15 has been washed away in perspiration.

Down the cliff path come two young men and the cultured long-limbed, boyish figured beauty, a visitor from the city, here for the season, who raises the temperature wherever she goes. A man's Panama hat, a cotton tee-shirt, silky, long loose pantaloons. Across the shingle to the sea, fighting the heat. There she sheds every stitch, except the Panama, then bronze from head to toe, she wades in, slowly savouring the luxury of her immersion, until there is nothing except the Panama above the motionless water – part of the heat haze – part of the mirage.

At the back of the house, behind the barn where the hens live and the olive oil is stored in the huge barrels, is the little motor which pumps water into the cistern. There is a sterna somewhere below the ground, but the water is brackish, suitable only for showering and washing, but it is welcome, nevertheless. Drinking water is transported in large plastic containers from the village by the house owner and her donkey twice a week.

When we have showered and washed off the salt of the day, we set forth into the dusk; an evening drink, joining in a little laissez-faire philosophy with Costa at the coffee shop, a meander along the waterfront past the house where the communal baking oven still stands. Once darkness has fallen, small boats put out, carbide lamps hissing and glowing over the stern, luring squid within the reach of the spears, like wreckers lured unsuspecting ships onto treacherous rocks. Along the shoreline too, small clumps of lights spring up. Householders have moved onto the beach, setting up microcosms of their bedrooms to escape the oppressive heat indoors. There they lie, out in the open, by the sound of the sea, waiting on their mattresses to catch whatever stirrings there might be in the stillness. It is too hot to sleep through the night.

Rising in the early hours we cross the courtyard and as the house is so secluded slip naked into a sea as black as squid ink. As we start to swim, fluorescence like diamonds spilling out of a black velvet pouch, streams from fingers, arms and legs, leaving light-filled tracers in the welcome coolness of the water. Even after climbing ashore, green sparks like miniature fireflies jump and flicker on our bodies. A quite unusual phenomenon exaggerated by the heatwave.

It is time to move on and as we leave the otherworldly isolation of the village, the seriousness of the heat makes itself felt. Driving across the plain of Lamia, we open the car window. The effect is like standing in a Sheffield blast furnace when the melt is poured; a gale of dry heat. The plain has become a fan-oven.

Lamia itself provides no respite, its large main street from hillside to the plain where the sea meets the land. We wrap towels around our heads and soak them with the contents of the bottles of drinking water we have with us, in an attempt to ward off dehydration. Hastily we consult the maps and opt for a revised route over the mountains where, relatively speaking, the air is cooler.

CHAPTER 19

The mountains of Evritania

July 1987

It's true! One only has to look at the map. It is obvious that to turn right very soon after Lamia and head for the hills will be the wiser route! In this particularly brutal heatwave, there seems to be no alternative! Especially when we are hoping to hop on a ferry to Cephalonia, for yay look, there is a ferry on the map from a place called Astakos; a direct line across the map to Cephalonia, and who cares about obstacles such as a few mountains!

"We'll strike off West," I say in a faked American accent. "We'll stop for lunch at Loutra Ypati, I think Loutra means springs, there are bound to be cafes and tavernas there."

"Too hot to eat," grumbles the driver. We park and from the car the place with its slender green trees looks cool and welcoming. But we know it won't be, we don't need to open the car door, for the windows have been open throughout the journey.

"Wish we had one of those swanky new Mercedes with Air-Conditioning!"

"Well we haven't" snapped my husband, it is the day before our wedding anniversary and there is no need for that bolshy tone, I think, but don't say out loud!

"We'll fill the water-bottles and wet the towels again after lunch," I speak calmly.

"Let's just get a drink, I couldn't eat anything."

"Lime juice and lager would be great," say I, remembering the wonderful cooling pints we used to drink on Lindos beach.

"Are you hallucinating?"

"It's too hot to look around this place. I agree just the nearest coffee shop will do."

This turns out to be a Turkish Delight shop, perfect for ice-cream and soft drinks and we have to be grateful because while the funeral bell tolls from the Church, everywhere else is quiet. Even the restaurant is closed.

"There is supposed to be a wonderful waterfall here which is why I chose this place to stop. It's simply too hot to go and look for it, even the wind is scorching me, and I am seriously spooked by that tolling bell."

We worry about Max and his friends, on their separate journey back to Athens, although they are great and experienced travellers it is not an experience we would have wished on our guests. We are glad we have the option to drive up into the hills. Later we read in the newspapers of 700 dead throughout Greece. Victims of the heatwave.

It is a stunning route; climbing ever higher we gradually reduce the excess temperatures. Whizzing past in the heat haze the huge pines and scrub giving way to amazing mountain passes until the whole route after passing the mountain town of Karpenissi suddenly gives way to a vertical drop into the valley and man-made huge reservoirs below, which we can see we will reach via thousands of hairpin bends.

Great Pindus mountain peaks have graced our route, over 2000 metres, Mount Iti, and Mount Tymfristos to name but two but we are to drop down from these heights to less than 200 metres.

At the bottom, we stop at a café where a bus is parked, just as we cross the bailey bridge, rumbling across the first dry river. We have a quick drink joining the bus driver and his passengers. And then on, and on, until after crossing over the reservoirs we climbed perhaps higher than before, but the softer outline of Mount Tymfristos has disappeared and now we are in a greyer country which stays with us until we reach Astakos, a long, long way yet!

This journey will haunt us until we revisit, we are passing the entrances to the 'secret' Agrafa, possibly the most fascinating of all the mountain and remote areas which we will visit in our journeys. Passing the vast tracts of water of the man-made lakes, eventually we will come to Agrinion. Like most people who get totally lost in this large agricultural town with no signposts, (no-one who does not know the town passes through it from east to west, so why sign it, says Greek logic, everyone is going through south to north,) we rate it a dull town.

Although the map says not far now, just 33kms, it is, of course, the longest 33kms of the day, we are so tired and hungry.

But we are in for a wonderful surprise.

Astakos, Mitikas & Paleros

Astakos is a pleasing town and it the ferry boat agency does have a boat heading for Ithaca and Cephalonia two days hence, for which we are able to make a reservation. Undeniably the hotel is too expensive, they must have seen how tired we are, and of course, they know there is no alternative within miles!

The volta this evening is a joy to observe, the hotel is good, and we are happy. The volta compares with those enjoyed in Heraklion or Chios - the milling chattering of happy families in Crete and a volta accompanied by young blades in souped-up automobiles on Chios. But here it is farming families from the small market town.

We will shortly find out that this is an agricultural area as the following day when we drive north to Mitikas and Paleros it all feels very rural with livestock on the beaches.

The blue, blue Ionian Sea is just too inviting in a small cove, perfectly clean white pebble but a strong smell of goat which was better at least from pig or cow which it might have been, but we don't swim! We find Mitikas in the middle of a traffic crisis which with only one narrow street, let alone a main street might be a common occurrence. There is evidence of attractive waterfront tavernas with about three hotels and a bank, some shops but a temperature of 115 degrees F carries us forward to Paleros.

Directly opposite the mountains of Lefkada and with equally impressive mountains rising from the back of the town, it has a feeling of a lakeside location rather than a small seaport.

At first, we are disappointed but after dismissing the busy town beach as being no good for swimming we find a quiet little fish taverna called The Garden, which is delightful and the fish the tastiest I have had on this long trip. We question the English-speaking Greek sitting at a nearby table. He assures us his small town is both historic and packed with tradition.

"Do you know that we had a very famous battle near here, Queen Cleopatra from Egypt was staying near here at Actium. Think about it! A Roman called Mark Anthony was having a romance with an Egyptian woman called Cleopatra and another Roman guy called Octavian didn't like what was going on! So, they started fighting right here in Greece, with large armies! And you should be here when we do Greek dancing or one of our little theatre productions!"

We couldn't see the correlation between the two events, but it was handy to have the information. We find Paleros to be much larger than we expected with a modern commercial town above the port with shops and restaurants but the long beach which had scavenger birds on it is nasty. So, no more swimming, although we do find better soft sandy beaches away from the harbour.

In fact, business summons us, and we hasten back to Astakos to make some phone calls to the UK. This evening is not as special as the previous evening, the meal is not as good and although we go to bed early anticipating a 7 am rise to catch the ferry for Ithaka, we fail to sleep well, the noise from the lively town is just too disturbing.

Years later we are to return to find a pleasanter coast, welcomed by tourism with its proximity to the developing Preveza airport at Actium and a busy sailing hub for small yachts setting off an Ionian sail.

CHAPTER 20

Ithaca and Cephalonia

July 29 1987

We awake to clouds, no less, although they soon clear and with the car packed up, breakfast eaten, we sit on the seafront and paddle our feet in the sea.
Already it is hot and there is no sign of the ferry, so we walk on to the Café Bar where the Greek, back from America makes us a special fruit salad as though he divines it is our twenty-second wedding anniversary! The little ferry boat SS Ithaki comes in and quietly offloads its cargo, there are no big commercial vehicles and Simon has no difficulty backing on the hire car allowing us to sit back for the voyage, without stress and enjoy the deep blue Ionian Sea on an air-conditioned boat.

Vathy

Arrival in Ithaca follows a pattern, small islands to pass by as we sail into the harbour, outlines of hills, trees, more sea and the day we arrive there is a sorrowing drama caused by a forest fire, but well under control by small airplanes.

Vathy is the tiny island capital, sitting at the end of a long and sheltered bay, more like a fjord, with a narrow entrance, the village with probably less than 2000 inhabitants, mostly rebuilt in the Venetian style after the 1953 earthquake. At first, it seems as if the Captain will have difficulty negotiating his blue and white pride and joy into the narrow bay, but practise makes the arrival as perfect as it is possible to be. We hadn't wanted to come, we are tired, and it has been some time, at least eight days, since we were in a place where we might bump into clients – we had almost forgotten what they might be! But the exquisite calm and beauty of the bay soon overtake our senses and we seek somewhere for lunch.

Here we find even the taverna has pretty plates, (Crown Derby style, no less) and we begin to feel we should be staying more than a night.

Kioni

We drive on to Kioni to the office of the tour operator hosting us for the upcoming night. Big mistake! Inside we encounter James and Miriam who are restlessly seeking attention. Before the rep can attend to us, they round on us condemning the company for letting out such primitive accommodation, as though it is our fault! This puts the rep, in this dusty and untidy office, in a difficult position and unwilling to admit that his clients might be disillusioned for a good reason, he gathers some keys and whisks us along the quayside to, yes primitive, but by Pelion standards, the spacious Kioni waterfront accommodation.

The location is charming. This little port is smaller even than Vathy. We walk along the waterfront and examine the small tourist shop which had it sold clothes would have had my order, such is the state of luggage disorder after three weeks travelling.

Planning to turn the car around we take the right turn, where Simon blatantly drives on and on, in full view of all the locals even after being told to go left; then we encounter an even greater loss of face, much to the locals' amusement who could see it coming! We are confronted by a huge motor-yacht which has come into the tiny port of Kioni. They locals knew all along that we were about to run out of road!

At first, as it loomed into sight, we think it must be the big house we had seen on the corner. Clearly, this large boat (it was registered in Gibraltar) has come in not knowing the waters and its owner Johnny is angrily scolding his crew, while his blonde and his guest, another woman, look helplessly from the upper deck.

"There's TV drama in this mooring!" I said.

"Blonde, guest, American no less, look how it's fouling up the mooring rope!"

"Watch it! Now they are demanding that the Brits shift their little yachts, and he is still trying to anchor!"

Finally defeated Johnny gives orders to sail out to deeper water. "No real damage done."

And there the big monstrosity stayed. No one came ashore for dinner. But we have a wonderful Anniversary meal with a bottle of Robola wine brought by the rep with the welcome news that our accommodation is also free. What luxury!

We leave Ithaca after a delay of the ferry boat's arrival allows us to take in something more of the atmosphere of Kioni, inspecting more properties, some very good, others less exciting and certainly poor in Frikes. After lovely Kioni we found Frikes lacking the atmosphere of the two other tiny ports, although the dark valley bottom guarded by two mills is a fertile home for tangerines and melons. We learn there that there are plans for a sailing centre to be set up here. We turn up the hill for the thrilling drive back to Vathy along the saddle with views dropping down to the sea on the east and on the west. No wonder Odysseus could not stay away from this magical island!

Cephalonia

For the last three weeks, we have been in relaxed mode but now as the ferry approaches Cephalonia, we are conscious that this is where hard work will begin. We are about to meet the directors of the prestigious villa rental company, who we hope to represent, and Cephalonia will be a prime sales product of our programme.

I'm not at my best, I had had very little sleep the night before, a party of rowdy Italians had partied on the waterfront well into the small hours and if I am totally honest our own lavish wedding anniversary celebrations had added to the discomfort felt in my head. Indeed, I had tried to grab an hour or so of sleep in the shade on the beach where we ate lunch, but the wash from the ferry pulling in somewhat destroys that idea.

We arrive in the laidback town of Agia Effimia and seeing nothing to delay us set off up and along another stunning coastal ridge, running geographically parallel to the one on its close neighbour Ithaca. The view down to Myrtos Beach is exhilarating, perhaps a thousand feet below.

Fiskardo

Once in pretty Fiskardo unspoilt by the recent

earthquake and reminding us of the Dodecanese, we are shown to a trio of tiny studios. Knowing that we will be meeting the directors for supper we are uncomfortable with our reaction to this property. Frankly, it is very grotty indeed and very smelly, probably some of the worst Greek accommodation we have stayed in and at its advertised price, very expensive. Fortunately, it is to cost us nothing and furthermore that evening we are treated to a lovely meal, and another bottle of the amazing Cephalonian white wine, Robola, which brings out the best in the conversation.

We didn't sleep too badly despite the ethnic character of the room and its ponging shower and loo! The next morning, we swim early from a small and unexciting beach and hope we can concentrate on the quality of the accommodation rather than the generosity of our hosts.

It is, however, the pattern of this pretty village; it appears the British visitors are happy to accept the simple accommodation in return for the friendly and excellent service from the individual owners which is reflected in the Greek word philoxenia, meaning literally 'friends of strangers' and which in the 1980s and 1990s comes to represent Greek hospitality.

It makes us long to create our own programme where we can have more control on standards. Indeed as we develop our own programme, (obviously we will name it Filoxenia Ltd.,) where we do deliberately choose accommodation for the warmth of the hosts, we also come to recognise that comfort, even a bit of luxury is necessary, but as we were once informed by a Greek hotelier, "the more aristocratic you Brits are, the more you are not just prepared to rough it, but expect to suffer!"

We experience another round of villa inspections, not surprised in this aspect that Fiskardo is much the same as Kioni, basic and simple houses made comfortable rather than luxurious but with outstanding service from Katerina, Ireni or Marika. Afterwards we wander around the village and then leave this little forest of sailing masts, balanced on blue seas, and the backdrop of ochre and white houses. We drive over the hill, slowly as the roads are certainly not for racing along!

Assos

In time we wend down the narrow road with its many hairpins to tiny Assos nestling at the foot of a mountain, guarded by a round peninsular, wooded with silver pines and topped with the walls of an enormous Venetian fort. Before we settle in the village, we cross the isthmus and press on up for the view which could give us vertigo but fortunately, we fight it and find the sight rewarding. Beautiful isolated beaches

beckon under steep cliffs, probably only accessible by boat and the village sparkles invitingly.
Then finding the castle area empty and unim-
pressive, we take a photograph of the stunning
village below and then we return down.

The village that looked so enticing certainly is, but as we take photographs dense dark
clouds loom on the mountain. *Nobody could imagine that thirty years later the darker clouds from
the storm of biblical proportions (there is no other
suitable description) dubbed Medicane Ianos would
devastate this tiny place with a massive rock fall
swept down to the waterfront in September 2020.
The Ionian as we would increasingly find has had
far more than its share of disasters.*

Fortunately, these clouds pass as we settle
under the shade of an enormous plane tree at
a very good taverna in Platia Parisian, (named
for the generosity of the French who rebuilt the
Venetian buildings after the damage inflicted by
the 1953 earthquake). We are enveloped in the

beauty of this tiny place and its delicate location astride the isthmus which leads to the castle peninsular. Surrounded by oleander and some of the delicate pink flowers it emanates idleness, except for the pink gravel path which leads down to the beach beckoning for a swim.

Myrtos

Onwards we have more agents and owners to meet so without even glancing at one of the few shops we find ourselves on the road passing Myrtos Beach way below us.

We are tempted. Is it too far?

An American sees us hesitate as we get out of the car to take photographs. "Go for it, it's well worth it but better to walk than drive, and the colours are best seen from this height! I think it is the white pebbles beneath the water that gives you the brilliant azure, turquoise and ultramarine."

We thank him and agree the walk might do us good.

"And for me essential," I say patting my stomach with a wry smile.

"Yes, too right," he says, "we can't resist these salads with their wonderful Greek olive oil and moussaka! Although come back in twenty years and I bet you my last dollar that there will be a wider and safer road built here down to the beach."

For the time being, we decide to walk; and we find a huge magnificent white beach of all type of pebble until it became white crystalline sand with a turquoise sea beyond compare of anything in our experience.

Argostoli and Spartia

Then after a truly wonderful swim and the long climb up we have to make great haste to Argostoli, a sad town with a view, a causeway over the sea lake, a market where one would expect a dock and very poor housing in buildings damaged in the 1953 earthquake.

Having located the agent's office, we are told we are not expected yet so after doing some shopping we make our own way to Spartia for another aspect of Greece. Rich and wealthy Greece, once upon a time, because no buildings are standing down here although there are some Venetian ruins and garden walls and gates left alone as if to emphasise the tragedy.

We are beginning to get a feel for the enormity of this disaster. Because Fiskardo was more or less spared it is not until we see the vast rebuilding programme with– there is no other word – nasty concrete replacement buildings in Argostoli, once a stunningly beautiful town of Venetian houses, monasteries and churches, that we can comprehend the damage done by three consecutive earthquakes in August 1953, all at least 6 on the Richter scale or more, the worst measured 7.3. Our imaginations can scarcely cope with the horror and despair the people would have felt.

Yet as I write I am trying to stay positive during our worldwide Covid-19 disaster: the loss of friends to the disease, the knowledge that just in the UK the recession will be the worst for a hundred years, although the good news is that the Greek Government and tourist industry are hoping to start opening the tourist infrastructure in June before opening hotels in early July. Our generation has for 75 years (we have just marked the seventy-fifth anniversary of Victory in Europe after WW2) grown used to the fact that most disasters are in places far removed from our life, and even these awful earthquakes which virtually flattened Zakynthos, Lefkas and Cephalonia were at a time in our modern history before-package tourism.

But Assos, as we find out, which we had admired earlier in the day, was rebuilt by the French in the style of the Venetians.

Our accommodation is, thankfully, the best we have experienced since we left Itilo in the Mani. We are beginning to tire of the simple rustic approach. And the dinner on the terrace of the Pomegranate Tree is also of quality. Our view is of Mount Aenos, for the first time since we arrived, as the cloud has lifted, and the peace and space overtake us. We hear only a goat bell, a barking dog and the odd sleepy cicada until a solitary motorbike en route to Argostoli wakens our reverie. Relaxation, a contrast indeed to the last few days and this lovely restaurant is in a new house built in the old style and run like the famous Stephanos' in Corfu town or Mr. Angelou on Leros, a place to be a guest.

Our parting gift from our hosts, the directors from one of the tour-operations, Greek Islands Club, whose large programme we had inspected in our few days on Cephalonia, is a first-class cabin on the night ferry taking us to Corfu. Pure Filoxenia! Delivered with the ebullient flair one of these young men is known for, he pops up from behind the Purser's desk, wearing a Purser's hat as we board 'The Ionis' proffering this very welcome first-class ticket! Ten days of exhausting high temperatures and being on our best behaviour whilst absorbing a very diverse programme meant we are happy to travel onto Corfu where we feel we may be under less pressure.

It also means together with the generosity shown with much of the accommodation and many of the meals being given freely, we leave with a warm glow of satisfaction whereas when some of the programme has been below our usual expectations it could have been one of disappointment. It is also a lesson in viewing the holidays offered through the buyer's eyes rather than through a glossy brochure. Some properties had been outstanding, others perhaps lacking in creature comforts. It will mean training our sales staff in our UK office very carefully.

CHAPTER 21

Corfu and Parga

August 1987

As the sun rises the ship comes alongside the coast of Corfu: Kavos, Messolongi, Benitses, Ayia Deka, Corfu Town, the fort, Venetian port – what a magnificent façade!

Would Argostoli have looked like this? I cannot get these poor residents of Cephalonia out of my mind. How can you cope with devastation that fells your whole life? But for us it is onwards and upwards, climbing a steep flight of steps in the morning heat, into another tour operator's office. This time not quite so slick and Greek-owned. We say we can make our own way to the villa in Aghios Stephanos, we don't need to follow them up the north-east coast. It will be a place of memories which come flooding back. The island immediately seems more populated and many of the buildings are new - infill.

Ipsos, N.E Corfu

At Ipsos we stop! And Soula remembers Simon, (everyone always remembers Simon!) But how the Hotel Mega has changed! Even the bougainvillaea has been reduced to a stump and the façade seems rebuilt. The jetty is exactly the same shape but totally reconstructed.

We quickly realise the clientele has changed. It is obvious that most people are nursing hangovers with a breakfast beer. On to Andreas' Pig and Whistle taverna, and Michael's house, at least they have not changed! The house now has been smartened up with a lower floor where the olive press once was. Once up and round the corner it is as if the blue cannot really begin until one reached Barbati. There are a few smart villas and a few more around Nissaki.

Aghios Stephanos, Kerasia, Kassiopi, and N.E Corfu

Then here we are at the small unobtrusive turning for Aghios Stephanos and we find it is just the same road down, perhaps it doesn't feel so far, perhaps more of it is tarred? There is now quite a little community of ochre roofed houses, all very select. There are now five tavernas and the one we remember is now called the Gallini, unrecognisable except for the wisteria now in a second flowering and the plane tree, eucalyptus and bougainvillaea all grown so much larger but jogging our memories and foliage, so lush and rambling that it hides the façade.

There is a new supermarket with swallows' nests inside the shop and a massive tub of basil outside. But of the little fishing bay, there is no sign and now there is only a modern small resort without, in our opinion, the genuine warmth the village once had. Villa Angelina up in the olive groves is, without doubt, the hardest villa we have had to reach and with plenty of live-stock around, rats perhaps and certainly sev-eral scorpions! But it is well furnished and has a very tempting 'welcome pack' which provides a tasty lunch for us, before going down to the lovely Kerasia Bay for a swim. Here there is still the Albanian coast beyond, four or five caiques tied up at the jetty near Nico's Taverna.

There is a forest of pine trees behind the pebble bay with some woodland trees along the shore and there is still a precious peace it may not be possible to hold on to for much longer in Corfu; although between Kassiopi and Barbati are still the same unspoilt villages and tiny un-spoilt bays.

Evening finds us in Kassiopi on the water-front after dinner, rather than relaxing under the wisteria at the Gallini in Aghios Stephanos. It is an eyeopener. The harbour stage remains the same, the tree setting within the taverna, where Heidi danced as a four-year-old is the same. But a whole town has been recreated and built, a symbol of greed – and this is where Nero once spent his holidays!

Wow! Another day and the morning on the beach at Kerasia is interesting with a great many tourist cruisers for company, and there is a lot happening although some brave souls are paragliding. We set off for Nissaki after lunch at Nico's at Kerasia. On the way, we walk around the Rothschild headland and wonder if Princess Margaret is on the beach? And where for that matter is Neil Kinnock? The tiny bay of Kaminaki does not have as many people on the beach, simply because it is such a tiny beach and the taverna is closed.

When we drive on to Nissaki, again, it seems very much busier than our memories, but through the thick of the tourists it is recognisable as the place we once knew.

What is more, Agatha recognises us! Agatha the owner of the main taverna has played such a part in our children's lives in all our many holidays in Corfu, over five consecutive years. She asks how our children are. We explain now they are older they have other obligations.

We recreate these past holidays; a tourist boat adds to rather than blocks our view of the little Villa Eleni across the small bay. It is from here that we moved during that cool damp Greek Spring and where the children had left their wildflowers pressing under the damp doormat! Now it is summer-time, waiters and Agatha dash in and out of tables, huge flasks of lager and beer seem endlessly passing our table, there is a smell of chips and fish frying. But it is worth every minute of our time here to refashion our memories.

Bellavista, Palaiokastritsa and N.W Corfu

We had hesitated about returning to Corfu, we know in the ten years since our last visit that the tourist industry has grown exponentially and going to Palaiokastritsa, this is the one place I really hesitate to revisit.

It stands for so much, our first honeymoon adventure and later the beach where our tiny children brave the shallow seas.

But it turns out to be a truly beautiful day, the kind of day we are sad when it draws to a close.

There are few other better places in which to end a day than at Bellavista overlooking the wonderful Ionian Sea high above the sparkling village of Palaiokastritsa.

Arriving from the north and Aghios Georgios, after a stunning drive and climbing up from Makrades, where we are overwhelmed with vistas which take our gaze for mile after mile, from east to west, from north to south we feel we were experiencing the whole of Corfu.

Now we are looking down to the Monastery of the Panaghia of Palaiokastritsa from the renowned Bellavista. Views that make your heart sing! Views that thousands have enjoyed through the years, and as the sign says, 'the Kings of Greece, the Kaizer, Tito and Nasser'!

Relax, stay, just savour this view, you deserve it! We do need to relax for between our wonderful excursions we pack in an extraordinary number of inspections of varying grades of accommodation. Our look around the many villas in Aghios Stephanos last night was protracted, although the villas are good quality and additionally many are reasonably priced.

Then this morning up on the north coast failing to find the representative from yet another tour operator we decide to locate their Sidari accommodation on our own. We know Sidari from our many holidays with the children. We have prepared ourselves for a change, but we had not expected Sidari to have grown so much. The once tiny village is more like a small town and although we can recognise some of the landmarks the atmosphere of the place has totally altered. We can remember the three remote beaches, including the Canal d'Amour with its amazing soft sandstone formations. The tunnel through the rocks, through which we had swum, has worn away and the formations are quite different. Nor are we overly impressed by the apartments and studios. Some of the accommodation is too much at the budget end for our Greco-file office to be interested in and we are even less impressed with even more budget accommodation at the north-western end of the island.

However, Aghios Stephanos West does redeem itself a little with a huge and magnificent sandy beach.

Nearby Arillas which has more character has less of a beach. We drive onto a promontory and look out to tiny islands across the sea; are they inhabited? I finally locate them on one of the several maps we have brought with us: The Diapontia Islands, Othonoi, Eriekoussa, Mathraki. Sadly, they are out of our reach! It is necessary therefore to drive on to Aghios Georgios for our swim and to convince ourselves of the value of this family orientated area; this last beach allows us to look at the whole area with a more rounded vision.

Our last day in Northern Corfu brings the welcome news that our son Oliver has passed his driving test back in Yorkshire, on his first try! We drive into Corfu Town in the evening to celebrate as the light, brilliant yellow catches the soft stone of the mellow tall houses, thin Venetian pillars of chalk, a kind of Portland stone maybe. We walk past the taverns, "Dirty Dicks" and "Spoty (sic) Dog" happily surprised they are here still, as Corfu island has modernised quite considerably.

In our exploration, we have to remember that we have left the hire car, now in its 'hometown' after its many adventures, back on the park for Kapodistriou.

We steal a glance at the now-famous jeweller's Ilias Lalaounis, prices beyond us now, and are glad we bought the linked silver bracelet from the great man himself, a decade or so ago. We had entered the shop for a small silver ring and left with the ring and the matching bracelet, unique in the way the six bangles interlinked. Sadly, stolen from me when we stayed in Ludlow, Shropshire many years later.

We do some business with the agency who supplied our hire car and own up to the small damage incurred when we backed the little red car into the bollard on the quay in Igoumenitsa, so many weeks ago now, a lifetime away in experiences! Spiros simply smiles and calls to his colleague also called Spiro who laughs aloud.

"It is what we expect," he says. "Hire cars seem to take far more knocks than their counterparts in private ownership, especially red ones," he adds with a chuckle.

We thank them profusely and leave walking back along the street towards the square of St. Spiridon. We feel we must adopt the Greek custom of lighting a candle for the island's saint.

I feel grateful and also for the achievement of our son Oliver who passed his driving test as we walk into the OTE office (The Telecommunications office of Greece) to ring Oliver and congratulate him again. But the booths are occupied, with a long queue and we feel the wait will be too long.

It was often hard to ring home before the days of mobile phones and those at home did not expect to be in contact frequently.

It is time to eat and we know we must find the Lucciola, the wonderful inland restaurant we first found on our honeymoon. Over the years we have eaten here so many times it is like a homecoming. The garden is still lovely, and we eat artichokes with mushrooms followed by cod with white wine sauce, it is still lovely.

Casa Lucia, Corfu

Casa Lucia, Corfu

Conversing with Denis who has developed Casa Lucia alongside the Lucciola with his wife Val, we convey our plans for our travel business and say how we are concentrating only on what is good in Greece. He says they are now concentrating on the cottages at Casa Lucia exclusively and we make a note.

It does, in fact, become a centrepiece for

the tour operation we are not aware at this moment that we will establish in the future.

Our little car huffed and puffed up the dreadful track to the Angelina cottage at 1 am. I almost wish we had walked by the light of the full moon. Incongruously the strains of "Scotland the Brave" drift up from the posh houses in the bay below.

We sleep long and awake late. We have to pack and vacate our comfortable villa with its uncomfortable form of livestock. I think if Nicos and his family at the taverna had not been so hospitable we would not have stayed here! There are days when I wish these research trips were not dependent on us having to accept so much complimentary accommodation but to do them without would be almost impossible. As the companies grow larger, we do of course find that we have more say of where we stay, and 1987 of course was only our second year of operation, our first of being a licensed travel agent.

Southern Corfu,
Kavos & Maltas

Our final night in Corfu is to be spent in the south-west.

We leave Aghios Stephanos with time to visit Kerasia which is very busy, horribly busy in fact. Back on the main road Kouloura and Kalami look as they ever did but there are signs of mass building at Kalami.

In busy frenetic Ipsos, we stop to say good-bye to Soula who again greets us most warmly and insists we come back next year to stay. We smile and say we will try but we know we could never cope with the crowds on the narrow Ipsos beach. We remember all the fun we had with Michael Wegg and the friends we made over five consecutive years. We drive straight through Corfu Town without stopping as far as the Miramare Hotel. We remember it from our honeymoon.

Everywhere is busy but it is mid-August and as Soula has kindly warned us, all the Greeks are on holiday as it is coming up to the Panaghia festival. Not surprisingly we allow ourselves a sophisticated drink at the Miramare before leaving its cool shelter for the other world that Kavos has become.

We are horrified how much tourism has encroached on this southern coast although Lefkimi has hardly changed. Still the same flat waters of the river with the attractive caiques moored on the banks. Kavos is still approached through the long cool avenue of olive groves but rather than being a haven of light, an oasis after our long drive, it is an electric monument to modern tourism.

We momentarily baulk at the thought of looking up our friends, George and his wife, who we have not seen since our holidays with the kids. The road and the heat combined make it seem too much trouble. Immediately we are immersed in the closeness of humanity which is part of modern holidaying and in the eyes of many part of the fun.

We have always been loners, even our Yorkshire home is situated at the top of a steep hill!

Now, thankfully still able to edge our car through the ambling crowds, buried deep in the concrete jungle and ghetto blasters until we come out onto the familiar beach.

Yes, the beach is full and busy with activity but somehow the taverna doesn't totally contradict our memories, and there is still a smell of good food with the building surrounded by bougainvillaea.

George and his wife welcome us, full of woe! "Look at us! Oh, how I wish we could back to the old days!" Bit by bit he tells us of the despicable behaviour of the young Brits and Germans, who out of their minds with alcohol or drugs seem to have no shame, and which they must now endure. "They urinate everywhere, they even copulate in our garden."

Again, we are sorry to say goodbye, because we know we won't come back. *(Writing this I look up the names on the internet. I think I can still conjure up in my memory, the name of the taverna, and then George's surname, and think I find a new property, with excellent reviews, a smart taverna and ac-*

commodation and think yes, although the taverna
might still exist perhaps George and his family have
moved on and re-created the high-end establishment
it always was.

So often through our travels in Greece we find
family businesses have moved with the times, made
the best of their family estate, often originally mod-
est but over the generations helping it to grow and
become something impressive, against all the odds.)

We drive across the southern tail of Corfu to Maltas. We are due to meet a founder director of Sunvil Holidays here because many of the considerable number of properties we have been inspecting on Corfu have been under their wing. However, John has gone to Parga and we are left to form our own opinion about this charming rural place.

Well, put it this way, Maltas is both superb and awful: dreadful rats, hard small beds, indifferent food but the dancing in the taverna that night is excellent and good fun, above all the hospitality we are shown is first class.

The clash of expectations about a holiday destination where a wonderful beach and lovely quiet and scenic hinterland weighs heavily when either the accommodation or the food is disappointing and is increasingly something that we are constantly aware of, now we have ceased being a customer, and have become a provider.

On balance we decide that Maltas is the kind of simple destination to which holiday-makers would adjust, accepting the rough with the smooth. Maltas has a freedom and a spirit that is not found often these days.

We will make a report about the rats when we got home. As to hard beds this is pretty normal in holiday destinations and after a day lying on the hard hot sand, on what is an exceptional beach, the body is able to relax anywhere!

But each year as we travel towards the millennium standards improve so that around the time of the Athens Olympic Games in 2004 most places adhere to normal European standards.

Corfu Town

Our drive back to Corfu Town takes us across the central plain of the island and over Ayia Deka. The second highest mountain on the island and its peaky shape is very attractive and the route up and down offers wonderful views, over the fishing village of Benitses below to the Epirus mountains, again the hills are beckoning for this is the way we will travel tonight when we reach the mainland, and then ahead of us, we see the town of Corfu to our right and the lagoon of Khalikilopoulos, the Albanian mountains beyond and Mount Pandokrator.

It reminds us why we love Corfu so much. "Sad though," says Simon, "none of it is enhanced by the pylons, they are everywhere we go nowadays in Greece."

There is a festival when we reach the town, and we park down by the Corfu Palace Hotel and walk towards the festivities.

The Procession for St. Spiridon had gone by and only a brass band and some cheerleaders remained. We are told they are celebrating the Venetian Litany of the St. Spiridon when the holy relics of the saint are paraded around the town. "We saw another procession," I say, "when we were here one April with the children. Do you remember we saw the Royal Family that day?"

"No, not with the children. That must have been on our honeymoon in 1965," corrects Simon. "The Royal family was deposed in 1967, if I remember rightly."

"Well, perhaps that was when we saw the remains, in August 1965."

We mingle with the remaining balloon sellers and there is a jovial, colourful air. We are happy to wander and absorb but we find ourselves drawn towards St. Spiridon's church. We buy trinkets and incense and I decide on impulse to brave the crowds and go into the church to light three candles, one for ourselves, one for Heidi and one for Oliver. We are missing them.

It is a pleasant church with none of the finery of other churches we have seen, but with a reverent air. It is impossible to see the casket containing the relics for the throng in the church and I pass slowly through towards the exit in common with others including priests and nuns I finally escape through the entrance. I have had difficulty placing our candles in the candelabrum but do achieve it, and hope ours doesn't end up in the large heap on the floor.

We make haste to the Lucciola. We have rung Denis when we first arrived in the town, asking if we can take up his offer to see the cottages at Casa Lucia. But the time it took to draw attention to ourselves at the Inn we need not have hurried.

We are very impressed by Dennis' cottages

but on first meeting his wife Val (who became a good friend) seems less impressed by us!

This is an important moment in our life. Sometimes you carry out undertakings unaware that what you are doing will lead to a turning point in your life. We had no intention during that event of becoming a tour operator, but our enthusiasm for this couple and these properties is subconsciously sowing seeds for our transition to serious work in the travel industry.

The little 'hotel' a similar concept to that of the developing Portmeirion in North Wales, the vision of a talented architect and engineer. We are drawn into the greenery of the estate and a vivid blue swimming pool which is central to the colours of the beautiful garden. The cottages are furnished with antiques, desks, oil paintings, comfortable beds with two pillows and each cottage with an exceptionally well-fitted kitchen.

One house the Red House enjoys furnishings in a nautical style, another is luxury in white. If Val and Dennis will let us, I am sure we will be able to do good business with them!

I say enthusiastically, "this is just what we have been looking for! Somewhere where the detail has not been compromised and where the comfort of guests is paramount!" We don't immediately realise it but the seeds for Filoxenia Holidays have been sown.

Now as we leave Corfu by sea – as we sail in the proudly named "Theodoros Maria" alongside the twin peaks of Pandokrator to the north and in the south Agia Deka, the harbour walls are ancient and unwelcoming. The ochre-coloured houses above the quayside are dilapidated and crumbling under the weight of the heat haze, the sea is not as pristine nor so blue as it is in the morning light. It reflects our sadness at our departure from this exquisite jewel, Corfu, or Kerkyra as we learned to call it.

One or two caiques are beyond, a ferry boat readying itself to pass us port to port. Above us, an incoming flight is lining up to approach the airport, perhaps the flight of our friends from Yorkshire. All too soon, for we are savouring this repeated journey to Igoumenitsa, in all the excitement of approaching this mountainous wedge of land, we are about to dock.

Parga, Coastal Epirus & Paxos

It feels appropriate that our thoughts can revisit our arrival on the Greek mainland, if with sorrow for this day that I write, 19 May 2020, is the date on which we had flights booked to return to Greece for a four-week trip, and which due to the Covid 19 Pandemic and the foreign Office ruling we have had to cancel. Although we have rebooked for the autumn, I think it is less than likely that we will be able to travel then. Older people are being wrapped up, so to speak, in tissue paper and stored gently in their homes, unable to socialise except for the strictest guidelines, discouraged from going to shops, or anywhere for that matter, except for taking daily exercise.

So, Greece remains a dream, a memory and a fading goal. Greece itself which can congratulate itself for having far fewer cases than other European countries is emerging from its lockdown, with the beaches open, sunbeds spaced at the correct social distance and with cafes and bars and then hotels to open shortly.

You know how it is but thoughts of a holiday in Greece usually include visions of tiny islands in a sparkling azure sea. But the Greek mainland too has a vast coastline with villages, beaches and fishing ports, many of which have less tourism than the islands. In addition to the antiquities and classical sites, mainland Greece offers some wonderful touring and walking country with spectacular mountain passes, huge gorges and acres of deciduous forest and now the road takes us inland through a valley, through marshlands thick with waterlily and bamboo, yet another facet of Greece.

Parga

We arrive in Parga, at seven o'clock, a little

town of great charm and character on the Western coast of Epirus, almost opposite the tiny island of Paxos. A castle dominated rock separates the islet filled harbour from the vast sandy bay of Valtos, while the village tumbles chaotically down either side of the hill in a collection of little square houses and narrow alleys ending in the harbour promenade of tavernas and cafes.

We have been told that as a touring base Parga is ideal for exploring Epirus, with such oddities as the Necromanteion, where the ancients communicated with the dead, the river Styx and there are some unchanged hill villages in the foothills of the Pindus mountains.

The Hotel Bacoli, with a very attractive mountain view, rather than a sea view is lovely and cool. We order wine to be ready for our friends hopefully following us after their flight into Corfu and walk down to the town.

It is quite different to what we expected: a floodlit fort, small steep-sided streets up to the castle, little arched alleyways host some good quality gift shops.

There is no sign of the long sandy beaches, no doubt we will find these tomorrow. We find a fish taverna on the seafront which we like the look-of, away from the busy harbour and by chance realise this is probably one of the better places to eat.

We meet Tom and Joanne, with their teenage children, Anna and Martin, at breakfast the next day, together with the Sunvil representative who will no doubt have a programme of properties lined up to show us.

"Not today," I tell her firmly. "We are going to the beach, if nothing else I am going to finish Zorba!"

Thereby we flop out, six of us finding a reasonably quiet bit of the beach beyond the castle. No sooner have we staked out our 'patch', as close to the sea as seems sensible than a crowd of Italians come by and park themselves in front of us!

"Typical," says Tom. "They are known for their gregarious nature, there is plenty of room on the beach, but they feel safer in they can 'camp' in the vicinity of others!"

"They would sit on you if they could!" replies Simon. "Friday is Panaghia, 15 August, and we have been advised to avoid the busier places."

"Then clearly Valtos Beach will be out."

That evening we find another good restaurant in the square and follow it by a 'sticky cake' at the Zacharoplasteion on the waterfront. We explain to our Yorkshire friends that we must take a trip across to Paxos the following day.

"Don't you guys ever rest?" asks Joanne.

"It's a sea trip, we will relax on the boat!" But the trip is fraught with oddities.

Anti Paxos & Paxos

It is the 13 August, but not Friday! But we understand in Greece it is Tuesday the thirteenth, which is unlucky, and today this is a Thursday, so all is well!

Yet the rep had booked us on the Anti Paxos boat, not the correct boat to Paxos itself. But that turned out to be to our advantage because the Thomson rep directed us to a water-taxi speed boat which showed us the glorious glistening white beaches of Anti Paxos with their luminous green and blue Caribbean-coloured waters and then literally sped us on up to Gaios, the tiny capital of Paxos.

A little square right on the quay is charming, with the traditional tiny church with its signature belltower and everywhere the buildings smothered with bougainvillaea.

It is all nicer and prettier than we had expected, but also more crowded. There are souvenir shops lining the square, but it seems a pity that cars are allowed to drive across the wide marble-paved square with its gaily painted little houses and red-roofed buildings, plus some much older buildings probably going back to Venetian times.

However, it is a classic Greek island with more houses to inspect and another representative to meet. Something is telling us it is probably time to go home, we are getting tired, yet many of these owners and representatives do become good personal friends.

We make a mental note not to travel again in the heat of high season. The houses in Gaios are out of the village and it certainly isn't a pleasant experience to climb fifteen minutes uphill to reach them.

The regular caique whisks us back to Parga and we stroll slowly up to the castle in the evening where we dine on a terrace after looking at an art gallery, with an appealing backdrop of the floodlit shape of the acropolis and tall cypresses in the bay.

We are alerted towards the Kastro by the sounds of pop music after breakfast on the 15 August, the Panaghia Festival. In the late afternoon we walk up the steep street to the castle to investigate. It is indeed a modern pop festival.

The people of the small islands who climb up steep paths or steps up to the Churches of the Panaghia on their knees will decry this awful stoop to modernism. Each year we travel to Greece we feel uncomfortable that tourism is encroaching on centuries of religious observations.

Ammoudia, Necro-
manteion, Loutsa

The next day, anxious to keep cool, we set off

down the Epirus coast. Again, vistas of the sea below to the right, barren Epiriot mountains to the left and above all sandy soft landscape, hardly stable for roads or village foundations. At Ammoudia we find a great plain where in the flat valley the rivers Acheron and the Styx flow into the sea. There is a wonderful beach here with headlands almost enclosing the sea, the beach and the plain.

Believe it or not, it is too hot for a swim, the effort needed to change and walk across the sand is simply too much and we decide to explore the Necromanteion at Mesopotamo, but when we reach this interesting looking hillock rising from the plain, it is closed for the Panaghia!

Ever onwards the road takes into the mountains because the coastal road is signed 'road under construction'.

(In later years we find different parts of this stsretch of coast is constantly under reconstruction, due to the unstable nature of the land in this area.)

We are soon in groves of silver poplar and willow and onto marshlands and we realise we are in the Amvrakikos Gulf, where we can spot rare fish and sea birds. What a magical place to explore another day. Then we head back before we reach Preveza itself where the pine trees meet the bougainvillaea and now with endless sandy beaches on our left-hand side, we drive back to Ammoudia.

Preveza is just one place which will have to wait for another year to visit!

How many years before these small seaside hamlets become thriving holiday resorts like Kavos on Corfu? We note the names, Kanlandi, Kastrosykia, Ligia and others, we love the roadside oleanders, the rocks and towering mountains. Emphasising the shifting sandy earth, there are many tunnels built through the headlands on this beautiful coast road; this stunning undeveloped coastline may just be saved by its instability.

The following day we return south, bringing Tom and Joanne and family with us. The Necromanteion of Ephyra is open, we are impressed with the Polygonal masonry. Is this the location of Homer's "house of Hades" in the Odyssey? *(The authenticity of this site has recently been questioned.)*

Given the age of the dark cave arched over and the almost unimaginable labyrinth that ancients confronted it is hard for all of us not to be spooked.

Back in Parga, Joanne, never one to miss a party, has gathered together as many people as she can call by name and has headed for Vasiliki at Anthousa. Joanne's planning ensured they organised, we ferried! So much for the romantic village evening for two.

In fact, the evening is good, ten people and a Greek wedding which floods the place out. It doesn't seem to occur to us that we Brits may have gated crashed the wedding!

Tom and Joanne are thrilled to be taught Greek dancing by the owner of the hotel and we enjoy meeting their Athenian friends.

At Loutsa on this Bank Holiday Sunday there is turquoise sea, white rolling waves, clean fine sand but only three tavernas, not enough space for the many people on the huge beach and we can't find room at the taverna with the thatch roof and flowers outside. We walk back to the Panorama, uphill where we eat kalamari and salad, the trip is growing to a close. We want to leave time to sunbathe.

Back on the beach, a young boy plays footie with a large watermelon in the sea, making sure it will be cool enough before it is cut into for a refreshing lunch. We plunge into the waves which are great and high and fierce and enough to cool our overheated bodies. Quickly towel dry and back over the sandy hillocks lined with myrtle and oleander, the great Pindus hills in front of us I never know how one's feet know when it is the end of a wonderful journey. Slowly our feet are lifted, one after the other as we make our way back to our little red hire car.

A slow drive back to Parga, final vistas to keep ingrained in one's soul to see one through the long British winter.

Joanne and Tom wave us goodbye, 'you are far too soon, stay and have a beer,' they say knowing full well that Simon doesn't drink alcohol and we had all only just finished breakfast.

It is a good thing we are early, again the boat deck for cars is full when we arrive at Igoumenitsa and I am searching for the Greek Tourist Board's letter of Bona fide when one of the sailors recognises Simon and bursts in gales of laughter, beckoning Simon onto the ship. It is the same crewmember who had been on that outward journey, six weeks ago, he remembers the Englishman who had stupidly backed his shiny new hire car into a bollard!

Fortunately, we had a few drachmas free for a generous tip! An amazing itinerary, three and a half thousand kilometres driven over a huge part of the Greek mainland and the several islands explored.

PART 5

SPIRIT OF GREECE

This title seems very apt at the moment! Today, 24 May 2020, is the first day for many weeks that we dare to hope that we may be able to go to Greece in 2020, at least for an autumn visit! They, (in particular the CEO of AstraZeneca) are talking positively about the possibility of vaccinating Britons against Covid 19 in September and October. Just

how we will be able to change our late summer flights is not completely clear. But it is the first time that I can sip my weekend lunch time ouzo with a degree of hope, nay even excitement rather than sorrow. The Oxford team that is producing this vaccine are confident, that just like the influenza vaccine that vulnerable and older people are given each autumn, will protect people from the debilitating symptoms of the disease, even if it fails to protect others from catching the disease of Covid 19 from others. But for us, it is enough to think of a life which will begin to feel like 'normal'.

CHAPTER 22

*Paxos & Southern Ionian
islands: Zakynthos & Kythira*

May 1988

Although our first visit to Paxos was only a year previously as a day-tripper, we are back a year later.

We are destined to visit Paxos several times. Not quite as much as we travelled to Corfu or will travel to the Peloponnese but probably many more times than we will visit individual islands in the Dodecanese and certainly more than the other groups of islands, the Sporades, the Saronic or North-East Aegean.

Our meeting with individual agents, in this case, the charismatic Grammatikos brothers, meant we would eventually set up a full programme here.

In 1988 the biggest problem we encounter on our journey there is whether we can get the car onto the tiny car ferry travelling from idyllic Sivota to Gaios.

"That was fun, wasn't it?" remarks Simon ironically as we get off. "The ramp is right in the prow of the boat, so from the quay to the prow it is so steep that I couldn't see how straight I was in lining up the car. I was looking right up to the sky and when I reached the tipping point on the prow I hadn't a clue how I was doing! It felt as though the car would tip on one side and I had no idea how to get into the space. The boat is so small there is only room for about three or four cars anyway."

"It looked even worse reversing when you were driving off, you were in the lap of the Gods!"

Lakka

We drive directly to Lakka, and by chance, Mark Ottaway is the first person we meet as we arrive in the little town. It seems a pretty fortuitous sort of day as we reminisce with him about our exploits in Karpathos and we have to break away from ouzos on the waterfront to find our apartments.

We are pleased with the accommodation. It is spacious, cool and overlooking the exquisite Lakka harbour, which is surrounded by greenery between sea and hill, cliffs would too grand a word.

After an indifferent dinner, we have become accustomed to mainland food always superior to island menus, we move to the bar where we carry on our conversation with Mark and crew at Spiro's until we drop out and go to bed around 1 am! "It happens to be my birthday tomorrow," says Mark. Will you join me and Clovis then? It'll be a good night! And I think you'll love our house. It has amazing harbourside views from that headland over there."

It does and becomes just another part of the determination growing within me to create our own house in Greece. There is a lot of good accommodation to see on Paxos and with the temperatures becoming higher we work hard, regularly climbing steep paths or steps as we criss-cross the island inspecting properties.

The end of the day invariably sees us relaxing with a final glass of wine, perhaps contemplating the geranium in a white tub, dancing to the beat of the mistral, half asleep, where yachts' mast lights also execute ballet steps against the black outline of the harbour shore as though they are headlights making their way down a Greek zigzag mountain road. The balmy evening air, the scents from the sea and the jasmine creating the perfect soporific atmosphere.

Gaios

The next morning, we struggle up to pack prior to departure, then to be told that the ferry is cancelled. A short delay to our schedule is not going to make too much difference, it is part of the trials of travelling to the islands. It will also give us a chance to explore the tiny capital of the island Gaios this evening. Having walked around and down the waterfront protected by the islet of St. Nicholas, which geologically seems to fill a fiord creating the effect of being on a river rather than on the coast, we sit in the pleasant town square.

Dusk falls, the wind drops and the fishing boats now chug out against the backdrop of the larger boats still marooned until the morrow, the old tub Kamelia, *(nowadays the name has transferred to the Kamelia Lines, for the two modern ferry boats plying the Ionian to Paxos.)* the Anna Maria and the Aspasia all add colour, blue and white, green and red, to this lovely place with its Venetian architecture. And with the square opening to the water, there is a definite tiny feel of St. Mark's Square in Venice!

CHAPTER 23

Zakynthos

May 1988

There is a regular ferry from Killini in the north-western Peloponnese to Zakynthos, an island which is well worth exploring, and not only for its excellent sandy beaches on the south-eastern peninsular.

Visit the lovely beach of Gerakas, where huge Loggerhead turtles come ashore to nest; but please do respect the instructions at the Conservation Information Centre above the beach, as this highly sensitive area is one of the very few breeding grounds left in the Mediterranean for the Loggerhead, the Caretta Caretta; the other nesting beach on Zakynthos, Laganas, having already been ruined by tourist development.

There are now several locations where the turtles have nested particularly on the western coasts of the Peloponnese and we have seen these handsome creatures from time to time, but only once do we witness the tiny wee things making their way down the beach to the sea and this is on Zakynthos.

It is important to say that this is not a pursuit that is recommended, the species are easily frightened and best left to their own devices well away from tourists' eyes. These wonderful reptiles less than the size of a thumbnail grow to around 36 inches, usually weigh over 250lbs and can live for over 50 years. Watching these tiny things inch their way across the wide beach to the sea is nothing short of miraculous.

Writing this we are marking the day for two reasons: it is now the end of May 2020 and but for the Covid epidemic we would have been in Greece, and could have been at the tiny fishing hamlet of Karavostasi in Itilo Bay where in 2019 dining at the waterfront fish taverna the waiter came over beckoning over the wall of the decking right below us, he pointed out a beautiful turtle gliding through the sea, less than two metres from us. But two metres also reminds me that this is the distance we are supposed to keep from our fellow kind and one of the Government's chief advisors has admitted driving 260 miles from his London home to self-isolate with his family, at a cottage on his parents' farm. And even driving out from there to Barnard Castle because he wanted to test his eyesight, after suffering from Covid 19 whilst here in Durham, a drive of 60 miles with his wife and small four-year-old son in the back of the car. And was it his wife's birthday?

Not surprisingly a huge number of people who have stuck to the rules are very angry. For some who cannot easily get outdoors to enjoy the amazing weather we who are more fortunate are able to do, it must have felt that there are rules for those who set the rules and rules for the others.

Overall Zakynthos surprises us, with restaurants in the hills and the sterling effort made by the town officials who painstakingly recreated its stunning Venetian buildings using concrete to create replicas of the original buildings again mirroring Venice's St. Mark's Square, destroyed in the 1953 earthquake. The mountain village of Keri on its own peninsula is with its own interest although nowadays most visitors head for Limni Keri which is not a lake, but a rather lovely pebble beach and for a sunset, the lighthouse beyond. Not part of the itinerary is Navagio beach with its famous and rather ugly shipwreck. Since landing on this western beach in 1981 with mechanical failure it has been intriguingly rusting ever since, to the increasing delight of curious tourists. Rather than competing with the hordes of day-trippers from the small cruisers, we are told it is better to view the beach and its famous talisman from above. But this would need to be another day, if we return.

It is on Zakynthos that we have reason to be grateful to the Hertz reputation for efficiency when an over-speeding Mercedes and its German driver, (wearing nothing but a posing pouch), side swipes us on a narrow bridge. The shock of the accident is compounded by the torrent of abuse by the speeding driver who also whips out his camera and starts photographing the rubber left by the two cars in their sudden shrieking stop. "Das ist yar spoor," he screams pointing to the tyre marks in the road whilst trying to claim he had the right of way. An old Greek in a nearby cottage, clearly no fan of the near-naked German man, tries to help by claiming he saw it all and we were in the right – what fun ensues! A single phone call to the Athens office sorts all the problems and at the end of the journey when we returned the car, filling the accident report form is painless, with no unpleasantries. But our initial tale of woe continues as we cautiously drive the damaged hire car back to our beautiful amazing modern villa, lent to us by the tour operator whose programme we are reviewing on the island.

It is worth contrasting this magnificent complimentary villa with the standard of accommodation offered by the same company a year earlier in Cephalonia. It is becoming obvious that Greco-file is making its way in the world as a company committed to prestigious holidays! It is to be our first night here and we are glad to be arriving in good time with great black thunder clouds looming from the north. It has been a hot day when we arrive at this new base to find the lane to the villa blocked by a gang of navvies with a large tarmacadam machine and wet asphalt along the length of the long lane.

They look at us with incomprehension when we try to explain that we live down the lane, in our limited Greek. We are sure it is obvious they know what we are saying but what could they do about it? We move the car a safe distance from this outrage when suddenly the heavens open and a deluge of tropical proportions descends. Silently we change into the skimpiest of summer clothing (including my favourite 'Mykonos' strappy top!) Carrying our shoes, wrapped in newspaper along with our usual respectable clothing, toothbrushes and all we needed for the night, we walked barefoot through the prickly, once dried, summer undergrowth, avoiding the new tarmac leading to the stunning modern house, our temporary home in which we had hoped to luxuriate.

We are absolutely wet through as we turn the key in the front door. We behold a sumptuous living room, white marble floors, white walls and an inviting white sofa. Our feet are literally caked in light brown mud, our bodies drenched in water. Fortunately, we have included a towel in the newspaper package and in the best way we can with the help of the newspaper and then the towel we scrape off most of the mud and tiptoe to a sink in the kitchen. Here each helping the other balance we wash a foot at a time, throw our skimpy clothes into the sink, look at each other and burst out laughing!

In time newly showered, clad in a lovely bathrobe, which has been conveniently hanging in the equally luxurious bathroom we look in the fridge and kitchen cupboards and find quite enough beyond basic supplies for a light supper and breakfast tomorrow. Sinking onto the soft sofa with a beer each, once again we count our blessings and that night we sleep well.

Morning brings a fair sky, temperatures slightly lowered when suddenly we hear gunshots. When they quieten Simon draws back the shutters of the full-length window on the upper balcony and steps outside. Nothing is to be seen or heard. He then looks down at the veranda and finds it peppered with lead shot. "Right, that's it. We're on the move," announces Simon. "We'll go back to Zakynthos town and find a travel agency and find the days and times of the ferry from Aghios Konstantinos to Skiathos."

This has always been part of our plan but not at such haste. "Who do you think was shooting at us? Was it hunters?" We know about hunters in Greece once the summer season is over and don't approve because small birds such as thrushes are targeted.

"Or," said Simon, "perhaps the tarmacadamers have returned for a bit of fun? Not all the locals appreciate tourists." That was the first I have heard anyone infer inhospitality and I am shocked.

"Do you think we can risk walking back on the tarmac?"

One thing is certain with our suitcases still in the hire car and no prospect of getting them and supplies easily into the villa there seems little point in remaining on the island. Almost certainly the men will return to tarmac the whole road today.

In town, on the waterfront, the tourist office said there are no ferries from Aghios Konstantinos to Skiathos. We are sure there are. We try a second travel agency in town. They say the only ferries to Skiathos go from Volos. We go for a coffee.

"They wouldn't have local knowledge out

here in the Ionian," Simon says, "I know there is a boat from Aghios Konstantinos to Skiathos, I saw one come in when we were there just three weeks ago on our way to Meteora from our arrival in Athens, obviously we need to be on the Eastern side of Greece to get an agent with a good knowledge of the Sporades time tables."

"We are out of our minds! Just tell me why when we are in the Ionian, are we even thinking about going to the Sporades? Our flights were into Athens and we are returning from Athens."

"Well, it was you that suggested we saw as much accommodation from as many tour operators as we can this year, continuing from the whole mass we saw last year on the Sabbatical. We'd have been daft not to take up their so generous offers of accommodation, clearly, we will improve our portfolio with Greco-file; Greek Islands Club and Sunvil have most of their resorts in the West, Laskarina in the Aegean."

"Well here's an idea! Do you remember that hotelier near Nafplio in the east, Yannis at the Hotel Minoa, he has a travel agency, he can check the ferries to and from Skiathos? We will ring him up! And since Tolo is roughly on our way we'll stay the night."

And so, our long co-operation with Yannis and Maria Georgidakis begins. Slowly at first, Greco-file is a lowly travel agency; but sitting after dinner with Yannis at the tables in front of the hotel, the sea lapping only feet away from us, he asks us of all our travels over Greece, Corfu and the Ionian islands, the Dodecanese, the Saronic islands, Pelion, Thessaly, and now the Peloponnese which is our favourite area and we had to admit that our recent tour of the Peloponnese ranked very highly.

Hotel Minoa

"Yes," I say, "after Corfu," my love for the Corfu we had known in the 1960s and 70s would never wane, "the Peloponnese, which does remind me of Corfu before the tourists began to swamp it, yes it's a wonderful place. Perhaps it will become our favourite!"

"I am glad you said this. I thought you might. Just remember my wife Maria has her own travel agency 'Yannopoulos Travel' if you want to take your business further, we can help you in every way. Yannopoulos Travel is an old business. The original travel agency in Nafplio was begun by Maria's father, and working from the old Customs House, dealing initially solely with maritime shipping." As Yannopoulos Travel increased its business into general overseas and domestic travel then the office developed in the central Syntagma Square.

"I have been thinking about it! It has a name already – Filoxenia, friends of strangers."

"Wonderful name," enthuses Yannis. "Filoxenia, the dictionary word for hospitality!"

By 1989, a year later, plans are well advanced. Rather than objecting, all the tour operators who had hosted or encouraged us as Grecofile, are very supportive, particularly Noel Josephides and Dudley der Parthog of Sunvil Holidays. That is the rather strange and lovely thing about specialist tour operators offering foreign holidays, especially those who were members of Aito (The Association of Independent Tour Operators), we did socialise but particularly we supported and helped each other.

CHAPTER 24

*Grecian Journey from the
Gerania Mountains to
Kythira and back to the
Peloponnese via the Mani.*

August 1989

T he Petrol Pump attendant just outside
Neapolis at the very southern tip of the
southern Peloponnese tells me that he
has many friends in England.

"Where?" I ask. "In Bognor Regis," he replies. It seems bizarre standing here in the road-
shimmering heat, equating this swarthy muscu-
lar man with Bognor. King George Vth's alleged
epithet for that south coast town floats disjoint-
edly into my head. I wonder if indeed he has
heard such a derogatory swearword for this gen-
teel town, but clearly, I will never be able to ask
him!

He interrupts the reverie to tell me he is
a football coach and mentions a name. "Do you
know the team?"

"I've heard of it," I say to please him.

Schinos, Perachora
& Loutraki

We had set off from Athens a few days previously, heading first for the south-eastern corner of the Gulf of Corinth, or to be pedantic, the Gulf of Alkionidon. The area here around Schinos, although remarkably close to the capital, is very untouched and a dirt road takes us along the coastline through big pine woods, ending at a small port and lagoon.

People are often amazed when we say we love Attica, but along its many coastlines spreading west and north, east and south, away from the growing conurbation of Athens are pockets of countryside, forest and seaside fishing villages, small communities untouched by tourism and the commercialism it brings.

These are places explored only by a few travellers and discerning Athenians, most likely those who were raised here and who had like the majority of Greeks emigrated to the capital to seek their fortune.

Here in a tiny taverna by the lagoon, a men's luncheon party is still in full swing at five in the evening. They supply us with drinks, refusing all payment. We buy them a carafe of wine. A rake thin old man gets up to dance, alone, lost in his rhythms and his pleasure. The music becomes more boisterous and did the waiter leave a pile of plates mistakenly at the end of the table? No matter, suddenly they are no longer whole white pieces of crockery, but broken plates smashed to pieces in the enthusiasm of the dance.

"You don't see that often," Suzi says. "I thought it was illegal, or certainly frowned upon."

Happy souls, - wise men content with their lot – or perhaps they are Athenian business-men, the smart cars parked on the road suggest this.

Reluctantly we leave them, wondering what the wives will say when (if) they get home that night, and we cut across country through Pisia, (marking mentally the ancient site of Perachora to our right, with no time to visit, made famous by Dilys Powell in her wonderful book 'An Affair of the Heart') and on to Loutraki, and the Hotel Pappas where we overnight.

This attractive seaside town has a long promenade, and a vast number of hotels, from the sumptuous to the old and slightly decadent as befits a spa resort. The place is famous for its spring water and its spa baths where treatment is offered for all kinds of rheumatic, arthritic, gynaecological and blood complaints.

In the fin de ciecle grandeur of the hotel Agelidis Palace, we take morning coffee on the terrace overlooking the sea while a loud mezzo soprano accompanies herself on the piano in the salon – that's entertainment! The lonely dancer by the sea and the opulence of Loutraki's premier hotel hardly seem to belong to the same country, let alone the same era; but the fact that they co-exist both so out of context with the fashionable images of modern Europe highlights the contrasts of Greece.

We leave the Hotel Pappas, just west of Loutraki, which with its welcoming seaside rural position and first class taverna under the pine trees has served us well. We head south, somewhat reluctantly, over the nearby Corinth canal, and will travel the length of the Peloponnese, across country to Argos and thence by the old coastal road, I say old but in fact, this was not fully paved with tarmacadam until the 1980s, down the Eastern side of the Peloponnese.

Arcadia

Below Leonidio we drive inland where the road reverts to part dirt road through ragged gorge-filled mountain country beginning our steep climb with our first sighting of Moni Elona, the monastery hanging like a limpet on a ledge on the side of the limestone cliff. Spectacularly sited against the pink hewn rock high above the green gorge- as much as a feat of architecture as the Meteora monasteries.

Moni Elona, Arcadia

Only perhaps here they had cheated because the road winding up the mountain, winding being the operative word, brings the traveller almost to the back door! Tight hairpin bends, amazing drops thousands of feet to the gorge below, straight off the side of the road. In places, the road just falls away literally leaving a crater or gap that might lead to Hades. In our case we keep onto Kosmas, high on a plateau of pine trees. After this pretty little mountain town with its plane tree-shaded square we begin a smooth descent on a rough road which will shortly be completed. As we leave this village with its gushing lion-headed springs below the church, a cracked bell solemnly chimes out the hour through the last heat rays of the afternoon.

We count at least six kafenions or tavernas, the houses built of large blocks and some have the pointing etched out like a primitive painting. An old man in his pale grey-blue sweater, flat cap and checked shirt and moustache all tone matching, stops to take in the scene. It's a place to linger.

It is only later that we learn that Kosmas was razed first by the Ottomans in the Greek War of Independence in the early nineteenth-century and then again in the twentieth by the Germans in WW2. In both cases, the hardy mountain people provided a centre for the Resistance.

Little are we to know, awestruck as we are by this wonder, that this area and the coast below, around Leonidio would one day become a place we could call home!

Neapolis & Kythira

Eight hours after leaving Loutraki, including a two-hour break for lunch, and our encounter with the Anglophilic petrol attendant we find a bed in Neapolis, that southernmost point in the Peloponnese. Two towns which for most of our travels have retained their authentic Greekness but which despite their similarities are poles apart.

Neapolis, like many places mentioned in this story, is a place we will return to often, again and again, but which many years later the visit in 2016 will become ingrained in our memories as the place where we heard that the UK had voted to leave the EU and became synonymous with our despair that the Europe, we felt so attached to, would be snatched from us.

In 2016, on the 23rd June, - Britain votes in a Referendum and votes to leave the single market, to leave the European Union. And here we are at the southern-most point of Greece at the southern and eastern point of mainland Europe when the news came through on my iPhone radio in the middle of the night, that we have voted out. Turning the TV on in the hotel bedroom only confirms our fears and with a huge ache in the pit of our stomachs, we eventually make our way to breakfast. "What have you done?" asks the hotel owner as we creep sheepishly to a shady courtyard where we toy with a minimal breakfast. It is a question that we will be asked all day. Neapolis does not have many British visitors and there are no other Brits to glare at accusingly, instead we slink guiltily back to the room, pack our cases and go down to the ferry port. Do we look so British? Why is everyone looking at us?

The stevedore loading the cars looks at us, takes pity on us and lets Simon drive straight into the hold of the little ferry boat, without negotiating the tricky ramp up to the upper deck. We find three seats in the shade, facing aft, and then realising that once moving we will be directly into the sun changed to three other seats. The normally short journey to Kythira seems interminable. A passing dog crouched to pee about twenty feet from us. Glumly I watch the puddle expand and then form a narrow stream heading very slowly to the way of our bags. It signified the mood of the day.

Once on land, there is the normal scramble off the ship. Drivers pushing past old ladies and children to get first to the hold, laid-back holidaymakers giving space but not adverse to swinging round to give any Brit who has voted the UK out of the EU a nasty swipe with their backpack. The day isn't going to improve.

We drive to absolutely stunning Avlemonas, all white and blue and cubist. There we made a conscious decision over iced tea and chocolate cake: this is an island we had sweated to reach and the EU aside, there is nothing we can do except try to enjoy this precious visit. Once in Kapsali, our lodgings located, we hang on to that thought, but in the roasting afternoon heat, carrying large cases up multiple very steep steps on an outside staircase that is only half in the shade, staying positive is not easy. To quote a modern phrase: it is what it is.

We are in beautiful Kapsali, our fourth trip, but it is many years since our last visit, and we are overjoyed that very little has changed excepting everything is better! Here is the Greece of forty years ago; alive, agricultural, living communities as yet resisting the corrosive effects of an avaricious tourist industry.

But on our first visit to Kythira back in 1989, as Vassilis Charos, whose family have been farming olives, among many other interests since 1600 says: "Our family company, Kythira & Co, has been directly responsible for the relatively recent revival of Kythira and the development of its tourist business."

"Not that this is excessive," he continues, "and there are firm plans to develop only in a controlled 'eco-tourism' fashion with small family-run hotels or villas whose architecture is in the style of and in keeping with the island."

We tell him forcefully that we hope these high ideals are translated into reality in the years ahead while privately doubting the survival of aesthetics against the lure of quick money, having seen some of the planning disasters that some village mayors have managed to push through to their own advantage during their terms of office.

In 2016 amazingly we found that most of the tourism, such as it is, is still centred in the village of Kapsali with its visually stunning Chora and the little seafront community where most visitors stay. Here are sufficient facilities, tempting tavernas, coves and beaches for those who wish to unwind and stray no further.

In the centre of the bay is the great Avgo (egg) or Aphrodite's Rock. According to legend, when Zeus castrated his father, Cronos, then ruler of the world, he cast the bloody member into the sea, this gave birth to Aphrodite, goddess of love who rose out of the Mediterranean at Kapsali. The spot is marked by the mystical Aphrodite's rock and we are told an ancient temple is dedicated to the goddess, whose Doric pillars can still be found in the nearby church. We never find them.

Much of the rest of the island deserves exploration. Many beaches remain unsullied simply because it requires effort to find them and to get there. Tiny coves such as Melidoni; or the white, white sand of the beach of Diakofti, which in the 1990s was a Caribbean-like hideaway with its aquamarine sea and tiny blue-tabled fish taverna right on the sand but which by 2016 had dissolved into a massive concrete jetty for the new ferry port, offering more shelter than the existing wind-racked harbours of Kapsali and Aghia Pelagia.

It's curious but I get more evocations from the original Diakofti, than anywhere. One corner of our English garden with a fig tree and a bay tree always triggers a memory of its pristine bleached sand and shallow turquoise and aqua-marine waters. The hinterland too is charming. On route to the caves of Aghia Sophia, we halt for lunch under the huge plane tree in Milopotamos where the little taverna offers home-made tiro-pitta and the most delicious kolokythopitta – a filo pastry pie made with zucchini, aubergines, onions, peppers and cheese. Below the square is an attractive river-bed full of ducks and lined with Eucalyptus trees, syphoned off from the river are a series of ducts or mini-canals forming a trough of running water for communal laun-dry.

Two beautiful young girls dressed identi-cally in blue and white striped dresses with big wide white collars, bring their washing down. Standing together, they giggle away, slap, slap-ping the wet clothes against the smooth flat sloping slabs of stone that edge the little canal, beautiful in their first awareness of their womanhood.

The Byzantine and Venetian settlement of Kato Chora of Milopotamos is often missed by visitors, but what a treat for those who scramble around the rough paths, lined with sea-cucum-bers and wild-flowers. Greeted by the gate of the Venetian castle, dating from 1565, with the winged lion of St. Mark proudly visible over the arched entrance intrepid visitors enter through the walls without formality and although it is a huddle of tumbledown ruins we find two-storey houses, just within the walls where the families of the soldiers lived in Medieval times. What we are not prepared for within the castle walls are the Byzantine churches, mostly locked but we are told containing wonderful frescoes. We have to content ourselves with looking over these walls to a deep gully below and beyond the Ionian Sea and imagining the soldiers protecting the island from the pirates roaming these seas.

Beyond the village, the road to the caves deteriorates from potholed cement to dirt and stone, descending steeply into the ravine we had seen from the castle. The caves are usually only open in July and August, so it is advisable to check in the square at Milopotamos before setting off. We park, wisely before the bend ahead of the path to the cave which is reached by walking into the bottom of the ravine and then ascending the other side by a precipitous path.

The cave entrance is a small church and the system itself has many fine formations. We proceed by torchlight with a young Anglo/Greek guide explaining the geological history and the effects of volcanic action and earthquakes forcing up layers of black asphalt and causing vast strata slips. A worthwhile expedition, lasting about an hour.

It is wild and windy (a characteristic of the island) as we leave Kythira for Neapolis after our first visit. Heavy seas and crosswinds sweep the Martha, a small battered but friendly and dependable tub, past the end of the jetty at Neapolis, thwarting the docking. After three attempts fail, with experience and clearly past practise, the Captain brings her in bow first then swings her stern into the wind under the lee side of the jetty.

There is no proper ramp here for the vehicles to disembark and we all shamble ashore with even more shoving, pushing, bumpy chaos than usual.

Clearing the Eastern Laconia (Epidaurus Limera) peninsula, we head out over the southern plains of the Peloponnese, below the tail end of the huge Taygetos mountains, which dominate this part of Greece. The plains here are full of orange groves replanted with the summer fruiting Valencia oranges, much prized for their juice. The Greek variety of oranges do not ripen until December but go on fruiting until March.

Gythio, the gateway to the middle peninsula of the Mani, but also the ancient port for Sparta, (from where Helen made her getaway to Troy with her lover Paris), is a transient town. Over the years we will use the tavernas lining the waterfront or join the backpackers working their way down the Peloponnese, waiting for the less regular boats to Crete and Kythira, or to head back to Athens.

Another trip to the Mani

So, we are back in the Mani. Each return visit throws up new treasures, new delights, perhaps if we returned every year for a lifetime, we would discover some new facet.

The wind seems to sweep even cleaner the swept-bare mountainsides of the Mani. Late light strikes the tall architecturally unique tower houses of the old villages. They stand as pearly grey stumps, dwarfed against the bulk of the mountains. At Stavri we find the Tsitsiris Castle, a cunning conversion of old tower houses into a rustic hotel. We are the only guests! Waited on hand and foot by Aspasia, a charming catering student doing her practical year as part of her course at Nafplio Catering College.

The hotel is the work of the five Tsitsiris brothers, four of whom in live in Athens, one runs the hotel. The exterior is designed to tie in with its tower house neighbours and the interior is all rough stone walls and ceilings, rooms like monastic cells with chunky rustic wooden furniture. There is apparently a thriving winter trade when shooting parties assemble and log fires are lit in the huge fireplaces.

Next door is the village store, an amazing emporium selling everything from nails to salt cod, diapers to donkey saddles, chef's knives, buckets, webbing belts and almost everything else. It has its own brand of locally distilled ouzo with hand-printed labels on the bottles and locally made retsina sold by the kilo at a few cents. This area of the western coastline of the Mani from Gerolimenas up to the caves of Pyrgos Dirou and beyond to Areopolis and Itilo, is worth extended exploration, with its wealth of tower villages, caves and exquisite, often difficult to find, tiny Byzantine churches. Indeed, there is evidence of fifth and sixth century Christian Basilica styled churches in the Mani. This means the area was probably Christian during the late classical period, then a gap in further evidence until in the tenth and eleventh centuries when there is a plethora of church building which to this day enhance the Mani countryside.

There is the oddly shaped 'frying pan' Tigani peninsula which stretches nearly a kilometre out to sea before expanding into a great crag with as yet the mostly undiscovered treasures, ancient and medieval fortifications. A cart-track leads from Stavri towards Aghia Kiriaki. From here it is a two-kilometre hike through rough country to a castle with crumbling arches, great cisterns and the remains of a Byzantine church, possibly one of the earliest in the Mani dating from the nineth-century.

It could well have been the cathedral for the Byzantine bishopric of Mani recorded in the time of the Emperor Leo the Wise AD 886-912. But Tigani's history goes back much further than the Christian era. A cross-wall two metres thick at the south-western corner is typical of the masonry of the Greek bronze age around the thirteenth century BC. Much excavation work needs to be done before the medieval and later secrets of the Tigani area are revealed.

To investigate all the Byzantine remains in all the little villages and all the secret places of the Mani, such as the sombre intimidating headland of Cavo Grosso, with its pirate caves and huge sea cliffs, will take many visits. Some of the best churches (many of which are in a parlous state of disrepair) are in the little villages reached by ancient tracks on either side of the new main road.

On the seaward side don't miss Kafiona, Kouloumi and Erimos. Kafiona's St. Theodore's twelfth-century church has thirteenth-century frescoes unique in Byzantine art, while it is claimed that the church of Aghia Varvara (St. Barbara) at Erimos is one of the finest Byzantine churches in Greece.

Ag. Varvara, Byzantine Mani Church

Turn off the main road at Lakkos, where we drive through an olive groves through the small settlement to a ruined megalithic church. From here you can see the dome of Aghia Varvara. Unfortunately, on our visit, repeated enquiries fail to elicit the keyholder to the church and we have to leave this gem of Byzantine architecture sitting proudly alone in a little field without being able to see the frescoed interior.

Perhaps one of the churches which previously stirred our imagination the most is the near ruined "Trissakia" – the three churches. A few years earlier our photograph of the frescoes exposed to the elements, but still in situ on one of the walls, drew attention to our dismay of the neglect of this gem. On a subsequent visit, when we saw that scaffolding had been erected to help protect the masonry, and perhaps preserve the still expressive faces of those imbibing the Last Supper, we thought perhaps that our postcard had helped? A further visit rather quashed those hopes, as the roof put over the scaffolding to create the steel tent had blown off, probably in a storm; although perhaps efforts continue?

In the early summer of 2020, during the Covid 19 pandemic I worry that the Greek tourist season might fail and not provide the much-needed cash and resources for any necessary work or investment in future. All the headway that Greece has made, becoming a member of the European Union in 1981 and adopting the Euro in 2001, up to and including the Olympic Games of 2004 to come into the twenty-first century, threatens to come to nought. The burden of the debts that have been incurred with these efforts, with the following huge energy and determination during the first two decades of the twenty-first-century that the Greeks themselves and their government have made to deal with the resulting economic crisis and the refugee crisis, until by 2019 businesses and the people were reporting hugely positive results. Now, will all this be destroyed again, this time by the coronavirus? Of course, the Greek nation is not the only country to be devasted by this unheralded disaster but after all its struggles that have overtaken the country, really going back to the conclusion of the Greek War of Independence, the WW2, the Civil war, this must feel as though that this is one thing too much to bear.

All too soon the time for exploration is over and we are driving north up the new road to Kalamata and civilisation, then onto Tripolis, Argos and onwards back to Corinth, all without the benefit of motorways and thence to Athens.

CHAPTER 25

Chios & Limnos

September 1989:

We suddenly awake to the sound of a dull and rhythmic, thud, thud, thud vibrating through our heads. In the disorientation of half-sleep, it is reminiscent of being on a Greek ferryboat plodding its way through the night. As the room comes into focus, I recognise the rooftop apartment in the hotel owned by our friend Theodore Spordilis on the north-eastern Aegean island of Chios and the noise is indeed the midnight ferry approaching harbour on its first stop from the Piraeus on route for Lesvos, Agios Efstratios, Limnos and Kavala. Names and places to conjure with.

Agios Efstratios

Suzi recalls the sparseness of Agios Efstratios, arriving there once at dusk, even though we have to hold position offshore, the excitement on the quayside is obvious when clearly most of the population of three hundred people are eagerly awaiting their supplies from the ferry. Even in the twilight, we could see some of the houses are prefabricated.

A few backpackers disembark into a small packet boat to be ferried to the quay to enjoy the remoteness, the pristine beaches of this tiny island, recently ravaged by an earthquake and to enjoy fish meals and simple salads rather than the variety of meat dishes to which as tourists we are all becoming accustomed.

Chora (Chios Town)

The room at the Hotel Kyma and its spectacular rooftop veranda encapsulate much of Theodore's philosophy in this lovely old hotel with its plain wooden floors, fine marble staircase and the very latest in telex, fax and switchboard equipment. These are days before the internet was invented! Our own room contains in its bathroom, totally incongruous in this setting, a vast modern Jacuzzi style bath big enough to hold about four people and taking half the water supply for the whole hotel to fill. It is Theodore's pride and joy for he is obsessed with new technology.

The hotel's history is worthy of a book on its own, being built in 1922, by a rich shipbuilder and was seized soon after its completion to house the headquarters for the Greek Colonel Nikolaos Plastiras, at the time of the Asia Minor catastrophe in Smyrna, when thousands of Greek soldiers and refugees were fleeing from the city across the sea. Here among other decisions made was one to hold to account those responsible for the dreadful consequences of the fire and massacre in what is now Izmir in mainland Turkey. (Ironically Theodore is married to Güher, from Izmir, modern Smyrna.)

The real gem of the hotel, according to an eccentric English guest, (one of the sort who believes that if you speak loudly and slowly enough to the natives that they will understand!) is the marble staircase which he tells Theodore, slowly and loudly is: "Just like the one in the National Liberal Club in England."

Theodore, whose English is perfect, smiles and nods. His father was a Chian who was born in Odesa, Ukraine and returned to his roots to buy the Kyma, opened it as a hotel in 1963, having restored it from a ruined state. The hotel has been in the family ever since.

The second time the hotel was commandeered was in WW2 when it was seized by the Germans and used as their command centre and barracks. The heavy machine gun installed on the Kyma's terrace caused damage to the marble staircase at its narrowest point.

Chios at the time of our visit is not an island for the sunbathing tourist. The main port and town are workaday, but interesting, nonetheless. Most of the tourist development is centred around the sandy beach at Karfas along the coast, while inland the fortified villages of Pyrgi and Mesta with the sgraffiti decorated houses, the ancient ruined village of Anavatos and the eleventh-century monastery of Nea Moni are among the best-known sightseeing spots for visitors.

Mastic villages: Pyrgi and Mesta

Indeed, in Mesta it is possible to stay in village houses which have been restored by the Greek Government. That is if you can find them, the tiny Medieval village is constructed like a maze, some of the narrow streets are covered as in a tunnel and it is easy for the visitor to become confused and lose the single entrance/exit.

Pyrgi, a much bigger village with several noteworthy churches, like Mesta, is a Mastic village, and again is protected but not as obviously fortified.

The Mastic villages are concentrated in the area where the evergreen tree, a genus of Pistacia is cultivated. By and large, this is a form of agriculture unique to Chios and the products made from the gum range from alcohol to cosmetics, bread, spoon sweets and Turkish delight.

The villages were protected by the Ottomans to allow the Turkish Delight trade to prosper and to guarantee the ladies of the Harem remained happy.

In Pyrgi the extraordinary decoration employed on the walls of the buildings is of black and white geometric design and covers all seemingly blank canvases with an intricate pattern which exposes the black volcanic underlayer where the white plain plaster has been carefully and artistically chipped away.

   As well as pots of geraniums and trail-
ing bougainvillaea the balconies display long
withering strings of drying tomatoes, heralding
the long winter ahead. The most beautiful little
Byzantine church in Pyrgi shelters just beyond
a tunnelled street, where out of the dark of the
tunnel, Agioi Apostoloi, is framed and appears
completely golden in the sunlight. A trick of the
light maybe with sunlight coming from behind
the church as you approach through the tunnel,
but absolutely riveting.

Nea Moni

There has been extensive forest fire damage around Nea Moni which has detracted some-what from its tall cypress shaded enclave of peace and serenity.

Nea Moni however, has survived 900 years of plunder and earthquake. It was ransacked by the Turks in 1822. During the raid, women and children who had sought refuge there were slaughtered along with many of the monks. (Their shattered skulls are still on display.) Nea Moni was pillaged and fire badly damaged the exquisite gold mosaics which had been created by some of the finest artists in Byzantium.

At its zenith, Nea Moni housed some 800 monks. Today five old nuns are the sole occupants, but the surviving mosaics, the beautiful buildings and the idyllic setting are well worth a visit. A new, but rough road now cuts through from Nea Moni to the west coast of the island, making accessible many lovely, isolated, but largely pebble coves offering excellent swimming.

Emborio and other villages

It is possible to drive south to Lithi and cut inland over the island to the intriguing village of Emborio in the south with its black volcanic pebble beaches. There is an excellent taverna in the little port here, just on the right once you have negotiated the approach road to the village with its seemingly endless succession of sleeping policemen. The area is known in particular for its archaeological finds and brought to life by Dilys Powell in her book An Affair of the Heart.

Up in the north-west of the island above the more popular bays of Limnos and Limnia is Aghios Markella with its large monastery built on the seashore. A big Panaghia, religious festival, is held here each year on 22 July. It is difficult to see why until one crosses the long sandy beach to a point where a rock and concrete path or causeway traverses the base of the cliff for more than half a mile.

Its destination seems a mystery until a cross standing on a rock just offshore marks the point of a spring rising at sea level evidenced by the presence of much iron ore in the rocks. Further along, there is a much grander shrine with icons, an oil lamp and steps leading to a stone basin in the sea surrounded by railings. Here is the obvious rising of a much stronger spring where it is said (and there are eyewitnesses) that if you go accompanied by a priest or a very religious person, then the water will boil and bubble. However, if evil people are present then the water will never boil.

There appears to be no logical or scientific explanation unless the priest introduces something to the water that reacts with the chemicals and minerals in the spring; or, but this is much too coincidental to be naturally occurring, there is a vast thermal emission every 22 July.

Back in town, we sit on the waterfront at the Acropolis Kafenion which serves the best mezes in Chios: Zucchini, Keftedakia, ropa, feta, loukaniko, gavros marinada, tzatziki, dolmadakia, olives and bread. We are watching the volta, that huge social parade of people walking the waterfront, back and forth, where boy meets girl, where families exchange pleasantries and where the arrival of the ferry boat is eagerly awaited, and arrivals and departures are anticipated or dreaded.

The waterfront is lined with sticky cake shops, unsophisticated tavernas, shops selling preserved fruits and gum and liquor made from the indigenous and unique mastic industry. Alongside these are the shipping offices, (the wealth of this island derives from the big shipping families), banks and retail outlets for the young Chiots' status symbol – the motorbike.

Two blocks behind is an open area of interconnecting paved streets – a square around the central buildings which become a splendid daily market with outdoor fruit and vegetable stalls and, compared to the rest of the island, sophisticated delicatessen and butchers' shops. These are trading cheek by jowl with old-fashioned emporia selling caged birds, hens, pheasant, quail, partridge and a variety of songbirds, wicker baskets, brassware and fresh ground coffee.

We leave Chios on a sad note. A foreign guest of Theodore's at the Hotel Kyma has been struck by tragedy. A couple had arrived the day before and the male guest has died suddenly of a heart attack. There is great bureaucratic difficulty getting all the formalities completed for the body to be flown off the island the next day. Theodore works through the rest of the day and night getting an autopsy completed, the government papers signed, the attorney sorted out, the airline and flights organised, while his family do their best to comfort the man's wife.

He is frustrated in the early hours of the morning by a government doctor who refuses to come to his office 30 minutes early to issue a certificate. Thus, the body cannot be put on the morning flight to Athens and will miss the connecting flight to his home country. In the midst of all this, Theodore still takes time, as the midnight boat approaches, to drive us to the port, take our luggage to the quayside and see us on board. As we thud, thud our way north through the night on route to Limnos, we think of a good friend – and good hotelier.

Limnos

It is a beautiful island It is very much influenced by the army who are so well behaved, compared to British forces, as they wander around the main town of Myrina, like Lesvos on the map with its deep rounded inlets it is like a jigsaw piece. Some call it the Butterfly Island.

In the interior which, by the standards of many Greek islands, is barren and brown, the drystone walls are constructed with stones placed vertically, rather odd we think, given that one of us is a Yorkshire Dalesman used to creating long horizontal walls with a through stone every so often.

The port of Myrina is a charming place and as the ferry approaches, you can't help but be impressed by the jagged dark hills that stand behind the waterfront. Despite possessing a small population, it proclaims its status as an island capital and clearly can serve the needs of its people, who even if they wanted to would have difficulty moving speedily to a larger conurbation. The whole island creates this remote aura, this cloak of self-sufficiency and in spite of our short stay, we quickly adapt to its gentle rhythm.

Mornings spent on one of the islands glorious beaches, a leisurely lunch in the seaside taverna and a pre-dinner drink at the ouzerie. Its crowning glory is the Kastro, a castle, which is central to the two bays, the elegant Romeikos Gialos on one side and the port of Tourkikos Gialos on the other makes the whole town pretty walkable.

With its quaint corners, neo-classical buildings and attractive market, Myrina is weaving its way into our heart. We are sorry our stay on Limnos is short because we have been told the Thermal Springs, surrounded by plane trees and the archaeological ruins are well worth exploring, and like the town itself many of the ancient sites have been inhabited since prehistoric times.

It is the nature of our visits that we are on business and satisfying our clients' needs by checking out the accommodation where we book them also means back in a UK office to tend to the day to day necessities of running a travel business. "Here the beaches are the crowning glory of the island," said Kostas the taverna owner. "Although we have an airport, it is not a well-known destination and we are a long way from Athens, so the beaches never get busy as they do in the larger islands."

"I'm amazed at how attractive Myrina is, I came expecting to find a very flat island and of course it has no high mountains, but just the backdrop to the town of the castle on the peaky ridge of hills is very alluring and the architecture is also very striking."

"Yes, it is not the pancake of the island you are told to expect. And all over the island, you will find unusual sites and wonders, there is a real desert, and some salt pans, and it is very influenced by its volcanic geology. I can't stress it enough; the beaches are perhaps some of the best and unspoilt in the Aegean. You need to hire a car, are you planning to do so?"

"Well no," says Simon, thoughtfully. "Our son Oliver is due to come out sometime in the near future with a couple of our office staff and we thought we would leave the exploring to them."

"I can see even after our short time here that it's very wild and even mountainous in the interior. I wish we had time to explore and see the desert! And I was surprised to see a deer near the Kastro last night!"

"Yes, they were brought to the island in the late 1960s, someone thought they may be a tourist attraction, but if we are not careful, they may become a pest. If your son does come, tell him if he comes out of high season, then he should expect to see flamingos! And the excursion you are clearly not going to do is the trip to the Cape of Falakro, it is an exceptional phenomenon with volcanic rock formations. They are well worth seeing."

The town hosts young recruits from the Greek Navy who I must say are very well behaved. As usual, we know we have not allowed enough time for a first visit. We will need to come back.

Oliver's Return Trip
from Limnos

We have just completed our educational trip to Limnos, as young sales staff of a fledgling travel agency. We are flying from the island on Monarch Airways via Skiathos to collect other holidaymakers and to refuel for our return journey back to Gatwick.

The plane is on time, thank God we thought, little knowing what is in store for us. Our first hop is good, we arrive on Skiathos on time, we collect the other Sunvil Holidays passengers and we start to refuel then suddenly a catalogue of disasters begins.

The plane goes 'tech,' now I am not an engineer or particularly happy flying! I am disabled, I have only just started working in the Greco-File office and usually I travel with my parents. I am beginning to feel nervous with all the activity of the pilots and cabin crew running around. It is beginning to go dark outside and then suddenly the lights go out and then the air conditioning stops. We are in the dark and it is beginning to get hot on the apron of the small airport of Skiathos.

Eventually, after about two hours we are told we are flying to Athens to get the plane fixed. We land in Athens and we are told an engineer would try to fix the plane. We are told that the plane couldn't be fixed that evening, but they would try the next day, which means that we will have to be allocated a hotel in Athens overnight, which we are.

This is a hotel where you could stand on the roof garden and almost touch the undercarriage of planes as they make their final approach to land. The next day we are all taken back to the airport and told we would be flying back to the UK mid-afternoon which means we would arrive back in Gatwick early evening, of course meaning that we might miss our connection back to Leeds-Bradford. Even so we are told eventually that our plane can't be fixed in time; so, they are flying the chief pilot out to fly us back. The problem seems to be that we can only fly at 10,000 feet or below as the pressurisation of the plane cannot be stabilised and we will have to fly at this height. Consequently, the flight time will be much longer as we will have to take a different route to the normal air corridors to avoid the Alps where we can, which means essentially, we will be following the coast. The plus point of this new route is it is a clear day and we have some wonderful views of some of the most beautiful cities and areas of Europe, to which the captain helpfully draws our attention; Mt. Etna, Mt. Vesuvius, Rome, and up the Rhone Valley via Lyon to Paris. Eventually, we arrive back into Gatwick around 9.00 pm tired and exhausted and we rush off to the sales desk of Dan Air, our carrier back to Leeds-Bradford just in time to change our complimentary tickets over to the last flight of the day back to Leeds-Bradford.

We think "that was close" and having travelled for more than 36 hours we think we are home and dry, until there is an announcement: - "could the holders of ABC tickets please come to the front of the plane. We sheepishly make our way to the front of the plane and are told we can't travel as we are wearing jeans! It is not Dan Air's policy to carry passengers who wearing jeans if they are travelling free as supernumerary staff, which apparently is how we are classed. Rachel protests she has nothing else except shorts but remembers she has a skirt in her hold luggage. The plane is not full, and our main luggage is quickly located. Embarrassed we search our cases there and then on the tarmac, muttering that they must be picking on us, as eighteen years old, because they know we have complimentary tickets. We change quickly in the plane's toilets.

CHAPTER 26

*Nafplio and the villages of
Kynouria and Mount Parnon*

27 October – 5 November 1990

We are heading for Nafplio at the northern end of the Gulf of Argolis. The historic and first capital of Greece from 1823-1834 in the early days after the Greek War of Independence released the citizens from the oppression of the rule of the Ottoman empire.

Because of its position on its peninsula Nafplio faces away from the sea and provides the safest harbour on the coast of the Argolis. Consequently, it has a fascinating architectural and military history dating back to before Classical Antiquity. It was known as a trading post in the eleventh century and it has been occupied variously by Venetians, Turks, Russians and warring Greek factions during the wars of independence. The Bavarian Prince Otho, the first king of Greece, disembarked in Nafplio in 1833 remaining there with the city as the capital of Greece and seat of government until the following year when the government was removed to Athens.

Nafplio out of season is a bit like the declension of that irregular verb to travel. I'm a traveller, he's a tourist, they're on a package. One feels quite out of place flopping around in flip-flops and the more usual kinds of holiday wear. Those Day-Glo Bermuda shorts in the kafenion are decidedly not the thing. The streets have regained their tranquillity in this elegant Greek community, and it is well worth adopting the dress and manners of the indigenous population.

Entering the wide square, Plateia Sindagmatos, (Syntagma or Constitution Square) in the centre of the old town, one passes under a huge plane tree redolent with the sweet sappy scents of the autumn. Adjacent to it and forming the entire width of one side of the square is the recently re-roofed and repaired archaeological museum, a stately Venetian building dating from 1715, the town's arsenal in the eighteenth century. Beyond it is the ex-Mosque of Vouleftiko in which the Greek Parliament met for the first time after the Greek War of Independence in 1827. At the other end of the square, by the other mosque, which is now a cinema, is a traditional taverna, said to be the first restaurant in Nafplio. There is no fancy stuff here; plain wooden tables under a plane tree and a simple unpretentious neon-less exterior. A fat little man hustles for customers and we are ushered through the long dark passage to the kitchen at the back. The result is splendid fish soup, gigantes (giant beans in sauce) and pork from the oven.

Along the waterfront, some of the kafenions and gelateria are still open as indeed are several of the better shops. The community breathes a collective sigh of relief after the congestion of the summer. They can sit in their cafes and count the cost, the profit and the loss, swap stories of the summer hordes and look forward to their holidays. Out in the bay, the castle of Castel Pasqualigo on the tiny islet of Bourtzi seems to float in the water. The light is now so clear, unlike the height of summer when the miasma or evaporating salt-water forms a permanent haze in the heat of the day. The clear light is a great bonus highlighting foreground colour and seems to bring the distant mountain ranges closer.

The great Frankish fort of Palamidi on its rock buttress above the town appears even more dominant and at the same time to be fulfilling its protective role.

Yesterday was "Ochi Day" (October 28, celebrated each year as the day on which the Greek Prime Minister said "Ochi" (no) to the Italians who wanted to take over Greece. They subsequently invaded, followed by the Germans and Greece entered the Second World War.

The children of our good friend Yannis take part in the school and military parades and afterwards everyone makes for the waterfront and a mid-morning spontaneous volta takes place. Little groups of people debate, discuss, greet, gesticulate as they parade the waterfront pavement. The candy sellers with their awning-covered, carbide lit stalls do a brisk trade in dried figs, apricots, pistachio nuts and Turkish delight, while the cafes fill with people. Parents drink the bitter Greek coffee, children the freshly squeezed juice of the first of the ripening orange crop.

The next day we set off with Yannis and family to explore some of the villages in the Arcadia, the hinterland in the foothills of the Parnon mountains.

We take the road south following the eastern coastline of the Peloponnese, a road which did not come into existence until mid-century. We drive past Xeropigado, Astros and somewhere after Leonidio and Poulithra, we head inland, turning higher and higher on corkscrew corners, up into the hills whose upper reaches are bare scrubland.

The gorges and valleys below are full of fine forest trees, predominantly plane, sweet chestnuts, oak and tall silver popular, some ash and some wild cherry. The views are stupendous, over the forest and down to the Aegean Sea and across to the Argolida and the island of Spetses, Hydra beyond. We stop and gather sweet chestnuts from the trees, a treat to take home and roast! It is amazing after a few days rain how quickly the whole countryside has greened up.

Yannis says there will soon be the autumn blossoming of wild-flowers. We stop for lunch in the village of Peleta, with a large imposing church, preparing for a Saint's Day. The one taverna is serving roasting lamb on a spit. Yannis bolts inside and gets things organised. He emerges, "I've persuaded them to serve us half a lamb," he grins, self-important with his organisational abilities.

The lamb arrives, it's a bit stringy and sparse. "This won't do," says Yannis wishing to please his guests. "I'll send it back, I ordered the back half."

"Let it be," says Maria, his wife. "They need the best for the festival, who do you think you are? President Karamanlis?" The old men at the next table under the wall of the taverna listen to all this intently. They are well into their bottle of ouzo and being Greek men do not take kindly to one of their sex being lectured by a woman, wife or not.

Gruff laughs come out from under their outsized moustaches, "Here's to you Mr. President," they say, lifting their ouzo glasses in a toast to Yannis, as a plate of lamb, the rear portion of the lamb, is being presented!

This is the real Greece, the people, the offbeat spirit of place, away from creeping commercialism. But it is slowly vanishing as the country finally moves into the twentieth century, let alone the twenty-first. Let us hope that at least some people will survive with their rural charm and courtesy intact, the culture sustained, not swamped with commercial dross.

As this account of the first part of our travels throughout Greece draws to a close, we are presently in early June 2020, still in lock-down, albeit a less stringent version than it was in March, April and May. We can meet now in small gatherings of no more than six persons, outside in parks and gardens; we now can travel to other places but not stay overnight anywhere, or even go into others' houses. Shops will not open until mid-June. As few public toilets are open, and you can only use those in a friend's house when visiting if, in dire need, you are hardly likely to go far. Particularly as pubs and restaurants are still closed and as far as foreign travel is concerned no one knows when we will be let off the leash. Some flights are to begin next week but there is still doubt whether Britons will be let into Spain, or Greece for that matter, even if the Foreign Office relaxes the ruling that 'only essential travel should be undertaken.' Greece who, until this week, kept its cases and deaths to a minimum is also now beginning to report increased numbers. Was it not for the optimistic hope that because New Zealand is now reporting its cases as zero that other countries will eventually follow? Excepting some say this will be impossible to achieve, throughout the world, without a vaccine.

Then suddenly as I am writing this the U.K. Prime Minister makes the unexpected announcement, out of the blue that single-person households can create a bubble with one other household, and even stay the night within that one household and whilst in that bubble do not have to self-isolate. This news might defuse some of the sorrow, upset and anger that has accompanied much of the daily news and lifts the mood of many who have suffered so much during this pandemic. And so many have suffered/are suffering so much. No wonder when we work on this account, in an extraordinary way re-living the wonderful travels we have enjoyed, that we feel to have been incredibly fortunate.

10 June 2020.

Halki waterfront is as good as any place to discuss today's catch!

GREEK FESTIVALS, NAME DAYS AND FESTIVALS

The majority of first-born children in Greece are named after their grandparents and celebrate their 'name day' on the appropriate Saint's Day. Ioannis or Yannis, Costas or Constantinos, Georgios, Vassilis are universally very popular. Names are popular in certain areas and on certain islands: Thus, you will find much of population of Rhodes is called Manolis; Dionysus, Zakynthos island; Gerasimos, Cephalonia; Spiros, Corfu.

January 1 – Aghios Vassilou – St. Basil, celebrated by Greeks all over the world. January 6 – The Feast of Epiphany – A cross is thrown into the sea with blessings and to ensure good luck. Celebrated in many areas.

January 6/7 – Feast of St. John the Baptist.

Celebrated universally and on Rhodes for the mumming.

January 17 – Aghios Antonio – St. Anthony

January 25 – Feast of St. Gregory the Theologian

February 2 Feast of the Purification of the Virgin or Candlemas – the Candlemas of Salvation (Sotiros)

February 10 – Aghios Charalambos

LENT AND EASTER CELEBRATIONS turn certain Saint's Days into moveable feasts. In particular: All Souls Day (Several times a year) St. Theodore's Day (March 22) St. George's Day (April 23) St. Thomas's Day (May 11) St. Michael's Day (June 23) Zoodochos Pigi (May 8) March 25 - Greek National Day, Feast of the Annunciation of the Virgin Mary.

April and May

There are several EASTER FESTIVALS, Carnival, Meat Week, Meat Saturday, Cheese Week, Clean Monday or Shrove or Ash Monday. Palm Sunday, Holy Week, Ascension Day, Pentecost. Days change from year to year.

April 23 - St George's Day can only fall on this date if this falls after Easter, otherwise it must be the first Thursday after Easter. This is true of other dates subject to the Orthodox Calendar, (see above).

May 2 – Aghios Athanasios & Koukkoumas

May 21- St. Constantine & St. Elena

June 24 – Birthdate of St. John the Baptist

June 29 - St. Peter & St. Paul

Throughout July, August & September, wine festivals

July 17– St. Marina

July 20 – Profitis Elias – St. Elias

July 26 – St. Paraskevi

July 27 – Aghios Pantelimon

July 30 – Aghios Apostoli In August on Kos, re-enactment of Hippocratic Oath at the Asklepion.

August 6 – Feast of the Transfiguration

August 15 – The Assumption, Festival of the Panaghia

August 25 – St. Fanousios

August 28-29 St. John the Headless

September 14 - Name Day of Timios Stavros

September 20 – St. Eustace, the Martyr

September 26 – St. John the Theologian

October 3 - St. Dionysus Areopagite

October 18 – St. Luke the Evangelist

October 20 – St. Gerasimos

October 21– The Blessed Christodoulos

October 26 – St Demetrios

October 28 - Ochi Day – a national holiday

November 1– St. Cosmas & St. Damian

November 7/9 – The Archangel of St. Michael

November 14 – St. Philip the Apostle

November 16 – St. Matthew the Evangelist

November 18 – St. Plato the Martyr

November 21 – The Presentation of the Virgin Mary

November 25 – St. Katherine the Martyr

November 30 – St. Andrew the Apostle

December 4 – St. Barbara – the Martyr

December 5 – St. Savvas

December 6 – St. Nicholas, the Bishops Patron of sailors

December 9 – Conception of St. Anne

December 12 – St. Spiridon

December 24 – Christmas Eve

December 25 – The Nativity, Feast of the Magi

December 26 – St. Stephen, St. Panayiotis the Peloponnesian the Martyr, St. Panayiotis has 3 name days.

December 31– New Year's Eve

If you have enjoyed
this book:

I would be very grateful if you could take a little time to write a review on Goodreads.com or the Amazon site where you purchased this book.

Simply go to the Amazon or Goodreads site or use this link on Amazon: http://bitly.ws/aEIP

www.greco-file.com

*SYNOPSES OF JIGSAW
novels and memoirs TWO
QUARTETS which are as
easily read as a series as
independent novels*

THE GREEK LETTERS QUARTET
THE COMING OF AGE QUARTET

& a series of MEMOIRS OF GREEK TRAVELS:
NO ORDINARY GREEK ODYSSEY
      Book One: Where the Blue Truly Begins
      Book Two: The Mountains come down to
the Sea (to be published 2021)
      Book Three: We get to unpack the suitcase!
(perhaps to be published later!)

GREEK LETTERS, VOLUME ONE "BEFORE" In
1827, Samuel Carr, a naive Philhellene from a
Cheshire yeoman's farmstead is drawn into the
closing stages of the Greek War of Independence
on the Peloponnese. Totally out of his depth and
pursued by a wilful young woman he has met on
his voyage to Greece, he must continually fight
to conquer his inner demons. The historical detail and spirit of place will satisfy history buffs
and armchair travellers alike. Through romance,
tragedy and triumph, Susannah and four Greek
orphans will have a lasting effect on Samuel, and
will this be the beginning of a dynasty?

GREEK LETTERS, VOLUME TWO "AND AFTER" After the birth of Modern Greece following independence in the 19th century, Samuel and his companions journey between Nafplio in the Peloponnese and an emergent Manchester in Northern England, but is there a whiff of incest in the air?
Can love overcome and defeat blackmail by those who have Samuel's interests at heart?

GREEK LETTERS, VOLUME THREE "THE EYES HAVE IT" This is as much an account of an Edwardian childhood in Cheshire in WW1 as it is an adventure and travel romance prior to WW2 in the Greek Pindus and Peloponnese mountains. It is a lovely gentle story which develops into a love story in the heady and dangerous times prior to the second world war.

GREEK LETTERS, VOLUME FOUR "MUCH MORE THAN HURT" The last book in the GREEK LETTERS QUARTET, really is the last piece in the Jigsaw and reads well as the conclusion to the series. When Roz is caught up with the fascination of tracing her ancestors, it impacts on all the many characters in this Anglo-Greek family, bringing them all to make their own journeys through Europe and Greece. Roz's son's twins travel most over the continent; Roz has to question her own relationship with past loves, not just her son Andrew's father.

The years around the Millennium is an era of early climate change debates, of soul searching, psychological therapy, same sex relationships, of easy money and this family does not get off lightly.

CAST A HOROSCOPE, Coming of Age Quartet *Winner of a CHILL WITH A BOOK AWARD:* A story of childbirth out of wedlock, heartbreak and a difficult marriage; but also it provides a welcome to the Mediterranean world, prior to mass tourism, told initially through the eyes of a rookie airhostess in 1960 and then, with maturity, through the norms of 'respectable society'.
Do we always hanker after the freedom and excitement of our youth?

THE SCORPION'S LAST TALE, Coming of Age Quartet This is a psychological thriller, with many twists and turns. A journalist takes his family to Corfu at the time of the Greek Junta under the Colonels' regime in the early 1970s. Events become increasingly sinister and simply returning to their home in Pennine Yorkshire does nothing to improve matters. You probably wouldn't want to employ the "Nanny" the family met on Corfu but is she as bad as portrayed? Does it take a young boy to throw light on the situation?

BRIGHT DAFFODIL YELLOW, Coming of Age Quartet *Winner of a CHILL WITH A BOOK award:*

The seeds of one man's romantic trysts with four different women have germinated as he flees from the 1974 Turkish invasion of Cyprus. Who is this man? Why does he attempt to live incognito in the Lake District? What is he doing on the underground railway the day the train crashes at Moorgate Station?

THE GLASS CLASS At the beginning of the evening the question is can the Glass Class still throw a good party? But tragic consequences following an accident throw all their lives into disarray. Will a family tree, taking the friends back to the lives of their ancestors in the mills of West Yorkshire have the answers? A tale of intrigue set in Calderdale, West Yorkshire; Clwyd and Snowdonia, North Wales and Spetses island, Greece.

NO ORDINARY GREEK ODYSSEY Book 1: Where the Blue Truly Begins
The first book recalling travels to Greece begins in 1960 when Suzi, and later her husband Simon and their family, can have no idea where these experiences will take them. The first volume explores the period from 1960 when Suzi first stepped onto a Vickers Viking as a young airhostess up to the end of 1980s when Greece had very much become a central part of their lives. It is interspersed with observations on the sudden impact of COVID 19 on everyone's lives and travel plans.

NO ORDINARY GREEK ODYSSEY Book Two: Where the Mountains Come Down to the Sea. This second volume in the Memoirs will take Suzi and Simon on further travels through the remoter parts of the Greek mainland and more unusual islands. The fact that their travels are now a necessity for their growing travel business doesn't dilute the pleasure. To be published in 2021

NO ORDINARY GREEK ODYSSEY Book Three: We get to unpack the Suitcase – planned for late 2021

You will find an interactive map of Greece on our website: (About page)

At the beginning of this account of the first thirty years of our travels in Greece I asked a question "A way of life in the twentieth century but how much will survive?" To answer my own question: I think the combined impact of the Covid-19 pandemic and the huge issue of climate change will contribute to an immense change in society; in the way we travel, and with the finances we have at our disposal how we share it.

I can only conclude that we have been so fortunate to enjoy such a carefree and prosperous life and above all I wish that all can rejoice in the joy of travel, which is, after all a basic human instinct.

Afterword

When we retired Filoxenia Ltd was sold and although the name no longer trades, a substantial amount of our itineraries and the properties we used survive in the Inntravel programme!

You will find further pictures, (including photographs relevant to this volume of memoirs), information about our work and Suzi's books at www.greco-file.com

Printed in Great Britain
by Amazon

77869200R00242